# BEFORE WE WAS WE

Madness *by* Madness

with Tom Doyle

Foreword by

Dave Robinson

Virgin BOOKS

1 3 5 7 9 10 8 6 4 2

Virgin Books, an imprint of Ebury Publishing
20 Vauxhall Bridge Road
London SW1V 2SA

Virgin Books is part of the Penguin Random House group of companies
whose addresses can be found at global.penguinrandomhouse.com

Plate section 2 picture credits: page 7 (top left and right) © Virginia Turbett;
page 7 (bottom) © Chalkie Davies/ Premium Archive: Getty Images.
Maps reproduced by permission of Geographers' A-Z Map Co. Ltd. Licence
No. B8466 © Crown Copyright 2019. All rights reserved.
Licence number 100017302.

Mike Barson, Mark Bedford, Chris Foreman, Graham McPherson,
Lee Thompson, Cathal Smyth and Daniel Woodgate have asserted their
right to be identified as the authors of this Work in accordance with the
Copyright, Designs and Patents Act 1988

The publisher and authors have made every effort to credit the copyright
owners of any material that appears within, and will correct any omissions
in subsequent editions if notified.

First published by Virgin Books in 2019

www.penguin.co.uk

A CIP catalogue record for this book is available from the British Library

Hardback ISBN 9780753553923
Trade Paperback ISBN 9780753553930

Typeset in 11.2/17.1 pt Sabon LT Std by Jouve (UK), Milton Keynes
Printed and bound in Great Britain by Clays Ltd, Elcograf S.p.A.

# CONTENTS

# FOREWORD BY DAVE ROBINSON

In the dark days of the mid-seventies, when the likes of Yes, Genesis, Pink Floyd and their gargantuan, gatefold-sleeved albums were the hippest things on the block, it wasn't much fun being a pop music fan. The only records in the shops were those hand-picked by middle-aged gits from corporate record companies who were oblivious to all real music. We decided to take music out of the corporate boardrooms and give it back to the punters.

A change had to come, and it came through the formation of Stiff Records, The world's most flexible record label and Undertakers to the Industry, formed over forty years ago in September 1976. Stiff was very much the blueprint for the independent label of today, a rough-and-ready set-up founded on enthusiasm, naïvety, a touch of business acumen (although not too much, mind), a modicum of talent, flair, style and a good pair of ears and a batch of telephones.

In 1979, Rosemarie and I were planning to get married and needed a band to play at the reception. At the same time I had been tipped off by a few people I rated that I should take a look at a London 2 Tone band called Madness. I was told that they were right up my street. I always liked to see the bands live, but they didn't seem to have any up-and-coming dates and time was getting short, as I think that Chrysalis Records had seen them at least six times already. I knew that I only had a couple of viewings left, as Chrysalis normally took about eight visits to make any decision. I thought a bird in the hand is worth two overhead and booked Madness for our wedding.

They accepted the job, somewhat to my amazement, and I only had to worry that as they were known as rudeboys they might want to take some advantage of the situation. However as soon as they started up I felt that I had known them for a long time and the pieces were there for a great album. *One Step Beyond* immediately struck me as a title and direction. The fact that they got Elvis Costello up dancing added to the occasion. All the songs played that night seemed to resonate as social music from the estates of London and those stories needed to be told.

My wife was thrilled at my interest, needless to say.

Madness are one of the groups that have really given me the most joy in my ongoing career. National treasures in the UK now and still going strong formed in 1976. We had a great time together – and it was easy, as they were all talented in many ways and fitted into the machinery and staff of Stiff so smoothly. We obviously had our ups and downs but our friendship is still intact to this day. They had already been produced and got on well with Clive Langer and I encouraged him to add Alan Winstanley as co-producer so he could concentrate on the songs, his forte. That partnership has also come a long way.

# PROLOGUE

# BEFORE WE WAS WE

The shaky Super 8 camera film footage moves through the crowd of house party dancers and then finds the band.

We catch an initial glimpse of the crop-haired singer, wearing a second-hand two-tone tonic suit, before the lens passes over an unfamiliar bass player and drummer and lingers over the soul boy guitarist, throwing some enthusiastic shapes. Behind him, we can see the shades-wearing, sideburned saxophonist, blowing intensively while sporting a maroon baseball shirt bearing the number 17.

The footage then cuts to the keyboard player, enigmatically grooving away in the background, before returning to the singer, Suggs, whose name – like the pseudonyms of a few of the others (Mr B, Kix, Chrissy Boy) – may be unwittingly known to the partygoers from graffiti on walls all around north London. The frontman holds his microphone in one hand, a freshly lit fag in the other, and jerks his head from side to side in a manner that will soon become very familiar. The camera picks out the name of the band on the bass drum: The Invaders.

The date is 22 April 1978, a Saturday, and in 45 seconds of silent film, someone has captured the essence of the group that we will all come to know. The Invaders are still ten months shy of becoming Madness, and in that time, they will lose and gain a member or three – a couple much younger than them (and one still at school) – but in many ways, the blueprint of the band is already sharply drawn.

As an echo of a past more than four decades gone, the cine film vividly depicts a band born of a gang of loners, each one very much proficient in living in their own heads. All, though, are possessed with an outsider/chancer magnetic force that has slowly pulled them together.

The early history of Madness takes place in a London that is entirely unfamiliar now: public washhouses, few cars, the streets still pockmarked by World War II bomb sites and dilapidated buildings, many of them taken over as squats. The shared background of most of the members of the group, as we will discover, is one of disparate broken families who've spawned young urchins-turned-musicians so skilled in artful dodging that their tale is almost Dickensian.

From the fringes of a petty criminality that gave them their unique culture of stolen clothes, records and instruments, free travel and sneaked-in gig experiences, they began to form a sound, and look, that would blaze a colourful and original trail through the world of pop. By the time the solid seven-man line-up of Madness is complete, in 1979, they will look back and realise that for the past decade, growing up, they have all – sometimes unknowingly – been following in one another's footsteps through the streets of north London.

Not everyone in the band will have undergone the same route from opportunist toerag to pop star. But each of them will become as famous and recognisable as the other, spotlighting their unique characters and the special chemistry that made them Madness. At the same time, as a formidable unit they were, and remain, possessed of what Suggs calls 'comic malevolence', existing in an unexplored middle ground somewhere between *Monty Python* and the Krays.

Moreover, perhaps, come rough or smooth, rain or shine, their friendships will be set to last more than forty years. In fact, the strong foundations they cemented as mates, before gradually building their slightly intimidating gang-cum-band, will very likely prove to be the solid base of their longevity.

So, here then are the ragamuffin early days of Madness, 1970–1979. Strap yourself in. No arms outside the car, please. They're taking you for a ride and they don't call them the Nutty Boys for nothing.

Tom Doyle

## CHAPTER 1

# 1970

LEE 'KIX' THOMPSON: In 1970 I would have been living on the Holly Lodge Estate in Highgate. From day dot till '67, '68, when we moved to Holly Lodge, we were next door to Denyer House, off Highgate Road. But even in '70, I used to spend more time meeting old pals at Denyer. I'd walk the distance, the mile, mile-and-a-half from Holly Lodge to Denyer House, because that was where our playground was, Tammo Land. It was a big, bombed-out place the Jerrys done in the war. An old electrical plant, and they obviously had these pinpointed. There were unexploded bombs found in the ground there in the mid-seventies. Back then it had corrugated iron up around it to stop us urchins playing there . . . dancing about on fucking unexploded bombs. That was sort of my hangout.

Funnily enough, The Kinks did a video there for 'Dead End Street', down the alleyway, underneath this tunnel, carrying a coffin, past Denyer House in '66. So, they would have been walking past my house when I was eight or nine, and I'd never even heard of them. Then they filmed a bit down Little Green Street, in the little houses there. The doors are only about four foot high, because the houses are so old, and people were shorter then.

My earliest memory of taking something that wasn't mine was a lollipop, in the old corner shop down in Highgate Road. My mum and dad asked me where I'd got the money for it, and I told them that I'd pinched it from the corner sweet shop. They made me go back there and tell the shopkeeper, who was a sort of over-grown old Benny Hill-looking feller. He said, 'Good for being honest; there you go, have it back.' Why I did it, I don't know. What makes you turn into a dishonest person? I suppose some people see how far they can push it.

My mum was the complete opposite. She could not stand anything like that. She came from a very straight family. She was extremely straight and honest.

Dad was into warehouses and safe-cracking and 'parcels', as they call it. Finding the keys to a lorry, normally round about Christmas, with all the electrical goods and cigarettes and alcohol on. Which is normally an inside job, half the time. He had a lot of friends that came round who looked like the type of people you wouldn't want to meet down a dark alley.

I didn't really see much of him. I can count on my fingers the sort of things that he taught us. 'Do it at night and do it alone.' That was one of his things. 'Don't get caught. If you can't be good, be careful. If you can't be careful, watch out.' That old cliché. He was away quite a lot. The main memories I have were going away at Christmas and Easter and summer holidays, to Great Yarmouth, where all his family lived. Or swimming, cinema and going to visit him in Parkhurst.

My mum used to say, 'If anyone asks you, say your dad's working away on the oil rigs, earning good money.' What, with gelignite? Oh, he was on the oil rigs . . . I swear . . . I swear, Your Honour, he was on the oil rigs. It was too embarrassing for her. If I came home with something to put on the table, she'd half say, 'You shouldn't be doing this. You'll land up like your dad.' But yeah, we'd have it for supper that evening.

I was earning pocket money my way. I weren't going to sit on the corner, begging. Mind you, I did dress up as Guy Fawkes once, outside my local sweet shop. I was the only mug up for it, and I near enough got my foot burned off. Someone went and set alight to my shoes. Of course, you've got the Guy Fawkes mask on, but I felt heat down below. I had plimsolls on. I smell rubber, I look down, next thing, I'm stamping my foot. I think we made about five or six shillings or whatever.

My first court appearance was in the summer holidays of '69, when I was 11. First burglary. A house set back on Highgate Road. That was just walk in . . . literally . . . back when you could leave your doors open. I went in and just stole some bits and bobs. I know there was some jewellery involved. Terrible. Probably some mother's, grandmother's, daughter's.

We got caught, my mate Bob Townsend and myself. We were picked up, put in the car, because I had a pocket full of jewellery. Then I met who I assume was the owner, who was obviously relieved that she'd got her stuff back. But that was it. Our first appearance at Seymour Place Court for Juveniles.

**MIKE 'BARSO' BARSON:** I grew up in north Kentish Town, off Highgate Road. When I was born, in Edinburgh, my mum had just separated from my father. He went off with one of his students. He was an art school teacher in Edinburgh and one of the students came onto him. Sixteen, eighteen, maybe she was. He's married with two kids and his wife's pregnant with a third one. Anyway, he decides that this little hot chickadeedoo is worth more than his kids and his marriage, so he starts something with her. My mum's in the hospital having me, and then this young girl was pregnant as well, so he's suddenly having two, right at the same time. Then he leaves my mum while she's in hospital having me. He got into a scandal and he buggered off then. So, we moved back to London after that.

My mother initially started living with friends in the Euston area, in Robert Street, when we were very young, me and my two older brothers. It was right in front of this big housing estate and it was pretty rough round there. One time my brother was getting chased by a load of kids, because we were new in the neighbourhood. He went and hid in a big bin container under all this cardboard. One of the kids found him and started pissing on the cardboard. He's under there and there's all this piss coming down. So, it was pretty rough.

My brother had a friend and they both climbed up onto the slanted glass roof of Euston station. His mate was one of these crazy kids who was into daring. The glass gave in and my brother saw his mate fall to his death on the platform below. Nobody really asked him what happened and I don't think he said anything. He carried that around with him, that sort of traumatic experience.

I was pretty young then, and my grandmother gave my mother some money to buy a house in Chetwynd Road, near Highgate Road, quite close to Hampstead Heath. She thought the nature would be good for the kids. That's where I spent my youth, really.

Back in the seventies, I suppose there was much more equality in society, and there were beautiful houses that were not necessarily expensive. Kentish Town was totally different from now. It's really busy down there now, millions of parked cars. But then, it was quite spacious, and you'd get to know all the kids across the road. Everybody knew each other.

My mum was a teacher. Teaching difficult kids. She was stuck with three kids of her own, because my dad had fucked off, so she had to make ends meet. London County Council were offering reasonable pay and reasonable holidays and there was a push to get more teachers. I guess she wanted to teach art, because she'd always wanted to be an artist. She trained to do that, and then she turned out to be helping difficult kids, which is interesting, seeing as me and my mates all turned out to be difficult kids.

Primary school for me was Brookfield, near Highgate Cemetery. We had a very nice science teacher. She was somebody who seemed to really want to make it interesting, and she was interested in the kids. Thinking back now, I guess the kids responded to that and it was quite an enjoyable class. Whereas some of the teachers were just horrible and some were nutcases. One time this supply teacher was walking around with these high-heeled shoes on, and something happened that she didn't like. Everybody had to shut up and she was walking up and down with these shoes, *clack*, *clack*. Every now and then she would whack someone on the head. Even then, it became a big scandal. She was just completely barmy . . . and that's the fucking teacher . . .

CHRIS 'CHRISSY BOY' FOREMAN: All my life, from when I was born, I lived in this house on a street called Mortimer Terrace, NW5, near Highgate Road. A little cobbled street, and all these houses connected to a railway line. It wasn't council, it was owned by the railway. You would feel vibrations from goods trains. I lived in this bizarre house with my dad John and my mum Rita and my brother Nat. We had the basement, the ground floor and the first floor, and then there was two more floors with these spinster women, Freda and Doris, living above us. We didn't have a bathroom – we had a tin bath that we took down off the wall – and we all shared an outside toilet. On special occasions, I went to the public baths in Prince of Wales Road.

My mum was a housewife. My dad was a lecturer at the London College of Printing, but before that, he was a teacher. I once said to him, 'What do you think you are?' He said, 'A working-class intellectual,' which he sort of is. He was a folk singer, but not in the traditional sense. A lot of his songs were from music hall. One of them he sang was 'If It Wasn't For The 'Ouses In Between' by Gus Elen. It's really funny: about living in this house and the fantastic views it would have, if it wasn't for the houses in between. Y'know, 'Wiv a ladder and some glasses/You could see to Hackney Marshes/If it wasn't for the 'ouses in between'. He didn't sing 'My Old Man's a Dustman', but it was kind of songs that were like that. They were all very funny.

I used to go and see him in these folk clubs, or sometimes I'd probably have to go with him. He knew Ewan McColl and Ian Campbell and The Dubliners, who were a right laugh. To me, it wasn't like, 'This is fantastic.' But it was fun, those songs and everything. He played the guitar and he taught me 'Bobby Shafto's Gone to Sea', but I just wasn't interested. I wasn't really interested in playing a guitar.

My parents split up when I was 12 or whatever. I might have been older. The unusual thing was, my mum went and my brother and me stayed with my dad. I wanted to know why, and I never found out. Still, to this day, I don't know the actual reason why she left. She went and lived with some guy for forty-something years. The sad thing was that before my mum left, my dad used to walk down the road, whistling. Then when they split up, he didn't. But, after some time, I heard him whistling again and thought, 'He's gonna be OK.'

I was at Gospel Oak Primary School. I did really well in the 11-plus and they said I could go to any school I wanted. We looked at William Ellis, which was a grammar school, which I could have walked to. We went to Acland Burghley, which was a comprehensive, which I really liked, because there was no uniform. That's far and away where I should have gone. But then we looked at Dame Alice Owen's which was this fusty old school in Islington, where some of the teachers wore bloody gowns and all that. My mum had gone there when she was a kid, so I went there, and it was terrible, because it took me ages to get there on the bus.

Some of the teachers were kind of mental. We had this one teacher called Mr Copping, and he was just unbelievable. He would read the register, and he'd go, 'Bligh . . . Irish git,' and say all these things under his voice. 'Briggs . . . little queer.' We used to laugh our heads off. At some point, he was our form master and he took maths, but he just never used to teach us anything. We used to do all these things like turn all the desks round the other way or turn all the pictures around. I was a bit of a tear-away, and not that interested in getting educated. At home with my poor old dad, I had carte blanche to sneak out of the window and do whatever I wanted.

*

CATHAL 'CHAS SMASH' SMYTH: In 1970, I was 11. We lived in Muswell Hill on Windermere Road. Dad was a procurement engineer in petrochemicals, so he worked abroad a lot: Africa, the Middle East, Europe. Sometimes we'd join him. The rest of the time, Mum was left to cope with me and my younger brother Brendan. Dad would send money home, but I get the feeling it was never enough. He liked a drink and a gamble, which was the cause of a lot of the arguments between him and Mum. He could be gnarly after a night's drinking. We had the bailiffs round a couple of times when Dad was away and Granny bailed us out.

By '70, we'd lived in three places in Ireland, and in Baghdad. Which meant I was either leaving a school, starting a new one or not going at all. I was a shy, introverted kid and all this new school, new boy, new face, fitting-in malarkey was stressful. We never seemed to stay anywhere for any length of time.

Mum took me to an interview at this school in Finchley. The headmaster, Mr Coughlan, quizzed me, which was OK, until he got to maths. I couldn't get anything right. Not a fucking clue. 'No problem,' says Mr Coughlan. 'We'll work on that.' I figured there was no way I was getting into this place, but it turned out it was a fee-paying school, and once Mum said she could pay, it was a done deal. The headmaster then whipped out a form, which Mum had to sign, that allowed any form of punishment the school fancied doling out.

It was a Catholic boys' school and it was strict. A lot of the teachers were definitely not the full shilling. Punishments were varied, physical and brutal. You'd be dead-legged, whacked over the arse with a leather strap, punched, grabbed by your cheek, made to kneel in the corner of the class or be boxed round the ears.

Between lessons we had to sit at our desks in silence waiting for the teacher to arrive. You walked to lessons in silence. School caps had to be worn at all times to and from school. Hair cut two inches above the collar. We each had our rule book. Detentions and caning for any offence were standard.

My first day there was a disaster. Mum hadn't bought me long trousers – being summer she tried to convince me that everyone would be wearing shorts. They weren't. I spent the day being wolf whistled at. I felt a right fucking plum. To get home, you had to walk through a park to the bus stop. Passing by the pond that first day, I got pushed into it. I sat on the top deck of the bus going home, sodden wet, squelching and dripping water. I hated school.

By the time I'd learned everyone's names we were on the move again – that year it was Coleraine in Northern Ireland. 1970 was not a great year to have an English accent in Northern Ireland. It was in the midst of The Troubles. On shopping trips, you'd walk past soldiers with rifles at check points, or you'd be passing through sand bags and barbed wire just to get into Woolworths. It was weird: the same shops as in London, but like being under occupation. Paramilitary graffiti on houses and walls.

I suppose I must have had some good times there, but if I did, I can't remember any. I joined in a game of soccer once and quickly became the football. In cookery class, I got a pan of water poured over me. The nun said, 'Smyth, what are you doing?' I said, 'I had an accident, sister.' I couldn't grass or I'd have gotten worse.

After about a month of being bullied, I told Dad what was happening. He just said, 'Fuck 'em, stay home.' The year before, my mum had given birth to twins: my brother Dermot and sister Bernadette. So, I stayed home and helped Mum with the twins.

Northern Ireland was a far cry from Iraq. We'd lived in Baghdad in '68, which was beautiful. At night, on the banks of the Tigris, you'd see fires where fishermen would be cooking their catch. You'd hear the call-to-prayer every morning, which I loved. But, for some reason I never understood, we didn't go to school. We spent most of our time in the Al-Alwiyah social club, an old colonial throwback. In the mornings, I'd go with Dad down to the bazaar to get baguettes and chapattis. It was our morning routine. I loved the bazaar. A cacophony of tinny radios blaring out Arabic music; stalls selling carpets, jewellery, copper pots, herbs, dates, pistachios, fridges and second-hand bicycles. Dad was working there constructing a chemical plant in Hillah. Years later, just before the Iraq War, it was in the news and identified as a suspected location of weapons of mass destruction.

Dad had a driver, Tamoor, and we had a nanny, Hannah. She snuck me off once – I'm sure Mum didn't know – and took me through a warren of back streets into this small temple. It was empty, except for this old man in a robe sitting there, looking a lot like Mahatma Gandhi. A holy man, I suppose. He beckoned me forward. Hannah let go of my hand and I went up to him. He gave me a gentle hug, placed his hand on my head. I'm not sure what he said to me, but I suppose it was a blessing. Odd, but it felt OK.

While these lazy days at the Al-Alwiyah club sound idyllic – nothing but swimming and ordering cold drinks – there weren't any other kids around. Just me and my brother. Dad would stock up at home with crates of 7-Up and orange Fanta. I did a lot of sitting on the balcony munching bread, drinking pop and day-dreaming, looking out over the city.

\*

GRAHAM 'SUGGS' McPHERSON: I was in Wales in 1970. We were in a small village called Port Lion which was really out of the way in Pembrokeshire. I was amongst kids who lived on farms. Coming from London and the urban environment I'd lived in most of my life, to be out in these fields, it was really a very extraordinary experience.

The background is that my mum couldn't really cope at that time. I'd started bunking off school, even at the age of six, seven, and my mum was just having a hard time herself. She worked in bars and sang. She was a great singer, and I know that for her, the main burden of her life was she had a really fucking good voice. She did very little recording, she just sang in bars. But for me as a kid, it was an embarrassment to hear my mum getting up and singing: 'Here we go, we're going to be stuck in this pub for another fucking three-and-a-half hours.'

We moved around, so there was a bit of Liverpool, bit of Manchester. My mum sang in the Blue Angel in Liverpool and The Beatles used to come in there. My mum said that she met this young girl called Priscilla White who was looking for a gig, and my mum said, 'Take my spot.' Apparently, there was somebody in there that night who spotted Cilla Black, and my mum missed out. But it was the story of my mum's singing career that these moments happened.

The big epochal moment for my mum was that she got offered a residency in a club in Paris. Somebody came to see her in the Blue Angel, and that's why she came down to London. But you couldn't have your passport until you were 21, and her father said she couldn't go to Paris. That really became the kind of burden that she carried for the rest of her life, I think. I don't doubt there were moments where she begrudged having me at this point.

In London, we were staying in people's flats, moving a lot. I remember probably four or five different places where we were living, mostly around Fulham, which is why I'm a Chelsea fan. Looking back, one house, it was a whorehouse, in Putney. There were, like, six rooms, and in every room, there were different girls, and there was always different blokes coming and going. I just assumed that was a normal part of life. Not for a second that I'm suggesting my mum was involved in that. But I think we were just living in very disparate places, anywhere she could get. So, for this kid to be running around, someone must have alerted the authorities to that.

The social services were getting involved in my life, and when I look back, there were some obvious choices. I was going to be taken into care, basically, or I could go and live with my Aunt Diana in Wales. My auntie became my mum for a few years. We used to go to hers for Christmas and summer holidays, so I knew the place. My cousins were like brothers and sisters to me. Then just one summer holiday, my mum didn't come back to get me. That particular summer holiday lasted for three years . . .

I was eight when I went to Wales, which was '69, so '70 I'm still there. Hay bales, swimming in the river, apple scrumping, torchlight processions, shooting rats with air rifles, riding and falling off horses. A really pure kind of country existence. You're just out all day, and expected to be out all day, no matter what weather. We were just all pretty poor kids, living in a very rural environment.

My Scottish surname didn't really occur to me until much later on, because my dad just wasn't around. He was a heroin addict and he ended up in Tooting Bec Asylum. My mum tried to help him a few times and couldn't, and he came and went a bit. She never really had a settled relationship after that. She was always just with this feller or that feller or Uncle Tommy or whoever.

She sang jazz, the old standards, 'Summertime' and all that sort of stuff, in various pubs and clubs in Soho. All those old maudlin sentimental crying-in-your beer things. 'Summerrrttiiiime, and the living is easy . . .' It was all of a bit of a mystery to me really. You just take it all in when you're a kid. You don't really see whether it's sad or happy. I think innately I knew that there was some kind of sadness in there. People drinking and singing their sorrows away. Some drink to remember, some drink to forget. But mostly you'd be hoping that someone would give you two bob and a pat on the head and a packet of crisps.

**MARK 'BEDDERS' BEDFORD:** In 1970, I was nine. Living in Archway in part of a maisonette, with my mum and dad. In the summer, you'd be up really early, and you just literally went out onto the street. All the kids did the same, and we'd play football or cricket. It was amazing, the amount of freedom we had, actually. It was down to the older kids to look after the younger kids. I have memories of the streets being very empty. Maybe just one or two cars in a street.

My dad was in the print. He worked in Fleet Street, on the machines, in the warehouses there. My whole family on my dad's side worked in the print, because it was unionised, so the union card went through the family. My grandad worked at the *News of the World* on Bouverie Street for about forty years or so. My uncle worked on the *Evening Standard* and the *Evening News*. He was mainly driving, delivering a lot of the papers.

I was taken as a kid sometimes, down to Fleet Street. It was a big treat on a Saturday night to be taken down there while the presses were running, which was really exciting. And they had wild times there. Because it was a place where there was a lot of casual labour, you got all sorts of people working there. My dad said that there used to be fights some nights, because people would turn up to work rolling drunk. People would gamble their money away. There'd be cards going on and there'd be punch-ups over losing money.

My dad was quite friendly with a comedy and music group called The Alberts, who knew The Goons. They were actors and comedians, but to make a few extra quid they did the newspapers on a Saturday night. Some of them used to turn up straight from the theatre. One night, my dad came into the locker room, and lying out on the bench was one of The Alberts, dressed as a sailor. He'd obviously been in some *Mutiny on the Bounty* production and he hadn't bothered to change. Another night, one of them insisted on driving the vans to and from the stations dressed as a Canadian Mountie, because again, he was working on a film or something, and hadn't changed out of his costume.

That really sunk into me as a kid. My grandad had a fantastic sense of humour, and so did my dad, and that shaped me very early on. My upbringing wasn't bohemian or anything like that, but it was full of characters and slightly different. My mum worked in a school, as a teaching assistant, for years. But my dad didn't go and work in a bank every day and then come home at five o'clock.

I was always interested in art and design, and that came from my parents. From when I was really young, my dad did oil paintings. My mum still makes stuff. They came from a working-class background, but they had those other interests. It obviously rubbed off on me. I thought, 'It's a good thing to be a painter or an actor or a *something*.' Something to – without being clichéd – get me out of where I was and see the wider world. I really felt that. I had that real desire.

DANIEL 'WOODY' WOODGATE: I was living just around the corner from Camden Square in 1970, in Stratford Villas, with my brother and my dad and his girlfriend, Annie Catford. Annie was one of our many au pair girls, then overnight she ended up with my dad. She was lovely . . . like a big sister to us.

We'd moved in there, my brother Nick and I, with my dad and his second wife, Celia Haddon, who's a journalist. My dad was a photographer and worked for all the newspapers in the sixties and that's how they met. She had some money, so she helped buy this huge great rambling house in Stratford Villas, and that's where we grew up. But, by 1970, my dad had divorced her and was living with Annie.

I still have dreams today of running all the way from the top of the house down to the bottom or sliding on the bannister. That's what we did most of the time – slide down the bannister and charge around and wreck the place. Dig up the garden and smash windows with footballs.

If it wasn't for Billy Butlin, I wouldn't have been born. Both my mum and my dad went to RADA. Cherry Butlin was in my mum's year, and she was having a 21st birthday party in a Mayfair flat owned by her dad, Billy Butlin. My dad came along, because he'd been in RADA a couple of years before. He was a bit older than my mum, and he went to RADA with all these incredible actors – Roy Kinnear, Richard Briers, Albert Finney, John Hurt.

So, that was my parents' little world. They went to the party, met, eventually got married, and then Nick and I came along when they were living in Randolph Avenue in Maida Vale. The marriage was really rocky, because my dad was always going away and photographing Twiggy and Joanna Lumley and all these other famous people, and he had flings with models and it was all a bit messy. Me and my brother were kind of torn between lots of arguments. My dad would disappear and then he'd come back, and then my mum would disappear and come back. They divorced when I was about three or four years old.

Out of the settlement came a really weird decision, which was that we were going to go and live with our dad. Because our mum was an actress, she was often in rep, so she would tour the country. I think the arrangement enabled my mum to go and do her thing, while my dad could go and do his thing, as long as we were looked after by nannies. My mum left; she didn't get custody of us. She was a weekend mum. My dad had met Celia Haddon by the mid-sixties, and they bought the house in Camden. But in the meantime, we still went to our little school, Robinsfield, in St John's Wood. In those days, there was no traffic, so it was a ten-minute drive.

My dad was a lovely, lovely, gentle man. But he did like to socialise, and we didn't know what state he'd come home in. We had all kinds of people from the showbiz world round our house – Eric Idle, Peter Cook, Spike Milligan. I'm sure Benny Hill came round to our house to have his picture taken. Everyone came round to be photographed.

On the weekend, Dad used to take us to have a kick around with a football in the park with him. He always used to do Sunday lunches. Those times he was like a proper dad and he was just amazing to me. But he had another side to him when he drank . . . dark, broody. He used to tell people exactly what he thought of them, as well, which used to get him into all kinds of trouble. Sometimes he'd come back a little worse for wear because someone had punched him. He'd be shouting at the au pair girls, and we'd be up in bed, going, 'Oh, fucking hell.' It was that feeling of waiting for him to come home and not knowing what he was going to be like, because he was a Jekyll and Hyde character. Never violent to us. Never, never in a million years. He was a beautiful man, but he had a terrible drink problem. So, it was difficult. It was always a bit tough.

When I was only a little tiddler, I had really long hair, but I loved the skinhead fashions, so I got myself a pair of Levi's Sta-Prest. But my shoes were just kiddie-style Wayfinders with a little compass in the bottom. A Ben Sherman, some braces and long hair. Back then you could really mix it up. As a kid it was just mad, very eclectic. That was the exciting and wonderful thing.

## CHAPTER 2

# OH, WHAT FUN WE HAD

**SUGGS**: When I got back to London, I was put in Quintin Kynaston comprehensive, off Finchley Road. Halfway through the first term, and it was mainly second-generation Irish or West Indian kids there. I was an ethnic minority, having a Scottish name ... The one feller who my mum settled with was Peter Chalk, whose son Andrew – Chalky – became my best friend when I got back from Wales.

Years later, when I wrote 'Baggy Trousers', I was thinking about my time at Quintin Kynaston and them Oxford bags that came out in the early seventies. The six-button waistbands and the platform boots and all that. People thought I was writing about Dickens or something.

The world of the grammar schools crashed headlong into the secondary moderns. It was one of the early comprehensives and they still had the kind of disciplinarian grammar school teachers in the tweed jackets. Then there was this sort of free-form hippie mob. It was the beginning of all that 'no competitive sport in the playground' kind of thing. We weren't even playing football. It was bizarre.

WOODY: I went to Haverstock School, close to Chalk Farm underground station. I suppose I came from a middle-class family, well-to-do in the sense that my dad had a big house in Camden. I wanted for nothing. I was classed as being intelligent, to a degree. I wasn't struggling necessarily, everything was going fine, and I should have really gone to Hampstead School over in Cricklewood.

That's where I wanted to go. But I was rejected on the grounds that the government had brought in a policy of getting more, let's say, upwardly-mobile family types into rough schools, to balance it out. So, I arrived at Haverstock, where the woodwork teacher had been stabbed the year before with a chisel by one of the students. You went to the toilets and people would go, 'Oi, mate, you got a fag? You got a snout?' and you'd go, 'Snout, what the hell's a snout?' 'Rainbow, mate, rainbow trout, snout? Oily rag, fag? C'mon, where have you been?'

It was really intimidating. You heard all these stories about people having their heads put down the toilet. It was really specific groups or cliques and they were divided ethnically. Everyone got on well, but when playtime came, everyone went in their gangs. You had large sections of the Chinese kids, the Asian kids, the Greek kids, the black kids. The black kids were so cool, because they had really big Afros and the combs and stuff, and they all looked like they were out of the Jackson 5. I knew someone from every single group, and they were just the best mates. I loved them all.

I smoked, so I was often round the bogs playing 'Penny up the Wall'. There was this bloke who used to appear in school occasionally. I'd seen him on top of the roof of a shed, bunking off. He had a sheepskin jacket and Doc Martens on, his trousers rolled up, and he looked like a cool character. I liked him, but I didn't often see him. That was Lee.

CATHAL: There were bomb sites dotted around London, and other places that were just rundown. We could run riot around by the Thames – the empty warehouses, Jamaica Street, all round that area. There was loads of just fucking around.

My memories are of Ford Anglias, and the roads being pretty empty. It was closer to the post-war era than it was to modern day. There was a quaintness, a quality of Englishness that's faded: Taffy, our whistling milkman, and the Esso Blue truck that came round with paraffin for heaters. We used lollipop sticks to scoop coins out of phone-box slots. My cousin Neil used to come to ours for tea and he was a skinhead – wore a Crombie with a silk kerchief in the top pocket, had all the proper gear. I really looked up to him.

In '72 we moved to Iran, to Bandar-e Mahshahr, an oil city on the Gulf. I went to an American school, but I knew nothing about Venn diagrams, the Battle of Bunker Hill, the Gettysburg Address. The teacher was a gentle, hippy type who kind of gave up on me, so I pretty much occupied myself reading. Our class was eighth grade – mostly girls, real beauties. We'd hang out listening to records: Cat Stevens, Elton John, the Carpenters, Paul Simon.

One day, I convinced one of my classmates, Mary Baker, that I knew how to ride a moped. So, she lent me her Peugeot. I fucked up completely – accelerated instead of braking – and me and the Peugeot ended up in an open drain. I caught typhoid, had a really high fever. Mum got our priest Father Mulligan to give me a blessing. Being delirious, I thought I was getting the last rites. Still, the injections the nurses gave me in my bum did the job.

I had a crush on my Farsi teacher. She looked like Sophia Loren, had fabulous green eyes. I can still remember every word of the Farsi song she taught us.

MARK: I got the grades and so I did the interview at William Ellis School in Highgate. It was very, very traditional. It probably hadn't changed since the thirties. It was all wood panelling and you waited outside the headmaster's study to be interviewed. Then you got shown in, and there was three chairs: one in front of the headmaster's desk, where you sat on your own; two for your parents, who sat behind you. Kind of intimidating, straight away. The headmaster sat behind a very large desk, a gown on, very learned. I found out later, when I went there, that he was actually quite a nice man, but he was very gruff. Mr Baxter. Sydney Baxter, so we called him Syd, always.

The interview went well, and I told him that I was going to be an airline pilot. I don't know why, but I just did on the spot. Then I think the clincher was that I told him I made aeroplane models. I was always interested in painting stuff and whatever. So, I think that connection somehow might have got me the gig.

It was run like a minor public school, even though it was a grammar school. Boys only and you had a very smart uniform that you had to wear all the time. I did Latin for three years – totally no use to anyone at all, whatsoever. But they had very good art classes. They turned their noses up a little bit about art, because they wanted to send kids to university. But I always wanted to go to art college.

The older teachers were very traditional. But then there were the younger teachers, who had come through the sixties, and, of course, all the teaching methods were changing. There was a lot more liberal teaching. A lot more fun, a lot looser. It was that kind of thing, where the older teachers might care about punctuation and stuff a hell of a lot. But these younger teachers didn't: 'Don't bother with punctuation. Forget it. It's some bourgeois fucking construct. Write down what you feel.' A real changing of the guard was going on.

There were some interesting alumni: Richard Thompson from Fairport Convention went there, and he taught the guitar to Hugh Cornwell from The Stranglers, who also went there. One of the older boys there was Max Bell, who went on to write for the *NME*. He looked like Bowie at the time, had the spiky Ziggy Stardust hair. So, he was really striking. Our future producer Clive Langer went there too, and our onetime drummer, Gary Dovey, and John Hasler, who would end up being the tie between us all.

The song I later wrote, 'Mummy's Boy', that ended up on the first album, was about a teacher at my school, who freely admitted that he still lived with his mum and dad. He was definitely in his thirties, forties at the time. He was a bit of an odd character, generally. He'd do really quite wicked, cruel things, to punish us. At that point, they could get away with literally hurling a blackboard rubber at people's heads. Teachers would throw stuff at you and you had to be really quick and get out of the way. We had another teacher who used to just give kids dead legs. If he didn't like what you were doing, he'd come up behind you – bang, dead leg – and you'd be limping. It was mental.

*

CHRIS: English was the only O level I passed, I think. See, the one thing about me that was a bit kind of smug was the teacher could go, 'Right, we're all going to read *1984*,' and I'd go, 'But I've already read it.' Because of my dad, y'know. From when I was a kid at primary school at Gospel Oak, I had a really good reading age.

For me, secondary school wasn't all bad. Me and my mates had a scam going on there for a while. Round the back of some of the classrooms, you could get out and there was the backs of some houses. One of them turned out to be the house that belonged to this couple, Fred and Olive, who owned a shop out front. They were a right pair of curmudgeons: 'Only two schoolchildren at a time.' Poor old Freddie had this funny wig.

Behind their house there was all these empty Coca-Cola bottles. In those days, you paid a deposit on a Coca-Cola bottle and you took them back to the shop. What we did was, we took the bottles from the back – can you see what we're doing here? – and went round to the front and got all the money back. Eventually, we got caught. They found dozens of flipping Coca-Cola bottles in our lockers. But, it's kind of what you call recycling these days, isn't it?

CATHAL: When we got back from Iran, I went back to my old school in Finchley and ended up in the same class. I got lots of hoots and cheers when I walked back in. I don't think they'd expected to ever see me again. There was one kid who took against me, Phillip. His dad was the head chef at a famous restaurant. Anyway, he was a lump and he went for me. Dad had bought me this book on karate by Bruce Tegner, which I still have to this day. I'd picked up a few moves from it and I suppose

I'd had enough of being bullied, so I side-kicked this kid in the solar plexus. I was quite surprised – probably more than he was – 'cause I decked him. So, I realised that if you acted a bit nutty, then people would fear you and give you a wide berth. Looking back though, I kind of regret it, 'cause you have to be careful what you pretend to be, or you might end up becoming it.

SUGGS: In London, there were fallen-down buildings everywhere. I suppose some of it was post-war. At the weekend, in the City, everything was shut, quiet and closed. If you went up towards Holborn, it was dead. Just fucking dead. There was this place called Gamages there, which had been a big department store. We used to mess around in these old buildings. There was always some old porno mags spread about on the floor. 'Whoa, watch out, there's a fucking hole in the floor . . .'

London was great in those days. Walking down Parkway in Camden Town and there's only three cars and they're all Austin Morrises. Empty buildings and bomb sites. You went down the bomb site. It was just an empty bit of ground with a hole in it and a big puddle at the bottom. A few prams and maybe a broken-down car. They were like the adventure playgrounds of my youth. All around north London, they were everywhere.

MARK: You could get a Red Rover ticket in London at the time for almost no money at all, and it gave you unlimited travel on the buses and tubes for a day. That was what we all did as kids, as teenagers. I spent so much time on buses in London in my early teens, just going around on my own quite a lot – visiting Trafalgar Square or visiting the Thames, and just walking round bits of London. That was imprinted, I think, on a lot of us: the sights and sounds of London. It's no surprise that they fed their way into the songs.

LEE: I had my paper round, had my little milk round. I'd always take along one of those little solid-state radios. I had to have my music with me. I don't know why, because it wasn't a big thing in the house. All you'd see on the TV really was *Top of the Pops* now and again, if I was in. But I was always out. I was always over Hampstead Heath, up to no good. I was out as much as possible. One of the first DJs I was into was Tony Blackburn on Radio 1. He was on 7am till 9am, which was perfect for my paper round. I'd have my one earpiece thing in, hearing things like 'The Tears of a Clown', 'Neanderthal Man' by Hotlegs, and of course 'Lola' by The Kinks, which was a massive inspiration. I didn't know what it was about at the time but I was just attracted to it.

CATHAL: Dad would listen to Terry Wogan on Radio 2 in the morning, as he made breakfast. He thought Terry Wogan was hilarious. I used to get *Disco 45* magazine, for the lyrics. I loved Marc Bolan, Bowie, Slade. Dad had a cassette collection, a mixture of Irish and country and western – The Clancy Brothers, Johnny McEvoy, The Dubliners, Johnny Cash, Charlie Pride, Dolly Parton, Loretta Lynn. I was into Johnny Cash big time, loved his voice.

Up on Muswell Hill Broadway was Harum record shop. In there, they had a line of booths that you stood in and listened to the latest singles. The first album I bought was T Rex's *Bolan Boogie*.

There was a youth club behind the ABC cinema in Muswell Hill where I first heard 'One Step Beyond' and 'Al Capone'. Then, at the weekend, it was Ally Pally for roller skating. Hearing the music so loud was great – 'School's Out', 'Jeepster', 'Brand New

Key'. Everyone would stamp their skates in unison to the drums in 'Jeepster' as we went round the rink. White Ben Sherman or Brutus button-down shirts were all the go. You had to make sure the pleat on the back of your shirt was ironed crisply.

**WOODY:** There were always Beatles singles in my mum's house. She had a big collection of them. But there were all kinds of artists, like Led Zeppelin. 'Whole Lotta Love' absolutely blew me away. So did 'Hey Joe' by Jimi Hendrix. My brother Nick started playing guitar and he picked stuff up so quickly. At ten, he was playing just brilliantly. He started to copy Eric Clapton, and do David Bowie songs, playing 'Starman' at the school concert.

**SUGGS:** I stole a couple of records. I stole *Imagine* by John Lennon out of Rock On in Camden Town. Imagine no possessions . . .

**CHRIS:** I used to hang around with these kids that were older than me, and they were sort of skinheads. We used to go to this place in Barnet where they had dances, and they'd play 'Al Capone' by Prince Buster and stuff like that. I sort of was a skinhead. At one point, I had a little suit and a little crappy imitation pink gingham Ben Sherman.

I witnessed some incredible music things growing up in London, though. I used to go to Parliament Hill and there was this little bandstand there, and one day in 1969 Pink Floyd were on. I've never witnessed anything so loud. Then, a couple of months later, I'm on my bike in Hyde Park with my mates. I thought, 'What's that noise?' The Rolling Stones.

Island Records used to do these sampler albums that would cost, like, 50p, and they would have all these Island acts on them.

I got one that had Mott the Hoople on. Maybe that's why I've got such varied taste. But then the first time I actually had some money, I went and bought Alice Cooper's *School's Out* album. The cover was a classroom desk and you lifted it up and the album was there, wrapped in a pair of paper panties.

I had a lot of singles. There was this brand of hair spray, and if you bought a can of it, you got a little voucher in the lid, and you could send off and get a single. We were in Boots and everywhere, nicking all these vouchers. Free singles would just come through the post.

MIKE: You could get a free Top 10 single, so we used to go in the chemist and open all the lids and take all the coupons out. I got 'Automatically Sunshine' by The Supremes, I think, and maybe 'Doobedood'ndoobe, Doobedood'ndoobe, Doobedood'ndoo' by Diana Ross. So, you'd have this little coupon and you'd wait till it got in the Top 10, whatever you wanted to get, and then you could order it.

MARK: A massive album for me at the time was Neil Young, *After the Goldrush*. It's a brilliant, brilliant record. At that age, I was so struck by its bleakness, almost. Or its beauty and its sort of fragility. So, there was all those different elements. But music was a monolithic culture in that period. Everyone saw *Top of the Pops*, so the next morning, you came into school, and you'd go, 'Did you see *Top of the Pops* last night?', and everyone went, 'Yeah, wasn't it brilliant?' You had that one side of you that loved The Sweet and Slade and Mott the Hoople. But then you also liked the more serious artists.

*

MIKE: I followed my brothers to Hampstead School in Crickle-wood, which was a bit of a crappy school, I guess. Everybody else at my primary, Brookfield, went to another school. They went to Acland Burghley, which funnily enough turned out to be a much better school, and that was in Tufnell Park, which was supposedly much more working-class. From Chetwynd Road in north Kentish Town, it was a bit of a hike to Hampstead School. I used to walk down to the train station, get the train to school, walk up the hill. But it was a bit of a walk.

It's funny with songs and memories. I mean, when I think of that song '(If Paradise Is) Half As Nice' by Amen Corner, there's this one moment when I was coming home out of Hampstead School, down Westbere Road. There was this little pathway just by a railway. These little stairways going up to get to the road. If I hear that song now, I'm suddenly back in that one spot.

I was listening to a lot of different stuff in the early seventies. Lindisfarne, Stevie Wonder. I mean, Elton John when he first came out was pretty cool: that cowboy album he had, *Tumbleweed Connection*. The Carole King album *Tapestry* was a big hit. I'd be going to parties at school and they were playing that, and reggae. Those *Tighten Up* compilation albums, particularly. Then, other things like 'Black and White' by Greyhound. Those hits were happening. And Motown was always there. Motown parties at school. There'd be a blackboard advertising the Tamla Motown party at lunch.

I've got a memory of being in the kitchen at home and listening on this little transistor radio to Radio Luxembourg. That song 'Sebastian' by Steve Harley was playing from across the North Sea, or wherever it was coming from, and it was coming and going, and sounding very sort of exotic.

Back in the sixties, one of the first records my brother bought was 'Little Red Rooster' by The Rolling Stones. He came home with that single and it was all totally exciting. I wasn't mad on it, I must say, at that time: but he was mad on it, and that was the thing. Suddenly he comes in with this new record, and it's a big stir in the house: 'Ben's got a new record.' You'd be well aware of it, and when he was out, you'd listen to his stuff.

Then my brother bought *Sgt. Pepper* . . . , and we were all sitting in the front room, playing it over and over and reading all the lyrics. It was great fun. Even now, when I start thinking about it, it's all connected to my youth, and it really touches you. And that's music. Music doesn't work with, like, the thinking mind. It works maybe more on an emotional level. So that it gets right, deep inside of you.

CHRIS: My dad knew Mike's mum, who's a very nice woman. She's quite left-wing, and my dad was probably in the Communist Party, and so they knew each other. Mike lived close by and he came round once with his older brother, Danny. I'm two years older than Mike, so I would've been about twelve and he would've been maybe ten. So I only really spoke to Danny.

MIKE: A lot of my mum's friends were socialists. There was quite a lot of socialism going around. It was all still coming from after the war, I guess. The Second World War confronted people with a lot of suffering, and it brought them together, and then they wanted to build something together, I think. Chris's dad was like that, so my mum knew him to some degree.

Older kids like Chris were definitely different, and he was halfway into a slightly older crowd than him. He was a bit of a 'wise', to some extent, in those days. Round his house, there'd be loads of records. Listening to records was a big thing back then. It was a big drawing factor for all of us. We used to hang out, sit in people's bedrooms. The old record player would be there, and we'd be listening to music and talking and stuff.

CHRIS: I used to hang around with these kids who were older than me who lived in Highgate. They were in a kind of yobby gang called the Highgate Hammers. We'd go up to the skinhead disco in Barnet. One time when we were coming back on the Tube, the police got on the train. Kids had undone the bloody handles to hit people with and so the coppers were going through the train, looking for offensive weapons. At that time, train guards used to have a seat that popped out for them. So, I thought, 'I'm going to sit here.' I popped this seat out and, Christ almighty, all these knives and things fell out on the floor.

After that I started moving away from these older kids, to – strangely – hang around with these younger kids like Mike and Lee. I might have had a bit of a reputation. I was quite unusual, with long hair, and an orange Chopper bike. Mike lived round the corner. So, us becoming mates was all about geography, really.

MIKE: I met Lee through my brother Dan. Somehow, he had a connection with him. But I guess we were all just living very close. Chris was living over there, Lee's living over here. I guess I knew all the local kids in those days. Some of them you resonate with more than others.

The funny thing was my brothers were hanging around with hippies, and I suppose 'hippies' relates to the sort of middle class, to an extent. But I was always hanging around with all these working-class yobs from the neighbourhood, for some reason or other, like Mr Lee Thompson. All my friends were those types, with Dr Martens. Getting into trouble and police arriving every five minutes.

Lee was always stealing. Always going a bridge further. I was always a bit like, 'OK, I've got this far . . . this is OK . . . this is good.' Then he would do something else, and I'd try to come to terms with that. Then he would do something else. So, I guess he was bringing a bit of excitement and I was all sort of Taurus: wanting to keep things on the ground and he would always be throwing in curved balls. We got in quite a fair amount of trouble.

At Hampstead School, I used to like art. I was always interested in drawing . . . from my mum, I suppose. Lee's dad was a burglar, so he was interested in burgling. My mum was an aspiring artist, so I was interested in art. Ever predictable.

LEE: Mike went to Brookfield primary school, same as me. I vaguely remember him, because he seemed about seven-foot tall, and just a little bit arty and different. He had two brothers and his mum brought them up to be very well-to-do, and I fucked all that up.

I wasn't welcome round Mike's house, because of his mum. I'd be whistling outside his window, and the bugger's still in bed. Always hanging about for him. Chrissy Boy was pretty punctual – I'd give it just a quick, loud whistle. He'd recognise that, open the window. Two minutes, then off we'd go, on our adventures.

CHRIS: Thommo used to come along and whistle and you'd see him standing below the lamp post. My dad always said he was a good friend, really, because he'd been kind of forbidden, but he still wanted to be our friend. I mean, Lee was hilarious. He used to ring up from telephone boxes. You could ring someone up and when they picked up the phone, you had to put the money in. But you had a few seconds, so with Thommo, you'd get a phone call, and he'd quickly say, 'I'matthebusstop!' and then the old pips would go. Lee and I were extremely close. Together all the time, doing lots of stuff together, just the two of us. We'd be waiting for Barso, 'cause he'd always be late. But then we'd just go and hang around together all day.

**LEE:** I suppose I was a real threat to their parents. Every mother's nightmare type thing. That was why I was forever whistling. Although Chrissy Boy's old man, he did have a bit of a soft spot for me. Still, he didn't want me around Chris and Mike's mum didn't want me around Mike. Fucking up their future.

## CHAPTER 3

# ALDENHAM GLAMOUR
# BOYS

**LEE:** We used to meet in a launderette in Highgate Road. It was warm, and you'd get your washing done at the same time. Plus, you could get a few quid out of the drying machine.

**CHRIS:** They had a timer lock thing on the door of this place so that it would lock at a certain time. We fiddled with this thing, so it wouldn't lock. We used to go in there, sit around, and rob all the machines. With the tumble dryer, you put some money in and it went down into this V-shaped metal thing and then into a box. We realised – because it was loose – that you could open the bit where the money went in, put a bit of cardboard in, and then you'd just come back at the end of the day and collect all the money. One day, I was sitting there, and I thought, 'You know what? That soap machine's just itching to be broken into.' I went and got a screwdriver and opened it up, got a sock and it ended up just filled with flipping 2ps. I said to my long-suffering little brother Nat, 'Go in the paper shop and say, "I've been saving all these up."' It's terrible really, because if anyone had put literally put 2p and 2p together . . .

LEE: You'd put your hand into the money box of the drying machine and just scoop up 5ps. Go and get yourself a Mars Bar or a bag of chips. So that was our meeting place.

MIKE: Yeah, it was warm, I guess, and somewhere to sit. Otherwise, a lot of the time, we were just standing on the street, hanging out, talking and stuff. We used to be in there all the time.

CHRIS: From the age of about twelve, I never paid to get in the cinema. We used to bunk into the Hampstead Classic or the Odeon up near Archway. Everybody went to see *A Clockwork Orange* when it came out in '71. Brilliant film. There was the ultra-violence, but it was really stylish. That same year, we went to see the re-release of *Dumbo* as well. *Dumbo*'s a fantastic film. I think we went to see that about three times.

One time at the cinema in Golders Green, Thommo climbed up a drainpipe, *whoosh*, like Spider-Man. We were waiting for him to get in and let us in. The back door opened and these two security guys came out: 'Hello, alright?' Thommo's up there, twenty foot above them. He had his jumper tied round his waist, and his jumper fell off. So, it kind of distracted them, and we all legged it.

We used to go around to the fire escape at the back of the Hampstead Classic, 'cause the door was a bit iffy. Then one day, they fixed that door. So, we worked out how to get onto the roof. It was really high. You went up and then you slid down the other side, and it was terrifying. Then you'd jump down into the women's toilets. One time I'm doing that, and there's all these flipping do-gooders in the pub below who must have seen us. So, we get in and the Old Bill are waiting for us, in the women's toilets. They went 'N&A.' 'What?' 'Names and addresses.' So, they put us in cubicles, but we could hear each other. Thommo was like, 'I'm Andy Mackay,' and they were going to me, 'What's your mate called?' 'Oh, he's Andy Mackay.' I said something similar to my name: 'Christopher Fordham.' But Thommo . . . I mean, Andy Mackay . . . the sax player in Roxy Music. The coppers took us to see the manager and, pretending to be really upset, I was going, 'Does this mean we can't come any more?'

CATHAL: I tried to get in to see *A Clockwork Orange* at the old Gaumont cinema in North Finchley. We'd moved there from Muswell Hill and it was that place I was thinking about when I wrote the lyrics to 'Our House' years later. 'Father wears his Sunday best.' That had two meanings, really. Dad spent most of his life in a suit. He was very much an office worker and he looked great in a suit. He was a right dandy as a young man. But it also made me think of *Love on the Dole*, because in the book they're always going to 'Uncle's' – as my dad used to call the pawnbroker – with their best suit on the Monday.

The funny thing is that whilst we travelled a lot, we still had a very earthy side to us. There was never that much money. Things went up and down and Dad used to on occasion go to 'Uncle's' with a ring of his or Mum's jewellery. You'd see these little redeeming dockets around every now and then.

Mum was the one who made ends meet, and that was hard on her: 'Mother's tired, she needs a rest'. And 'Our mum, she's so house-proud' . . . If you came in the house, she'd always go, 'Oh, it's such a mess,' and it'd be pristine.

**LEE:** Me and Bob Townsend broke into the singer Lynsey de Paul's house. She used to live on Swain's Lane in Highgate, just before the cemetery, these very Gothic buildings. Her place was very bohemian: lot of furs about, a lot of furry stuff. There was loads of musical equipment. We sat down and I think he had Sugar Puffs and I had Cornflakes. We just sat, having a meal. Then I think we was pretty good: we put the plates in the sink, and we left, just shut the door after us. We didn't take nothing.

On my fourteenth birthday, 5 October in '71, I stole two hundred quid from a locker in Whittington Hospital, which was a truckload of cash back then. It was a lady's that worked there: I don't know if she was a nurse or cook or what department she worked in. But I saw her put her belongings in there. She just said, 'Can I help you?' I said, 'I'm waiting for my mum that works here.' That became a saying, y'know. If anything dodgy was going on: 'Ooh, me mum works here.'

But what was she carrying that amount for? She probably wouldn't put it in a bank, kept it on her person or whatever. Not this day, unfortunately. I was flashing the money about, being a bit frivolous, handing it out to friends. I bought one girl a smock and my sister some clothes. It mainly went on clothes, and the fish and chip shop or something. And, of course, me mum. So, I got caught.

The police and the authorities ended up getting very pissed off with Bob Townsend and myself, so they sent us each to an approved school, a reform school. Not a borstal – you was out in the fields more than you was locked. It was like dormitories. Mine was Chafford School, near Harwich, and Bob went to Reading. That was probably the point where we both nipped it in the bud, because that needed to be done.

I think my dad had even given up sticking up for me. Y'know, coming up with various scenarios or whatever. He probably thought, 'You've got to wake up now,' because he realised obviously how much time he'd wasted. So, I broke the habit of a lifetime and started to plead guilty, and it was a relief for everyone in the area: 'Thank God they've gone . . .' There was a lot of mums that looked at us with one eye, side-on, from a distance.

I wrote 'Land of Hope and Glory' about Stamford House, which was a remand school where I was kept until I was shipped out to Chafford: 'If I hadn't mouthed it about/I'm sure without a doubt/I'd have missed this land of hope and glory.' The song was basically what actually happened to us. That's pretty much what it was like: cold showers, and if you weren't quick enough to get your milk and food, it would be snatched from you. That's why, I think, even now, I don't eat slow.

Chris and Mike came to visit me in Stamford House. I thought that was very sweet of them, very kind. I was really quite touched. They turned up and I was absolutely chuffed. But of course, when they left, when they could go out and have a jolly-up and I'm stuck in there, it hit home . . .

MIKE: It's funny to hear that from him, that he appreciated that me and Chris came to see him. Because he always seemed really independent and didn't need anybody. The impression you got of him was that he was tough and he wasn't bothered about it. I guess he was having a bit of a difficult time there. I think I was very blind to his feelings and wasn't very appreciative or understanding. I mean, at the same time, we were all very young.

SUGGS: By then, I was living with my mum in a sixth-floor flat in Cavendish Mansions, on Clerkenwell Road. That was extraordinary. When you were on the bottom of the housing ladder, it was like, 'You can have this flat, but it's the shittest of what we've got left.'

You got to the flat up these really slippery old steps and the landings were open. The flat was freezing cold, and there were just two rooms, so my mum would sleep in the living room. There was a sink and a toilet and a gas fire and that was it. But it was funny, because Cavendish Mansions was in a kind of horseshoe shape, and there were always people hanging out the windows. I've always got this vision like when you see those films of Little Italy or somewhere in the Bronx. People hanging out the windows, shouting at everyone in the courtyard, where we were all playing football and messing around.

If you wanted to wash, you had a bowl of water in front of the gas fire. Or you'd get sixpence and go up to Merlin Street Baths, which was the wash house where a lot of the women were still doing the laundry and the sheets and all that. There were maybe twenty cubicles you could have a bath in. The geezer used to come in with a spanner, turn the hot water on, and he'd give you possibly ten inches of hot water, and turn it off again, and that was it: you'd make the most of your sixpence. I'd go once a week at the very most, on a Friday, especially when I was getting into my teens, 13, 14, to at least have some kind of cleanliness if I was going out. All these people would be in the cubicles, whistling.

Steam and everyone whistling. Everyone happy to be in a bit of hot water.

**CATHAL:** God, Dad was a character. A bit of mystery to him. It's like, in recent years, I read Allen Dulles's history of the CIA, *The Craft of Intelligence*. I realised that most of the places he'd been were hotspots. We used to go Garmisch-Partenkirchen in Germany and it was a spy school for the CIA. It's kind of crazy shit.

**CHRIS:** When I was younger, I was not androgynous, but very long hair and sort of hips and flared trousers and very skinny . . . Around '71 or '72, we hung around with these two girls, Sue and Trudy, who lived in Hampstead. Sue had this lovely old house and her parents were really nice, and Trudy lived in a council flat. We were always hanging around with them. It was all like just kissing and going to the pictures or whatever. Me and Lee were always going up their houses, and I remember one night seeing the New York Dolls on telly on *The Old Grey Whistle Test* and Whistlin' Bob Harris called them 'mock rock'. I just thought, 'Flipping hell.' His comment really pissed me off, 'cause that was the most rocking thing I'd seen on there for a while. But I still liked *The Old Grey Whistle Test*. Well, it was either *Top of the Pops* or that, really.

**SUGGS:** Lee and Mike and Chris were from very working-class backgrounds, to a greater or lesser extent, but certainly in a very working-class area. There was a club called the Aldenham Boys Club on Highgate Road they used to go to, and they ended up in this gang called the Aldenham Glamour Boys, who I sort of knew. I was a few years younger than them, but I grew up hearing stories about the Aldenham Glamour Boys.

CHRIS: I'll tell you the origin of the Aldenham Glamour Boys. Listen closely, Suggs – because he's sort of obsessed with it.

What happened was, there was us little bunch, who used to go out shoplifting, and doing sort of vandalism. We used to walk through Parliament Hill, up to the top of Kite Hill, and set fire to rubbish bins, like you do. One night, we were kind of merrily doing that. It was foggy, and we heard these other voices. 'Who's that, who's that?' and we hear someone going, 'Oh, that's Tony Hilton.' Who we vaguely knew. These kids were called the Kiln Place because that's where they lived in Gospel Oak, which wasn't far from us. They weren't our sworn enemies, but they were like an unknown factor.

Then that night, the police arrived, having seen all these things on fire. We all got chased by Land Rovers through Parliament Hill, but there's loads of trees and things so you could hide. After that, we became this sort of big super-gang and we all started going to this Aldenham Boys Club. And then other people from farther afield came: they heard the rallying call. Somebody said once, just for a laugh, you know, 'Oh, we're the Aldenham Glamour Boys.'

MIKE: I don't know who coined that phrase, Aldenham Glamour Boys. It was anything but. Glamour it was not. But in there, there were layers of different ages of kids. I got beaten up in the Aldenham once. There was just some rivalry going on between somebody in my area, and some gang from Brecknock Road, and I suppose I got caught up in it. We were just in there, there was a disco going on, and I was standing in the hall. It was all dark and somebody suddenly jumped me from behind, and then they all started kicking and punching me.

There were rough elements. I mean, obviously this lot were pretty rough, or they wanted to make a name for themselves, I don't know. They were not the brightest sparks. Whenever there was violence, there was always certain types that were up for it. You heard of some guy getting stabbed one time, and it's like not everybody stabs somebody. It's only a certain type. If there was a fight or something, more normal people, you would say, 'Alright, cool down, cool down,' and they would cool down, y'know? But there'd be some types that wouldn't, and they'd got a screw missing or something.

**MARK:** I first found out about the Aldenham Glamour Boys because there was graffiti around, and some of them used to terrorise us coming home from school. One particularly guy called Alex Donnelly. He looked quite a lot like Ian Dury, in the sense of the big Crombie, a stick sometimes, big turn-ups, maybe a jean jacket or something. It was kind of like what Ian Dury would become.

**MIKE:** Me and Chris and Lee were into that sort of glam rock thing. Looking at album covers and going, 'Oh, what's he wearing?' and 'Ooh, look at that.' My mates were really the ones who liked to listen to records a lot.

**LEE:** I mean, with the Aldenham Boys Club, we were at that age where you were too old to go to youth clubs, but you were too young to go into pubs. There were some pubs, like The Bull & Gate in Kentish Town, that allowed you to drink underage, plus you didn't have to have ID then. There used to be a discotheque on the side of it, the Street Discotheque. Ah, the memories of that place. That's where I played my first Prince Buster singles. It was a right rough old gaff.

CHRIS: In the Aldenham, we used to wear jeans and jean jackets and we used to dye our Dr Martens. Y'know, spray them gold. Thommo would do things like that. One of the first things that I stole were these patches that you'd sew onto a jacket. One was the American flag in the shape of a peace sign. Lee's mum had an industrial sewing machine, so you could go through denim and everything. Me and Thommo got – nicked – some leopardskin fabric and we sewed this leopardskin onto the top of our Levi's. That was kind of because of Roxy Music.

I'd go through these phases. There were these things called loon pants, which were like extremely cheap bell-bottom trousers. They cost about a pound or something, these really tight black trousers flared at the bottom. Then we used to supplement our wardrobe by stealing clothes. There was a shop in Kentish Town called Chelsea Girl, and me and Barso both had the same jumper from there, a sleeveless jumper with kind of stripes on. Chelsea Girl was obviously a girls' shop, but the genders were blurred even then: we didn't care. You wouldn't care: if something looked alright, you'd wear it.

LEE: Personally, I was a bit gutted when the first skinhead era ended, sort of '71. It went a bit soul boy, boot boy and these fucking Oxford bags come in, that you could take off in, in a high wind. Crombies, shirts with those big, round collars on. Not button-down, they were completely the opposite. So, at that time, I started looking for my own type of clothes that I wanted to wear.

You'd always get your Levi's, you'd always get your Dr Martens. But I suppose ultimately, I didn't like that change to the soul boy look. It was a bit smarter, and I was a bit more of a scruff. Being scruffy allowed you to get into mischief without having to send your clothes to the dry cleaner's or get them damaged. I've never really been a smart dresser: I like casual. I feel starched in a suit.

I had some older friends, like this bloke Pete McGee, who I used to knock about with. Although they were not that much older than me, they were big fellers, especially Pete. He lent me a pair of Dr Martens once. They used to have Dr Martens with half-soles, up to a certain size. I was a size four, and I think the full-sole DM started at a five or a six. I probably could have worn a five or six. But anyway, they were too expensive. And I wouldn't wear the half, the wafer soles they were called, wafer-thin. He said to me, 'I've got a pair for you, Thommo,' and I was going to Madame Tussaud's that day with a couple of friends, Deaf-and-Dumb Paul and his twin brother, Steve, and Pete and a couple of others. He borrowed me these Dr Martens, and he must have been a size eight or nine, and I remember stuffing them with paper at the front and walking around with them on, just feeling like Coco the Clown.

You're at that age where you are image-conscious, I suppose. Or I certainly wanted to be different. That period after skin-heads, when the boot boy came in, the hair grew, which I could just about deal with: 'Yeah, I'll grow me hair.' But the clothing was all dodgy. Selwyn's was a shop in Kentish Town, and they used to do those flyaway collars and these greasy trousers that went outwards that I couldn't hack. I went through a bit of a period where I was running out of places to find clothes, so I'd go back to the Levi's and the DMs. Particularly faded Levi's that you'd put patches on.

At one point I had a pair of high-leg, steel-toecapped DMs. I cut the size of a sixpence – a 5p, the size of a button, or a Smartie – out of the toes and sandpapered it down and then wire-brushed the steel underneath. Then I got a brilliant white, snow-white pair of Levi's, and cut them so's they went just above the top of the ten-hole, and I'd wear glitter socks underneath. I had orange, blues, all different coloured socks, from this tailor's, Chris Ruocco, in Fortess Road in Kentish Town. These socks fucking scratched your feet. They'd tickle your ankles and that, but it was like, no, I'm wearing these. I don't know if they were men's, even. Might have been women's.

So, I'd wear all that, plus a long-sleeved stripy jumper that had black, red, orange, yellow, indigo and purple stripes about an inch wide. And a rainbow iron-on badge. It was great: you didn't have to stitch it on, just iron it and it stuck. Then to top all that off, a trilby. I haven't got any photos of that period. But that was my look. I must have looked a proper plonker.

CHRIS: I met my girlfriend, to-become-wife, at the Aldenham. Susan Hegarty. She was quite a hard nut, but one night, there were all these kids hitting her on the back of her head, and I felt really sorry for her. The Aldenham was a happy little thing, and then these kids started coming over from Highbury. Every week, there'd be a fight with the kids from Highbury. We'd chase them to the station, throwing stuff. So, come every Friday, there'd be police vans waiting. One night, the Highbury kids didn't come. The police must have been, like, 'We've got to justify our budget.'

We were walking around down by this block of flats in Gospel Oak and this police van came screeching in. I'll tell you, man, no one had done anything. The coppers just jumped out and they started whacking people and chucking them in the van: 'You're causing trouble.' And I thought, 'Y'know what, if I just put my arm round this girl, they'll think I'm some dopey love-struck teenager.' So, we went on the bus and I took her home, and I kissed her, and that was that. Then I went out with her and went out with her and went out with her, and eventually got married to her.

CATHAL: I had my first drink with John Hasler – cider, babysitting at 13, and my first joint. John was a big influence. I'd be round his place listening to Rick Wakeman's *The Six Wives of Henry VIII*, Led Zeppelin, Genesis, The Who. He got into wearing stacked heels and nail varnish, and it was like, 'Wow, what the fuck?'

I'd been to Dublin and picked up *The Dice Man*, a crazy story which really appealed to me. In it, the main character, bored with life, starts rolling dice to make random choices. So, I started doing it as well. At school, in a maths lesson, one of the options that came up was 'Crawl under the desks to the front of the class, then climb out of the window.' I ended up doing exactly that. As I was climbing out the window, the teacher, Mr DeMello, dumb-founded, was like, 'Smyth, what are you doing?'

'The dice told me to do it, sir.'

I never got any comeback from that.

I had a cushy thing going on at school: I'd started a little busi-ness making tea for the teachers. Three pence a cup, two pence for three biscuits. All official, next to the staff room. It meant I left lessons ten minutes early to turn the urn on. I could leave the school grounds to go to the shops whenever I liked. I'd bring hash in, skin up and then I felt pleasantly out-of-step with the whole place. Like things had flipped to my liking. Towards the end, I didn't take anything at school seriously. I couldn't wait for the weekend. Everything was changing.

**SUGGS:** Two floors down from me at Cavendish Mansions lived this family, the Bianchis. Somehow their dad had contrived to get two flats together. There were two flats on each landing, and he'd knocked them through. But if the council came round, he'd put a big cupboard up so they wouldn't see that he'd knocked through. He made out there were two different families living in these two flats, and there was just one. But it was like Narnia – you had to open the cupboard door to go through this hole into where they'd expanded the kitchen in the other side. There were about seven of them in there: three sisters, a couple of brothers.

The Bianchis had the newsagent's over the road, and I used to work there at the weekends, and steal fags and porno mags and all that. Mr Bianchi used to go down the docks and he'd buy water-damaged goods. So long as it was Italian, he'd buy it. The basement of the newsagent's would be full of rotting bottles of Chianti with the straw round them, or he'd get a load of underwear that was all mouldy. But then one time he got his hands on this shipment of parmesan cheeses. I didn't know what the fuck they were. They were these yellow things the size of a tyre. He's going, 'We're going to flog them.' There was a big Italian community round that little bit of Clerkenwell, and we were loading these up in the van, and they were slippery. One slipped out of my hand and disappeared, rolled away and exploded on a lamp post halfway down the road. He's going, 'That's fucking twenty quid gone there . . .' Every week, he'd be trying to flog something, down that part of the world.

LEE: Round about this time, I had my first taste of Bell's whisky. I'd had a few drinks with Mike, and we ended up going to this blues party – a lot of soul and reggae coming out of this house. So, we've gone through the front, open door, up the stairs. On whatever floor, there was a lot of music going on, but I carried on going up. There was a gas meter that used to hold coins back in the day. So, I've taken a metal rod that was holding down a carpet, and I'm trying to open this gas meter, which I've tapped and I know there's a few shillings in there. Then all I can hear is 'Thommo . . . Thommo . . . Lee!' I've looked down the stairs and there's Mike stood there, just a white head with about ten black guys around him. So, I've gone, 'Fuck!' Next thing I've found a skylight, so I'm up and out of there.

I ended up on the roof, hanging onto the tiles, going *screech* with my fingernails. Then I managed to grab hold of this lead downpipe with little nips on it. I've slid down that bastard and it's lacerating my hands. That sobered me up. I hit the deck and, y'know, it was like the *Tom and Jerry* cartoons, where they run through fences and bushes and that. I ended up having it on me toes with all prickles sticking out me, bits of rose and bit of wood. But then I thought, 'You bastard. Why don't you go back and see how Mike is? Why don't you help him out?'

CHRIS: In 1972, I turned 16 and left school. I ended up working for this gardening firm and I was getting nothing really – a pittance, like fifteen quid a week or something. But, I was just a kid.

What happened was, me and Lee, we were wandering through Hampstead, up to no good, late at night. There was a newsagent's, and there was an ad in the window: 'Gardeners Wanted'. We thought, 'That's quite a good thing to do.' I don't know why, we just thought, 'Let's get a job.' It was this gardening firm in Finchley called Your Gardens. The guy who ran it pointed and said, 'Which one of those is a weed?' We didn't really know, but somehow, we got the job anyway. It was going round, cutting people's grass, a little bit of maintenance and stuff like that.

I got a letter from the school, kind of going, 'We don't think there's much point you coming back.' I thought, 'Right, I'm 16 and on the scrapheap,' so I stayed working at this gardening thing for a long time. I can't remember what the hell Lee did. Thommo soon vanished off into the distance.

## CHAPTER 4

# FIVE-FINGER DISCOUNT AND THE AGE OF THE (FREIGHT) TRAIN

MIKE: Shoplifting was something that me and Lee and Chris all did. A lot of shoplifting. I guess there was a sort of feeling of like, 'Well, they're all rich fuckers anyway in them shops . . . nobody's getting hurt,' y'know? Breaking into phone boxes was another thing. I mean, a lot of the kids we hung around with from our neighbourhood grew up to be petty criminals.

I had trouble with it at one point. I had to try and extricate myself from it, because it seemed like it was just going to get worse and worse.

CHRIS: Poor old Barso. He couldn't run that fast, so he was always getting caught.

*

MIKE: I really didn't like crime that was hurting somebody. One time, we nicked a little scooter round the back of Highgate Road, by the crossroads. Somebody said, 'There's a scooter round the back there,' and we all turned up there to nick it. So, we got this scooter, took it up on the railway and we were driving around on it. I suddenly started thinking, and imagining this guy coming out in the morning to get on his scooter to go to work. And I started feeling really bad for him: 'What about that bloke? He's probably still got to pay for that thing, and it's going to get all smashed up and everything.' I didn't like that – some kids would just kick it, destroy it. Maybe those kids, they'd had difficult lives. It was not attractive.

Lee and Chris were not so much like that. But there were some kids who had a lot of aggression in them, I guess, and we were all hanging around together. Another time, we were walking up Highgate Road and we met two kids who said they'd gotten into robbing people, mugging people. Then they started undertaking one of their activities – fighting some bloke on the street, beating him down to get his wallet. I didn't like that.

CHRIS: Stealing scooters, that's what we did as a gang. Behind the church on Highgate Road, we found this moped, called a Puch. We thought, 'We're going to nick it.' Collectively, we decided to nick it. The next night, we nicked a Lambretta scooter from Parliament Hill Mansions, near Parliament Hill. I don't know how we knew how to get it going. Somebody knew a bit about them: 'You take that off and you join those up.' We got it onto Parliament Hill and they were pushing it and I was on it. Suddenly, *rrarrrr*, it erupted. Then we took it to the railway line near where I lived. We hid it there, and we said . . . it's a bit like the Famous Five: 'None of us will use it.'

But then our mate John Jones turned up at this party on this scooter, and we thought, 'Right, he's sort of broken the rule . . .' So, then me and Thommo were having a go on it. For some reason, we'd also nicked these white gardening gloves and we were both wearing them. As we were driving down towards Kentish Town, we saw this Morris 1000 police car, and it started chasing us. We went down, round the back, where the Forum is now, and there was this wasteland. The only way to escape was over this fence with barbed wire around the top. But, because we had these gloves on, we just went over it and we got away.

Then we must have just gone and got the scooter back. Not long after, we were on it going up to Holly Lodge Estate to meet Lee. Mike was driving, I was sitting behind Mike, and John Jones was sitting on the back – all of us on this little thing. We were going up the hill, *putt putt putt*, and what did we see in the distance? A bloody Morris 1000 police car. It revved up *rrrr* and it started coming down. We turned around and wobbled down the hill heading towards Lee who was standing under this lamp post. Then, Thommo jumped up and his little legs were off running, in mid-air, like a cartoon. Me and Lee could run really fast, and we ran and we ran and we ran over to the reservoir at Archway. Jumped over the fence, ran for miles, and we got away. Poor old Mike got caught, because he couldn't run fast. But, I mean, he was great, because he never gave us up.

MIKE: The Co-op in Camden was the main place for us to nick records. Other places had discovered that people were stealing albums, so the inner sleeve with the record inside would be kept at the back behind the counter, and out on display would just be the cover. But I suppose, with the shortage of staff or lack of training or something, in the Co-op, they just stuck it all in the racks. Lee turned up once, all excited, because he'd been to Camden Town and found this shop where they had the records in the sleeves out on display. That was the Holy Grail we were looking for. So, then we would all go down there and everybody would sort themselves a few records. The Co-op was a great shop . . .

CHRIS: We were like, 'Oh, my God, they're in the covers . . .' and we were just like nicking them left, right and centre. You'd go in a shop and you'd think, 'Right . . . I like that one and I like that one.' They'd be in different sections, so we'd get them slowly together into a little pile in one rack. We used to call it 'sifting a batch'. The first time we did it, we came out and we ran and then we were just laughing with glee.

LEE: In the Co-op in Camden Town, you'd get your Traffic, your Genesis, your Alex Harvey, your Roxy Music. Not too many, but not too small, or otherwise it would slip out from under your arm. Just a nice batch, ten to twelve albums. Stoop down, under the arm, come back out, quick.

MIKE: We must have done it a lot, because I had three hundred records or something and I'd never bought a record in my life.

That was the nice thing – you'd get records that you didn't know and you'd put them on and you might really like them. I'd spend hours at home, listening to all these albums. I remember that Genesis record, *Selling England by the Pound*, and there was a song, 'Firth of Fifth', on it. I learnt that on the piano and I could play the solo on it. Then, there was a flute bit, and I had a flute at one time, so I learned the flute part to that, as well. That was very enjoyable, listening, and slowly getting to know all those different tracks. It was that period where albums were like a proper body of work.

CHRIS: There was this other record shop down somewhere in Euston. Barso had gone and sifted a batch in there, and I knew, and I went and nicked his batch. He was so annoyed that he'd spent all this time, like, casing the joint.

We were pretty prolific. In the Co-op, there was this guy in there who had a sort of Homer Simpson comb-over and he'd be wearing a brown boiler suit. He was obviously a store detective, because he was always trying to change his appearance. The next day you'd see him in a suit. We used to go, "Ere, mate, how much are those?' and he'd be like, 'I don't work here.' We're going, 'Yeah? You're having a laugh . . .'

Once I nicked a copy of *Led Zeppelin IV*. But then when I got it home, I realised it had a Johnny Kidd and the Pirates album inside by mistake. It was like, 'Aah, bloomin' hell.' But then Thommo's mum went, 'Oh, I like this,' and we gave it to her. So, his mum had a Johnny Kidd and the Pirates album inside a Led Zeppelin sleeve.

Another way we worked out how to nick records was you'd get a large carrier bag and kind of puff it up, so it looked like there was something in it. Then you'd do this kind of mime and pretend you were carrying something heavy, so they wouldn't know once you had all the albums inside. At one stage we had an old Dansette record player we'd carry around, with nothing inside it, and you'd fill it up.

Then I got caught. I was with Lee. His mum made these bags. His uncle was always copying the latest designs and she'd make these bags with her industrial sewing machine. So, me and Lee were in Luton, with his dad, selling these bags in the street. His dad went, 'You go and keep look-out,' as he flogged the bags, like really quick. He might have given us some money for helping him. So, we went into a record shop and I decided to buy Golden Earring's 'Radar Love'. I thought, 'I'll get that, and I'm going to nick an album.' Y'know, the old classic thing of buying and nicking. Buy something, and then nick something. Buy one and steal one free . . .

Thommo was going, 'Don't . . . don't . . . there's too many people.' I was like, 'There's no one here . . . or they're all old people . . . what's going to happen?' So, I nicked the album, and someone went 'Oi,' and we ran. Some bloody members of the public grabbed me and Thommo. We were wearing these velvet jackets that we'd nicked when we got grabbed. Lee's went *rrrrrri-iiiip*, all down from the shoulder to the waist. But he got away and I got caught.

They took me to the police station in Luton, and there'd been a football match on. I had these cool black Ravel boots, with this thick crepe sole and the copper went, 'Take your boots off and leave them outside the cell.' I don't know if they thought I was going to kick myself to death. This big old copper came and knocked, saying, 'Were you at the football match?' I said, 'No.' He said, 'If you were, I'll fucking be back.' Then I heard him go into the next cell and kick the shit out of someone, because there'd been football hooligans at the match.

They'd rung my dad to make sure I was who I said I was. They said, 'You can go home. Do you want any train fare?' I said, 'No.' I thought, 'I'm not taking your stinking money,' and bunked the train all the way home. But I think I got a caution or something.

My dad blamed himself and I felt really terrible about it. Because he said to them, 'He's from a broken home . . .' So, then I kind of stopped nicking stuff out of shops. Had an epiphany.

MARK: I was living on a council estate in Holloway and surrounded by a lot of people of my age who had a bit of hustle about them. A bit of: 'I want to be someone.' Even if they were just local kids who were great at football, or they just dressed well. They'd have really good clothes, or they wore some piece of seventies fashion that you wanted: 'Oh, where'd you get that jacket from?' There was a culture of that. You were on the street, you were maybe working-class, but you were looking good or being good at something or other.

LEE: The first live music I saw was probably at the Roundhouse. You had the Roundhouse just down the road from Haverstock School, and I used to drink in there. In '73, I'd have only been 16, but you could get away with it then. You'd get a warm half-pint of bitter for like 15p, or a pint for 25p or whatever, and they'd have music on over there at lunchtime, which was a big attraction. I might have even seen Pink Floyd over there. Pink Fairies, Blodwyn Pig, Hawkwind, Mott the Hoople . . .

WOODY: When I went to Haverstock, we went in the Roundhouse pretty much every lunchtime for a bit of grub. We either went to Marine Ices for a little pizza or the Roundhouse for a baked potato. That's what we lived on, for years. I don't ever remember how we bought tickets for the gigs. I can't ever remember paying to go and see a gig at the Roundhouse, but I used to go there all the time.

The Roundhouse was very kind of hippy-dippy. There was this guy you'd see at all the gigs called Jesus. Everyone who ended up in the band knew Jesus. He had a kind of Dave Hill from Slade haircut, y'know, with the fringe and the long hair, but it was blond. He wore white robes and carried a tambourine, and everyone nicknamed him Jesus, because he looked like something straight out of the Bible.

**SUGGS:** Not that I'm obsessed, but . . . the other thing about the Aldenham Glamour Boys was that they would do things like get on the trains carrying all the new cars from the Ford factory in Dagenham. The trains would be coming from Dagenham and they'd stop at Kentish Town West. They'd just get in these cars, get the radios on, and then go off with this shipment of Ford Escorts. They'd end up in France or wherever and you wouldn't see them for a couple of weeks, and then they'd suddenly reappear, having had all these amazing adventures and been escorted out of some country with no passports or anything. They'd just fucking go.

**MIKE:** We'd jump on these freight trains that went over the bridge at Highgate Road. There was a railway signal, and I can't remember, but either when it went up or when it went down, it meant that there was a freight train there, and we used to like jumping on them. It was a bit of a thrill. So, when we saw the signal going up or down, one or the other, we used to run up to the train track from where we were. There was a little side passage through the houses and you could get up on the railway land. Then we would jump on the train and go to Willesden and places like that.

I really liked going up on the railways. It was like another world. In the normal world, there were certain rules and regulations.

Then you go up on the railway, and you're in, like, no man's land. A completely different world. It felt like a sort of secret, because nobody apart from us would ever go up to the railway line. It had a bit of a mystery about it, so we used to hang out up there, and then jump on the trains. I mean, it was horribly dangerous, really. But we were young and we thought we could handle it.

**LEE:** It was where the goods line crossed over with the passenger line, which had priority. If a goods train was turning up several minutes before, it would have to wait. Sometimes you'd have to jump it when it would be moving, which was fucking hairy. Our mate Paul Catlin was trying to do that one time, and next to where the rails were, they'd hit stakes in the ground which stood out about several inches; they were markers for I don't know what. He kicked one as he was running along the side, then he fell, and his arm was just a few inches away from the rail. That was very frightening. I grabbed him and picked him up and we carried on running to catch the train.

**CHRIS:** The goods trains went past my house, so we'd jump on them and open them up and steal things. It was incredible, because you never knew what was going to be in them. Once, we opened this train and we got an outboard motor. What a load of teenage kids were going to do with an outboard motor ... 'Yeah, but it's probably worth a few hundred quid.' But, I mean, how are you going to sell an outboard motor in this big box? There was this block of flats overlooking the track, and as we were carrying it down, somebody shouted at us out the window, and we threw the box into the bushes. Another time, the rest of them got a load of hot dogs and tried to sell them to the guy in the chip shop on my corner. Then they got a load of suits. They called them the Rod Stewart Suits, because they were these crappy suits . . .

We built a little bunker, out of railway sleepers, and we nicked these lights off the back of a train: these really old lanterns with oil and a wick. One night we were in this bunker and the police – like, proper coppers – came. They were like undercover or whatever, and they were like, 'What are you doing? Get out.' Then I read in *The Sunday Times* that near there someone had robbed a gold bullion train. I said, 'That's why they were flipping after us.' I mean, imagine if that had been us . . . How would we have sold that to the man in the chip shop?

We used to go wandering around on the line down near Tufnell Park and we'd get in the workmen's huts. They had these things called detonators, which were an incredibly primitive method of letting a train know that there's fog. They were these round things, like landmines, and they'd put them on the track. The train would go over them and they would literally explode and make this racket. So, we were always getting these yellow detonators and we'd chuck a brick at them and these things would flipping blow up. The workmen also had these horns, like an old-fashioned *eeee-ooor, eeee-ooor* thing that you blew. One of my abiding memories is Barso blowing this horn . . . it was hilarious. And he did this kind of Nutty Train thing. Even when we were kids, he did that sort of walk.

One time, we decided we were all going camping, by travelling on a goods train. It was mad really: we had no plan, and we didn't know where the trains went. Me, Mike, John Jones, Paul Catlin, maybe Thommo, we thought, 'Right, we're going to go on the goods . . . where it takes us, who knows?' We thought we were like hobos. That brilliant film came out at the same time, *Emperor of the North*, with Ernest Borgnine and Lee Marvin, about tramps jumping the goods trains. I said to my dad, 'I'm going camping,' and I got this little tent. He gave me, like, a fiver.

So, off we go. We get in one of the goods trains with the cars on. The cars had keys in the ignition, so we sit in a car, pull the aerial up and listen to the radio. We were all having a right laugh, and we kind of had the window slightly open. Then when we got to Nuneaton station, I heard someone go, 'Oi, there's an aerial up on one of them cars.' We were like, 'Shit,' and we all jumped out and ran. Suddenly, six kids jumped out of this train and went running out of the station.

We stayed up all night in Nuneaton and wandered round and then we stole a moped that had a steering lock on it, so it would only go in circles. This country bumpkin copper stopped us, and we all gave him totally fake names. But we were starving, and we found a bread factory. We creeped in, got this freshly made, hot bread. After that, I just came home, sort of in disgrace and said to my dad, 'Oh, the weather was really shit.'

Most of the time, we used to get on and go to Richmond or somewhere. Really, it was extremely dangerous. Now I think, 'Oh, my God, did I do actually that?' You'd jump off a train doing speeds, wearing your Dr Martens or your brogues, and your feet would hit the ground and it was like bang-bang-bang-bang, *doof*.

MIKE: We went to France on the freight trains, pretty much all the way. My brother had done that one time with a mate of his who was a bit of a wrong 'un. They'd gone round Europe and he came back with all these exciting stories about stuff they'd gotten up to, jumping on trains in Europe. So that became, like, one of the cards in our pack of things that we might do. We were going to go away for a couple of weeks, to see Europe in an alternative manner . . .

LEE: My memory's that it was October half-term, '74. Mike and myself and our mate Si Birdsall decided to get those old yearly paper passports. One of us left our passport at home. It was a fucking joke . . . I think it was Si Birdsall. We had to have it Red Starred down, because we were now in Ramsgate, waiting for the hovercraft.

MIKE: In Ramsgate, we slept in this park, in this fucking Viking-style boat. It had a tarpaulin on the back, so we lifted it up and got under there. Freezing cold, and raining. We'd read somewhere that you could hitch-hike at Ramsgate. Get into someone's car that was going on the hovercraft, and you could get to France for nothing.

We start hitch-hiking, but everyone was like, 'Fuck off.' There was not one person stopping for us lot. So, we end up going, 'Oh, how much is a ticket?' 'OK, we'll just pay for the ferry.' We get to Dieppe or somewhere, and we're sitting out in these train yards, trying to get a train, in the middle of nowhere. But we couldn't get one, so then we got a passenger train to Paris. We're thinking, 'There'll be goods yards there. We'll continue the trip from Paris.'

We bunked on the train, and then somebody caught us. Our plan was we would lie – if we got caught, we would say we'd got on the stop before. But we got fined. It ended up being the same price as a normal fucking ticket. Then, we arrived in Paris. All we had was our Dr Martens, turned-up jeans, maybe a little ruck-sack or something.

**LEE:** Up the Eiffel Tower, we found a load of beer. It was a franc or two to use the lift, and again, it was terrible, but we weren't paying. We'd sooner go up the back stairs; it kept you fit. We made it to the first tier, and that was knackering. I don't know if we made it to the second tier. But we made it to wherever the restaurants were, because we saw this door which this feller went in and out of once. When we opened it, we saw there was bottles of Kronenbourg 1664 beers in there. The first time, we went in all sheepishly, but the fourth or fifth visit, we were brazen: 'Come on . . .' But then we had to negotiate the walk back down, which took forever.

**MIKE:** Three o'clock in the morning in Paris, we're walking down these deserted railway lines, trying to find a proper railway yard. Finally, we find one, we get on a train, off we go.

It was a nice little train: it had these individual different car-riages, like a custom train. It had a round thing in the ceiling, like a bubble, and so we could open that up and look out. As the sun came up, we were starting to go through this beautiful French countryside, maybe hundred kilometres out of Paris. But the train kept stopping in these little villages, and they kept uncoupling one carriage at a time. We were like, 'Fucking hell . . . we're going to be next.' We had to keep moving and moving up the train, so we didn't get caught. But it was a really beautiful morning. It was the wine season, and we saw these French people with bare feet, like you read about, in these big containers, tramping these grapes. Strange to see that.

We ended up in these really desolate areas in France, in these big train yards, looking at these maps, trying to work out where to go. Sometimes the trains had this metal thing on the side. It'd be pitch-black at night and you'd pull out this little thing which would say where the train was going: Montpellier, Nîmes, might be hand-written on it, y'know? So, we're thinking, 'Yeah, that's the way to go. We'll check them all, then get a perfect destination. We'll get on the train, maybe have a little kip, and we'll wake up where we want to be.'

But then we spent a lot of time walking along godforsaken railway lines and in railway yards and getting chased every now and then. One time we were hanging around in these yards, trying to get a train, and it wasn't working. So, we jumped on this little shunting train; just a small train that had railings on the front and the back. We're hiding at the back, and somebody saw a guy coming out of the front and looking to the back of the train. And we're hanging off it. Then it slowed down, we jumped off, and we could see these blokes in the distance: 'Oi, oi,' shouting in French. I mean, what they thought we were up to, God only knows. Another time, this guy got a gun out, somewhere in the middle of France. Fuck knows where we were.

LEE: We zig-zagged our way down through France. Paris to Dijon, Dijon to Avignon, Avignon to Toulouse. Then we got rumbled by the railway police, all blacked-up and nowhere to go. Well, we hadn't had a wash for a week, and the clothes we had, we didn't have to wash. They hid the dirt and stuff.

We got put on a train back to England, and we mingled in with a school crowd who were there. When we were asked for our tickets, we just said, 'We're with this school.' But, I mean, I was

17 years old. How we got away with it, I don't know. Anyway, we got all the way back home from the South of France.

**MIKE:** I nearly got my head knocked off on a freight train one other time. There were a big gang of us and we were going to go away for the weekend. Up north on a sort of holiday.

**LEE:** We were going through that long tunnel where Hampstead Heath goes to Finchley Road & Frognal. Mike's talking and, *boom*, suddenly he's disappeared, and our mate took a hit.

**MIKE:** They were these double-decker car trains, and we were on the top deck, looking in, trying to see if any of the cars' doors had been left open. The train was starting to pick up a bit of speed, and there was a low bridge up ahead. We're standing on the top of the train, and me and my mate both got hit on the back of the head, and I was knocked senseless. I thought I'd been knocked off the side and fallen under the train. I had this idea that I was on the rail, and the motherfucking wheel's coming. I was thinking, 'I've got to do something . . . I've got to do something.' I was semi-conscious, y' know? And then I was seeing all this funny light in the dark, and I knew I was still on the train. But then I thought, 'I've got to roll off.' It's lucky I didn't roll off, or I'd have probably rolled under the wheel. Luckily then I woke up and I realised I'd just been knocked flat. But you imagine the brick bridge and the train going quite fast under it: that could have been like spaghetti everywhere if it had been going, I don't know, ten, twenty miles an hour faster. I mean, it was fucking mental.

So, the train slowed down and we got off at Kensal Rise. We're still a bit out of it: blurred, bleeding and everything. There's all these gardens, backing onto the railway, and we climb over a back wall. I mean, we're these yobbos, and we're knocking on these back doors. What these people must have thought . . . Imagine opening your garden door and seeing us lot out there. I think the first house didn't work out and then some guy let us in, I suppose because we were covered in blood and everything. Then we went to the hospital. But I don't know if we were alright really . . .

**CHRIS:** Luckily, I hadn't gone with them that day. They'd came to my house and asked if I wanted to jump some goods trains. I said, 'No . . . you can't take amateurs with you.' Barso had no discernible damage, but he was like, 'Argh,' and being sick into a bucket.

**LEE:** The train was probably only going twenty miles an hour. But, hitting the bridge, they were fucking lucky they didn't have fractured skulls. That was the end of the freight trains.

**WOODY:** The railway line that we called the Magic Line is a connection that all the band have. It's the overground train line that sort of circumnavigates North London: Highbury & Islington, Camden Road, Kentish Town West, Gospel Oak, Finchley Road & Frognal, West Hampstead and then all the way to Richmond.

Only recently, I was on a train and got talking to a guard. I said, 'I used to travel on this train all the time when I was a kid. We used to call it the Magic Line.' He said, 'Yeah, it's still called the Magic Line.' I said, 'I don't know why they call it the Magic Line.' He goes, 'Yeah, I do. It was because you never paid.'

**SUGGS:** Of course . . . it was the fucking Magic Line. I used to bunk off school and travel on it, 'cause I used to have friends in

West Hampstead. The irony was that I'd be bunking off my own school to go and hang around at my mate Chalky's school. He was at Hampstead comprehensive, so that was the connection with Barso and all of them.

One New Year's Eve, I was on my way to Hampstead to go to this party, and I had fuck all to take to it. My mum had won a case of whisky in a singing competition, and there were some blue pills on the table, which turned out to be Valium. I'd heard about the mods taking blues, so I took three of them and stuck a bottle of whisky in my pocket.

Anyway, the train stopped, and I thought, 'Right, we're here, time to get off.' I opened the door before I realised that the train hadn't even got to the station. I had white trousers on and a Levi's jacket, and I fell straight into this big fucking puddle. The train had stopped about four hundred yards from West Hampstead station. Then I had to walk down the line, get to the ticket inspector, and he's saying, 'Where's your ticket?' I'm saying, 'What? How dare you! That train went hours ago . . . I'm not even supposed to be here!'

After a good night out, my mum pulled me out of bed. I went, 'What?' I'd thought I'd got away with putting the whisky bottle back in the case. But there was only quarter of it left, with all diced carrot floating about in it.

MARK: We always said it was the Magic Line because it went everywhere we wanted to go. In those days they still had compartments on the old trains – one door and two bench seats. As kids, we'd get in there and unscrew the light bulbs and throw them out the window and all that malarkey.

\*

**WOODY:** The one thing that brings us all together is every single person in the band used that line. It was the connection. Kentish Town West burnt down in the early seventies. We heard that there was a fire in Kentish Town and, of course, these days, the line would be shut down for months or for weeks. There's no way a train could pass by. But back then, they cleared it in a day or two.

I have a memory of going through Kentish Town West and seeing smouldering embers. I mean, literally, we were travelling through smouldering embers. It was like, 'Bloody hell, that is really severe.' But, I mean, that was the seventies: no health and safety, really. But also, I kind of liked it. Because it was like, 'Get on with life.'

## CHAPTER 5

# THE WRITING ON THE WALL

**LEE:** Roxy Music were a big influence. Myself, Mike and Chris went to see them at the Rainbow in Finsbury Park when the *Stranded* album had just come out. We saw David Essex going in, with a blonde lady friend, and they were dressed to the nines. Our mate John Jones goes, 'He's got a bit of a flash car.' He had some convertible Merc and I can't remember if the roof was down or not, but I know we got in it. Inside, he had one of those new-fangled eight-track tape players. We thought, 'Oh, they must cost a fortune.' So, we ended up having several of his eight-track tapes away.

Then, we bunked into the gig. Supporting was Leo Sayer. I got on someone's shoulders – probably Mike's, because he's tall – and hauled myself up onto a window ledge, because I'd noticed it was on the latch. As I climbed up and looked in this window, there's Leo Sayer, putting his makeup on. He's got that clown's outfit on that he wore around that time. He had all the gear on and one red cheek. He turned round, and I went, 'Can you let us in?'

He was like, 'Sorry, I can't.' I'm going, 'We've come to see you, though, Leo . . .' Have we fuck! But he said, 'I can't, obviously,' and I descended back down.

MARK: Lee always told me that Leo Sayer mimed, 'I can't let you in,' in Marcel Marceau style . . .

CHRIS: Actually, I think it was me that climbed up and looked through the window. It *was* me, because I remember standing on the roof and Mike and Lee were in the street, and there's this big bouncer going, 'Get down here, you little fucker.' I mean, it might have been maybe we were both there, but I've definitely got a memory of climbing up the thing, opening this window, and Leo Sayer had that sort of clown face on.

LEE: Chris generally remembers what is what. On the Leo Sayer incident, I don't even remember him being up the wall. Roxy were promoting *Stranded* and he was probably banging his salt back home!

We had to find a Plan B, and so we decided to go higher up the side of the building, and we ended up climbing in and pitching ourselves up behind the trellis that was above the stage at the Rainbow. Just looking out at the crowd, hearing the music, and thinking, 'Sod this, I want to *see* the band.' So, we climbed down – I don't know how we got down eventually – and we got to see them do 'Psalm', which is the last track on side one of *Stranded*. They brought on twenty or thirty Welsh vocalists to sing the backing vocals on that, which was hair-lifting, goose-pimply stuff. I turned and looked at Mike and he was covered in dirt and bird shit after climbing in.

But, yeah, Roxy ended up being a massive influence on us. Especially that track 'The Bogus Man' from their album before that, *For Your Pleasure*. We played it a lot. It was just a track that was different; wasn't a commercial track for sure. 'The Bogus Man' was dark and moody and, later, we used to learn our dance moves to that song.

One time I was 'rubbings', they called it, with a lady friend, Marina, in the kitchen. The lights were out, I had this little record deck on, and me and her were petting. All my mum could hear, which she thought was us, was these heavy breathing noises. And, of course it's Bryan Ferry on the end of 'The Bogus Man'.

CHRIS: When I was working for the gardening firm, 'Street Life' by Roxy Music had just come out. I had a little transistor radio, and I was like, 'Oh, my God, it's fantastic.' It was so exciting then, when stuff came out.

Another band we sort of liked was Genesis, with Peter Gabriel. I mean, I probably liked them the most – knew all the lyrics and that. They played at Drury Lane, did this residency there, in January 1974. By now, I was getting quite old, I suppose – I was nearly 18. But we still all bunked in. I think we went about three nights, because Drury Lane, you could easily bunk in. It was all just old folk on the door: 'Eee, can I have your ticket?' Peter Gabriel was brilliant; he had all the masks and stuff like that. At one point, there was a big bang, and he's floating through the air, on wires. That must have inspired Thommo to be flying through the air years later in the videos.

LEE: I always liked bands who put a lot into their visuals. It was entertaining. It wasn't the normal, y'know.

It was Si Birdsall who first got to see The Sensational Alex Harvey Band, at Reading in '73, supporting The Faces. He said, 'Yeah, The Faces were pretty good, but if you get the chance, check out Alex Harvey.' Then Chrissy Boy said, 'That Alex Harvey's playing down in the West End.'

CHRIS: The gig was in the Empire Ballroom, Leicester Square, Monday, 11 February 1974. So, we go down – me, Mike, Lee and Simon Birdsall – and as we're bunking in the back door, we see this guy Mark Patterson that we knew, who was a bit of a geezer, and who had told us about Alex Harvey in the first place. Mark comes out carrying a mixing desk that him and his mate appeared to be nicking. We get in and we didn't know anything about Alex Harvey, really. He burst through this polystyrene wall with brickwork painted on the front of it. Then he did 'The Faith Healer'. I was like, 'Oh, this is brilliant.' I'd never seen anything like it, because they were so good. The guitarist, Zal Cleminson, did this solo version of 'La Cucaracha' and they had a quadrophonic speaker system thing and the sound guy was making it go round and round. It was an important night.

LEE: He put on this show, and it was like, 'Wow.' That is something that's stamped in your mind. It wasn't manic, it wasn't heavy. It was just different, and visual.

There's this great black-and-white footage of Alex Harvey, from a festival in Norway in '74. Must have only been a few months after we seen him. It cuts to people in the audience staring at him, and the looks on their faces is something to savour. They're like, 'What have we got here?' Because he's on form. He's had a few beers, but he's got them in the palm of his hand. He lets out a little giggle, as if to say, 'I'm going to fuck your little minds up. You're going to get it with both barrels.' He drinks from this bottle of beer and spits it into the audience, and then pours a load of beer in his hand and slicks his hair back like a Teddy Boy. Then he puts this stocking in both sides of his mouth, and does *The Godfather*, then slips this stocking over his head.

CHRIS: You look at Thommo, and it's Alex Harvey. A lot of the things, like when he put the stocking over his head.

So, anyway, that night we went to see him in Leicester Square, we come out, we're down the West End, and we run and jump on the bus to take us home. At the time, the bus conductors used to have these little bags they'd keep their money in, and this particular conductor had left his bag under the stairs. Of course, Thommo's straight over, going through the bag. The conductor came down and went, 'Oi!' The bus screeched to a halt and we ran away, and Thommo threw the bag back on the bus. We turned round, and there's these coppers, and they're like 'Right, get up against that wall.' Now, we had this scam going where we worked out that we could re-use old Tube tickets – we used to go up to Golders Green, because there was kind of deserted exits, and there'd be these old wooden things that collected the tickets. So, we'd just have handfuls of these tickets, and we'd use them on the Tube. This night, I had about twenty of these things in my pocket, and I'm thinking, 'If the coppers find them . . .' So, I tried to discreetly throw them on the ground, but they blew everywhere. One copper said, 'Pick them up, you little fucker, now.' I picked up all these things up and they took us down the station, and they separated us all up.

They kept going to me, 'What are you doing with these tickets?' and I'm just going, 'I found them, I collect them.' I was saying all sorts of bullshit. They were trying to break me down. Then, bizarrely, this copper came in and he went, 'If you don't own up, they can't do anything.' He sort of told me I was alright. So, we went home, but Thommo had to go and appear at Her Majesty's flipping court, as usual. So, I said, 'I'll come along as a witness,' and I got him off. I just said, 'Y'know, he was just mucking about . . . it was just playful . . .'

The best bit was that on the table in the court, they had the contents he'd stolen from the conductor's bag. Was it a load of cash? No, it was a half-eaten packet of Polos, and this dog biscuit that looked like a bone. Obviously, this bus conductor must have had a kind of spare bag. So, hardly the crime of the century.

MARK: I was massively, massively into Mott the Hoople. Their singer Ian Hunter's book, *Diary of a Rock'n'Roll Star*, had a really profound effect on me. At the time, when that book came out in '74, I would have been 13. There were two sorts of camps in music in the seventies, I always felt. There was the pop side, which even though Mott the Hoople were a rock band, they fell into. I thought they wrote really brilliant pop songs. Then there was the hippier side, like Pink Floyd. We were always playing *The Dark Side of the Moon*. It was an album that dominated that period as well.

But I think Mott the Hoople, for me, reinforced that thing of you could really be someone; you could really be in a band. Somehow, I found out that Ian Hunter had written this book, probably from the music press. Because from very early on, me and lots of kids at school were into the music press: we bought the *NME*, *Melody Maker* and *Sounds* pretty much religiously every week and read about all the bands we liked. So, I must have read there that Ian Hunter had this book coming out, and so I went to Compendium Books in Camden, which was near Camden Lock, and bought it. I read it, and just thought, 'Oh, this is it. This is fantastic . . . This life is for me, it really is.' It wasn't phoney, and I think, as a teenager, you can spot a phoney a mile off.

The other band that everyone was into was Ian Dury's band, Kilburn and the High-Roads. Everyone was into the Kilburns. I only ever saw them once, but I know that Chris and Lee went to see them a lot. I think Lee went because of their sax player, Davey Payne. The Kilburns played in all these pubs and that became the pub rock scene. There was the Moonlight club in West Hampstead, the Greyhound in Fulham, the Nashville in Hammersmith. But the main place the Kilburns famously played was at the Tally Ho in Kentish Town.

CHRIS: Lee and I used to go in the Tally Ho, well underage. We'd see these bands, like Ducks Deluxe and Brinsley Schwarz, and I can't remember who was on this one night, but they said, 'Next week . . . Kilburn and the High-Roads.' I went, 'Lee . . . anybody that calls themselves Kilburn and the High-Roads, we've got to go and see them.'

LEE: I wasn't supposed to be in there, being underage, so I was always hiding in the corners. It wasn't a sweat hole like some of the pub venues. The Tally Ho was all red velvet and had a good sound. I had a friend called Mick Aherne who used to work behind the bar, and he was about a year older than me. You'd never have that nowadays . . . But yeah, he was serving, and I think I had a few lemonades in there that were passed my way.

The first time I saw the Kilburns, I sneaked in through the window of the men's toilets: it was not much bigger than a big letterbox, so Christ knows how I squeezed in there. But I ended up hanging upside-down, getting caught on the nipples that hold the window bar on, and because of my weight – or weightlessness, really, being so light – I couldn't get off the hooks. Things were dropping out me pockets. Then this feller walked in, who turned out to be Ian Dury. You could hear the metal clanking of his irons, his callipers.

He goes, 'What you doing in here?'

'Oh, alright, mister,' I says. 'I've come to see the band that's playing.'

'Well, you won't see them in here, will you?' he goes, like, moody. 'Here, let me help you down.'

He helped me down, and I scuttled off like a rat into the night, into the crowd, and that was my first experience of them.

CHRIS: That night, before they went on, I saw Ian Dury in the pub car park. He had a bow tie on, and obviously I didn't know who he was. I said to him, 'What time are the band on?', thinking he was the barman or something. He went, 'I dunno, mate.' And then he gets onstage and I was like, 'Oh, fucking hell, look, there he is.'

At that time, they had this dwarf on the bass, and they had a drummer who was on crutches. His drum stool was connected by a chain or something to the bass drum pedal. The guitarist always looked very cool, clothes-wise. They really were like a misfit band, but I just thought they were amazing because the music was so good. They're definitely the biggest influence on what became Madness, because they did sort of rock'n'roll, they did kind of reggae, they did songs about London. They didn't do, 'I'm going to LA.' They were real. Dury was incredible, and he was always falling over. Once, there was a drum stick on the floor, and I thought, 'He's gonna tread on that and he'll go flying over.' But he had this guy, Fred Rowe, or Spider they called him, and he'd come and get him up. He was flipping something else, Ian.

**LEE:** The little feller on the bass was even shorter than me. The main thing for me was they had a saxophone, which I really had a soft spot for. I suppose I loved the overall fairgroundy, music-hall type sound that the sax player Davey Payne made. He had a tie that lit up: it had bulbs in it and a little battery pack on the side. Ian would throw things out into the crowd, like, odd bits and bobs, little presents – whistles, *boing*, and those little tin clickers they had in the war and stuff like that. I was quite attracted to that. That certainly rubbed off on me.

They were a real mish-mash. A bunch of misfits who all dressed in clothes from War on Want and your tat shop or whatever you called them then.

**MARK:** Songs like the Kilburns' 'Billy Bentley' had a massive effect on Lee. It was about London and it was done in an English accent, and it mentioned a lot of things that we did as teenagers – y'know, going to various places on the bus with our Red Rover tickets. It was a distillation of what a lot of us had done. But it was also just the gas of the idea that there's this guy who didn't have to put on an American accent. So, it really related to our experience.

**MIKE:** I went to see Kilburn and the High-Roads one time at Dingwalls in Camden. Pre-gig, we went into the bar and they were all sitting there, having a fag, and it looked really cool to me. I thought, 'Wow, must be great being in a band, y'know. It's something special.' For us, there was some sort of quest to find something special, or something exciting. There was obviously something psychological about it. I mean, we all came from broken families, pretty much. So probably that ties in with wanting to be special and wanting to be something different.

I used to love going to see gigs at the Rainbow. It was all done up like an Arabian palace or something, and there were stars in the ceiling. But rather than the bands, the main excitement was trying to get in there without paying. That was my speciality: 'Oh, there's a drainpipe over there, and if you go up there, you climb on that little bit, and you can go round there . . .' It was like mountain climbing, sometimes. It was quite an undertaking. We were always completely black after – covered with the grime and stuff. But we used to have these little routes and then there'd be a window up there that you could get through.

It was one thing getting into the establishment, but then it was all about getting into the arena, because they had security around the arena. This one time we sneaked into a Stevie Wonder gig, and we were in the establishment, but we were backstage, and we ended up right up in the heavens or whatever they called it: seeing Stevie down there, playing the piano, miles below . . . Then suddenly somebody came out and we hid in a little cupboard or something. But that used to be very exciting, and I suppose that was a big part of the excitement and the fun of it, was doing that.

Another big experience for me was I had that Bette Midler album, *The Divine Miss M*. I don't know what I would think of it now, but at the time I thought it was great. I guess I was not judgemental, just listening to whatever. But I remember taking acid one time and playing that album – sitting on my bed and listening to that *Divine Miss M* and all these waterfalls of colours and everything were accompanying the music. It was very beautiful. That was a beautiful experience.

MARK: It was very progressive times, the early-to-mid seventies. There was a great place called Talacre right near Kentish Town West that I used to go, from Holloway, in the summer holidays, when I was about twelve. The rest of the band knew it well. There was this famous adventure playground there, run by this guy called Ed Berman and this group called Inter-Action.

CHRIS: When I moved on from the gardening firm and I was working as a gardener for Camden Council, I worked on building Talacre, which was in Prince of Wales Road. I think it was a derelict old piano factory which had been knocked down and we built a little park there.

It was fantastic, because we had this massive area that was fenced around it in corrugated iron, so we were inside there just smoking fags and going round with a wheelbarrow, getting lead, and going to the scrap. Then, of course someone from the council went, 'People need to see what's being done in there: take the fence down.' 'Oh, no . . .'

There was the grimmest pub there, the Prince Albert. It was one of those pubs that had Alsatians on the roof. Like a *scary* pub. It was terrible really, because we used to get to work, then at lunchtime, go and drink about six pints. It was always that thing of, 'Your round, my round, your round, my round,' and you'd always end up square.

Prince Charles came and opened the park, which was funny 'cause it was in Prince of Wales Road. So, we're there and we're laying turf, toiling away. Opposite us were all our foremen and guvnors and bosses with their ties on and their hair all combed, dying to get an audience with him. But he just blanked them and he came and talked to us. He went, 'What are you doing here?' and I thought, 'I tell you what: that's a good pair of shoes you've got on,' because he had a really good pair of brogues on. I said, 'Oh, we're laying turf, Your Highness,' or whatever. He said, 'Urr . . . urr and how do you that?' I said, 'Yes, well, we stitch it together . . .' But, y'know, I thought, 'He's nice, talking to us.' He was cool.

MARK: When I used to go to Talacre, it was when some of the kind of sixties teaching was coming through and these playgroup leaders from Inter-Action were really quite radical. It was all about creativity: kids there with huge sort of saws, building things, and a guy playing a guitar and saying to the kids, 'Now you've got to pretend to be this, that and the other.' Pretty radical for the time.

CHRIS: At the end of 1974, this book about graffiti in America came out, called *Watching My Name Go By*. There was an article about the book in *The Sunday Times* and it was the first time any of us had ever seen New York train graffiti. So, then we started doing it in north London.

LEE: We saw in this newspaper supplement these subways trains covered in paint, and areas of the station covered in paint, and we thought, 'Wow, look at that.' Mike, being the arty chap he is, and Chris and myself, pretty much, we thought we'd follow suit. Having the railway right next to us, you had bridges everywhere. We done one brick wall, which is still there – Ingestre Road, Tammo Land, where the estate is now – and it's way up high. Of course, people have gone, 'How on Earth did they get up there? Did they get on each other's shoulders?' Of course we never: there was scaffolding up, that's how we got it done. That's still there, faded, from '74 or '75.

CHRIS: Simon Birdsall, who lived in Highbury and went to Mike's school, used to hang around with us. He'd write 'DD' on walls, or 'Daredevil', and I half-heartedly did 'Chrissy Boy'. But by then, I was going out with Susan, the girl who became my first wife, so I thought graffiti was all a bit childish. Lee and Mike were prolific though. Thommo had no fear of heights – and he'd do them incredibly well, over railway bridges – and Mike's very artistic. In this one overground station, Mike drew one of those old American streamlined trains. I suppose you had plenty of time to do it: the trains were only every 20 minutes and the stations were pretty deserted.

MARK: On the stations, I saw Mike and Lee's graffiti. I didn't know who they were, but me and my mates were always thinking, 'Fucking hell . . . look what that guy's done,' and it'd be something new every week. Mike's graffiti name was 'Mr B' and Lee's was 'Kix'.

Some of their earlier things were just literally marks; like tags, I suppose they call them these days. But some of the ones on the stations were incredible. The brilliant one was on Highbury station: an American train sprayed in yellow, purple and silver. It was like a perspective train, coming towards you, with 'Mr B' written on it. Because they rode the trains, obviously the railways figured quite a lot in their lives. So, I didn't know who they were, but it was intriguing to see what these guys were doing.

There was a lot of graffiti around – political slogans or 'Your karma's run over my dogma'. Stuff like that. Or even simpler things like that famous 'Clapton is God' in Drayton Park, which I used to walk past all the time. And you had the 'George Davis is innocent' campaign stuff as well, trying to free the armed robber.

CATHAL: My cousins Neil and Pat lived in Gospel Oak, on Mansfield Road, just up from the station. That's where I first saw 'Kix' and 'Mr B', sprayed on the bridge. It was before I'd met them. The first tag that I really noticed was on a wall in Archway – it was done with a paint brush and it said, 'Twitch for Sam Surfer'. For years, I wondered what it meant, until recently, when I discovered a song by Robyn Hitchcock of the same name, which tells the story. It turns out that Twitch was a girl and Sam Surfer was a boy she fancied.

When I got into graffiti with the others, it was at the tail end of their activity. I used to tag 'Seudo', 'Boz' and 'Chas Smash'.

WOODY: I saw really early Kix and Mr B graffiti. It was just literally the words 'Kix' and 'Mr B', on the railway bridges going across the road. I suppose me and everyone else went, 'How in the world did they ever do that?' And, of course, we know now: they used to literally lean right over the edge, and somebody held their legs, while they dangled over the edge.

SUGGS: Everyone was kind of into something. It was a feeling that everyone was just trying to get away from the status quo.

Some of them were going this way, some of them that way, and in the middle were Mike and Lee, who had a foot in both camps. They had both maybe not done everything correctly, but on the other hand, weren't out-and-out psychopaths. The sort of graffiti that Mike did was fucking art, as far as I could make out.

**MIKE:** It was a new thing, graffiti: I'd never heard of that word before. It was a completely new phenomenon. But what struck me was that they were all copying each other in America. They all did things that were very much similar, these big graffiti letters. I suppose, the fact that they were just copying each other, I found it very unimaginative. I guess we did some good things, because everybody's always talking about it. But yeah, we just did things that were a little bit different, a little bit more original than those big chunky letters. I was thinking, 'I'm not going to do that American chunky letters shit.'

**LEE:** Care of Woolworths and the odd auto parts shop, we'd acquire our spray cans and we'd go and do our bits. At first, we'd put our names up – Mike called me 'Kicks' and I think it was just because I was living for kicks. I got my own little spelling of the word, and that was it.

There were a lot of clever graffiti statements around. There was a particular one I liked: 'I'd rather have a bottle in front of me than a frontal lobotomy.' There was another one that said, 'I'm a hog for you, Deirdre.' A lot of the graffiti at that time was in south and west London, but we were sort of at the forefront of it in north London.

We got up on the roof of the assembly hall at Acland Burghley School and we just totally blitzed it with our names. I'm sure it's the same wood that's up there, so you can probably see it, still. Mike was good at doing locomotives and all things American. 'Sneaking Sally' was one tag. 'Daredevil' – or 'DD R EVIL' which I thought was pretty clever, that was Si Birdsall. 'Columbo' was another of his names. He'd always change his name in case we ever got caught, and then he's only done for one . . .

I've got a newspaper clipping from around that time about the graffiti that was going on in London, and the headline is, 'Not so much filth, more of an identity statement,' or words to that effect. And it was. We rarely done it on the side of someone's house. One time though was up in Hampstead – there was a spot which was painted beautifully white . . . white brick, and we ended up scrawling 'Kilburn and the High-Roads' all over it. Then, 'Columbo', 'Heads', 'Kix', 'Debbie' – who was a girl I'd recently started going out with.

I did graffiti my name on George Melly's garage door, though. He wrote a piece in one of the newspapers about it, saying, 'If I ever catch that bastard that wrote Kix on my garage door, I am going to slap his bum.' I bet he would have an' all . . .

MIKE: I guess they were nice drawings, sometimes. We did used to spend a lot of time on it, and I was very into it. We used to get special spray cans and stuff. In America they were all using car paint, and we sometimes went to car paint shops, but it was really shit: you couldn't get a really nice, solid colour. At that time in Woolworths, they used to sell this silver shoe spray that was a bit unusual, and that really used to come out like chrome. So, we used to get a lot of those. We'd be carrying out big bags from Woolworths, when we'd been in there on a shopping spree.

\*

**Woody:** Me and my brother, Nick, lived in Randolph Avenue, Maida Vale, 'til I was three or four.

**Chris:** Me outside Mortimer Terrace, aged about five.

**Mark:** We spent so much of our childhood playing on the street. Big kids taking care of little kids.

**Cathal:** I'm confident I will climb that mountain!

**Lee:** Gazing in the long grass. A young Lee ponders the joys of free spiritedness.

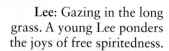

**Mike:** It's a bird! It's a plane! No – it's me and my older brothers, Ben and Danny, staying with our grandma in Petts Wood.

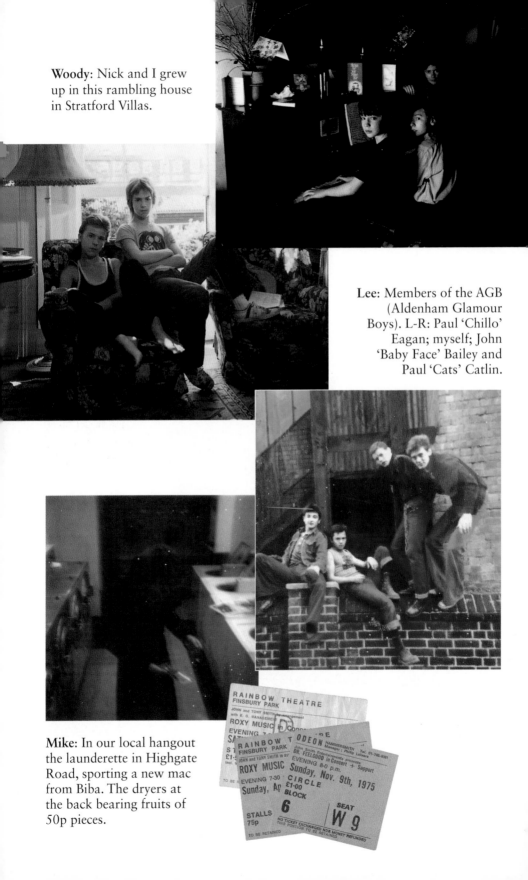

**Woody:** Nick and I grew up in this rambling house in Stratford Villas.

**Lee:** Members of the AGB (Aldenham Glamour Boys). L-R: Paul 'Chillo' Eagan; myself; John 'Baby Face' Bailey and Paul 'Cats' Catlin.

**Mike:** In our local hangout the launderette in Highgate Road, sporting a new mac from Biba. The dryers at the back bearing fruits of 50p pieces.

**Mike:** Me, John Hasler, Tony Hilton and Simon Birdsall (Cathal on camera, I presume) arriving in Cornwall, 'We're all going on a summer holiday'.

**Lee:** Si, Mike and the Great Monkey Tone Refreshment Break, Cornwall.

**Lee:** Up the Eiffel Tower with Simon Birdsall, sampling 1664. Jolly good year.

**Lee:** Debbie Thompson, Sue and Chris Foreman brave the Leysdown sea winds, Summer 1975.

**Suggs:** Very sturdy trousers, bought from Laurence Corner, the Harrods of Army Surplus.

**Chris:** Dogtooth Oxford bags, later taken in on a sewing machine, as worn on *One Step Beyond* album cover.

**Mike:** Me, Chris and Simon.

**Lee:** Myself and Si Birdsall outside the Hope & Anchor.

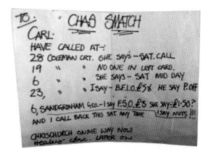

**Lee:** Myself and Cathal tried working as window cleaners. We were absolutely shit.

**Mike:** Hopping a goods train, 1975.

**Chris:** Susan and I cutting the cake. I was 19.

**Chris:** Mike, me and John Jones at my wedding reception.

**Chris:** Matthew and me, Mortimer Terrace squat, 1976. It's not a Rod Stewart haircut. I'd just got up.

**Lee:** Debbie and myself at Sore Throat gig, in the Hope & Anchor.

SORE
THROAT

**Mark:** I first saw Mike and Lee's graffiti on Highbury and Islington station, on my way to school. Firstly I thought, who are they? Secondly, they must be cool!

**Mike:** Of course after the spray painting, the deed needed to be recorded on the latest technology Polaroid film, in as natural a pose as possible!

**Mike:** On the railway bridge over Highgate Road, jumping on the freight trains headed West... Willesden and the great unknown!

**Chris:** Si and me hanging off a goodsie.

**Lee:** A bridge above Highgate Road. Chris and me playing up.

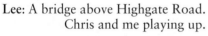

**Lee:** Chris, myself and Mr B pose for the 'Instamatic '74' photo.

**Lee:** Stop that train!

**MARK:** There was another great one on Highbury station that I think Mike did – this 'Paul Hangs Loose' painting, where he drew the back of the Kilburns' *Handsome* album. The original photo is this guy called Paul, and he's doing this sort of dance, and it just says, 'Paul Hangs Loose'. So that was written in really big white paint lettering and then there was a picture of this guy Paul that somebody painted. I don't know if it was Mike who did it.

**MIKE:** I can't remember that anymore, to be honest . . .
We just used to do them wherever we could. We used to like doing them on railways, or on the other side of the Tube track, because we imagined people thinking, 'Wow, they must be daring to have gone and done it on the wrong side of the track.' I guess it was a part of trying to find something different: it was like a different world, almost.

When you went up on the railways – because nobody was allowed up there, and it was all behind the houses and everything – I always liked that it was a sort of mysterious world, kind of existing outside of the normal world. We used to climb up into these other worlds.

Acland Burghley School is all built on this concrete on top of the railways and we'd go under there and be climbing around. There was this one bit, an embankment, and it was horrible, dirty and everything, and it went up and up and up. On the side was almost like a staircase and then it got really narrow at the top, and you'd climb through this little hole. There was a little wall, and you'd jump over, then you were back on the street. But when you were in there, it was completely a mad thing – a bit like *Harry Potter*, y'know. Everybody walks past that wall, but nobody knows what's on the other side. I used to find that fascinating; that idea of being kind of hidden.

One time, on the Tube, we found these hidden passages. Nobody would notice them or know about them. There'd be these little doors on the platform and you'd go in there, and suddenly there's all these secret passages. So, those sort of things always used to interest us, for better or for worse. It made us feel like we were a little bit different, y'know. That we were doing something that wasn't the normal.

I had a strong feeling of that when we were young, that we were a bit different, because of the sort of things we used to get up to. And I guess that rolled into the band, as well, and our attitude towards the music and stuff. The bands we liked were not necessarily mainstream. We always were drawn to something a bit idiosyncratic.

## CHAPTER 6

# HAMPSTEAD DAYS AND
# A CARRY ON CAMPING

**SUGGS:** The film *American Graffiti* was a big turning point for us all. We were all big fans of film in general, and everyone would go to all-night film screenings, showing Marilyn Monroe or Clint Eastwood films, or rock'n'roll films . . . *American Graffiti* being the big one.

On the outside of our firmament were these Hampstead Teddy Boy types – not the hard ones with the drape jackets, but just kind of like the ones wearing baseball boots and bowling jackets. Listening to that music, fifties rock'n'roll, was something that seemed to be happening around that time. You had rock'n'roll revival bands like Sha Na Na and Bazooka Joe, who Mike's brother Dan ended up in.

This was the whole precursor to punk. Rock had just gone really pomp, all Rick Wakeman, or it seemed. Then suddenly going back to fifties rock'n'roll made you realise, 'Man, that's what Alex Harvey and that are trying to go on about . . . they're trying to talk about *this*.' The main thing about *American Graffiti* is the music is as loud as the dialogue. It's very rare that you'd hear that music so loud. If you went to a discotheque, you weren't going to hear that. So, suddenly hearing these really raw fifties rock'n'roll songs, Jerry Lee and Fats Domino and all that, played fucking loud, it really was a revelation.

MARK: *American Graffiti* was a massively big film for all of us. We would sneak into late-night cinema showings, at the Screen on the Hill in Belsize Park or the Scala in King's Cross. They'd put on all-night rock films bills quite a lot, and *American Graffiti* was always shown.

We loved all that doo wop and just the look of it was amazing . . . people looked great. There were a lot of Teds around at the time and the Hampstead Teds in particular looked fantastic. They looked the part and they had all the gear: the guys had the quiffs and the baseball jackets and the girls had all the huge petticoats.

MIKE: There was *American Graffiti* and also *That'll Be the Day*. David Essex and Ringo Starr working in a fairground – in a funny way, it appealed to me at that point. Rock'n'roll was having a resurgence and it was pretty cool.

We started going up to Hampstead a lot, drinking in The Holly Bush pub or The Duke of Hamilton. Everyone was wearing creepers and this American hamburger place had opened there, and that was looked on as pretty cool. I don't know really why we ended up hanging about in Hampstead. I guess it was maybe girls that brought us up there ... knowing girls and then they said, 'Oh, we're going here, we're going there.'

John Hasler was a sort of mate of mine, and he was mates with Cathal. So that was the connection to meeting him.

CATHAL: John introduced me to Hampstead and I ended up meeting all these people. It was a really cool scene. I knew Mike's half-sister, Morag, who was part of this little clique in Hampstead, before I'd met Mike. It was the summer of '76 that I met Mike, Lee, Si Birdsall, Tony Hilton and Paul Catlin. That was a great year. I saw Bob Marley at the Hammersmith Odeon. He was abso-fucking-lutley brilliant, running on the spot as he sang and played the guitar. So light on his feet. When he played 'Get Up, Stand Up', the whole place erupted. Everyone leapt up and sang along. 'War' hit the spot too.

For me, getting in with a group of people – friends, a gang, belonging – it was a massive, massive thing. I suppose I idolised Lee and Mike and Simon: they were cool, they dressed differently. Mike had that kind of silent, *Rebel Without a Cause* gruffness. Lee was enigmatic, so you just had to look at him, what he was doing, what he was wearing. Lee, his sister Tracey and his girlfriend, Debbie – his wife now – they dressed so fucking cool. There was an amalgamation of rockabilly, skinhead and Roxy Music influences. Simon really carried off the braces, wraparound glasses, blue-painted DMs and American baseball jacket look. It was just a kind of melting pot of cultures. They were all cool, and I wanted to be part of it.

LEE: Myself and Cathal ended up being very close. I adored him, he adored me. To me, he was the blond-haired, blue-eyed Cary Grant.

He had this zoot suit, very smart, smoked Senior Service, untipped, like me old man used to smoke. He was quite different – very gentlemanly, very polite and everything. All the things I'm not that I probably wished I was. He sort of looked up to me. But we looked up to each other, I think, if that makes sense.

Hampstead was our watering hole, so we were drinking in The Cruel Sea, the Coach and Horses, The Duke of Hamilton, the Three Horseshoes and The Holly Bush. We were well into our own fashion – multi-coloured Dr Marten boots and all that. I embroidered the New York Dolls' lipstick logo on the back pocket of my Levi's, and I was quite proud of that. Roxy Music on the jeans leg, and then where your trousers were worn, I'd sew in leopard-skin, which was the fifties style, but again, Roxy Music-related. It was all things Marilyn Monroe and James Dean and stuff, and we added to that. I used to like woollen tank tops, but with long sleeves, not your normal tank top. The whole thing was a little bit fifties, a little bit sixties, a little bit seventies.

CHRIS: The Duke of Hamilton had this kind of basement, and a jukebox, and it was almost like a bloody youth club. That's where I first met Cathal. We used to drink light and bitter, and play the jukebox, and there were all these second-generation Teds there.

CATHAL: Hanging around in Hampstead, we were going to parties in these posh houses. You'd open the fridge and there'd be a whole salmon. I mean, I thought salmon came in tins: 'What the fuck's this?' And the girls were very attractive. We would basically gatecrash their parties.

Our mate Kit Gould had his own basement flat. This was outside our ken. But Kit's place was where I first got an introduction to an Aldenham Glamour Boy called Pete Kennedy, who I'd seen in The Bull & Gate in Kentish Town, having three fights, one after another and winning them. He turned up knocking at Kit's door and Kit was going, 'Shh, Don't let him in . . . don't let him in.' There was me, John Hasler and Kit inside.

He said, 'I know you're in there . . . I heard you.' Kit let him in and he picked up a guitar and went to smash it over my head. I had petit mal as a kid, and was on phenobarbitone, so I said, 'I've got a head thing, I'll get brain damage . . . you can't . . .' He wrapped the guitar round John's head instead. But that was it: there were two different groups of kids that we hung around with – the real serious ones doing the various deeds who ended up in prison, and then the ones that became the artsy crowd. Eventually, we all kind of split down the middle.

My petit mal . . . I can't remember ever having fits. But it was a bit like *A Clockwork Orange* – lots of going to hospitals for ECGs and getting things stuck on you: 'Open your eyes, close your eyes,' white lights flashing. I stopped taking the pills around fifteen. I thought, 'Fuck this.'

MARK: John Hasler ended up being the connection between us all. He was two years older than me, and at my school, William Ellis. He looked scary: he'd shaved all his hair off and he had a Levi's jacket, done up, and Levi's jeans and Dr Martens. But actually, when you got to talk to him, he was really lovely.

SUGGS: John Hasler wasn't averse to having a fight, but he wasn't a hard man. He was able to traverse those things that we were interested in, which were the wrong and the right sides of the street, and to not be afraid of either. Because the really bad kids were afraid of being bright or intelligent, or intimidated by it, and the really arty-farty ones were scared of the darker side of the street. I had that almost kind of greed: I didn't want to miss out on either of them, or I wanted to be able to handle myself in such a way that you could communicate with both sides. With the Hampstead mob, you'd need to be able to talk to them about the history of art, and on the other side of the street, you'd be talking about running round at the back of the Shed at Chelsea and kicking people up the arse.

CATHAL: The first acid trip I had was with John Hasler and Mike Barson. We were in The Holly Bush, and it was weird, but I could hear a conversation, like, thirty feet away, and Barso could, too. We never spoke about it until maybe twenty-five years later and realised we'd both had the same experience. In a way, that little black microdot changed my life.

MIKE: It was a very weird experience, hearing the *bu-bu-bu* of all the voices, and just being able to really focus on that one conversation. Acid can give you a very precise, real focus, I think, which is a bit out of this world.

Later that night I ended up at my girlfriend's house. She was two-timing me with a mate of mine – I was going out with her, and then she went and got off with him. Then she was saying, 'Oh, it was just a one-off, it won't happen again,' and then it did happen again. One time, she said to me, 'I've just got to go and say goodbye to him one last time,' and went off for, like, three days ... She was just really into boys fancying her, y'know: she was relishing the intensity of somebody wanting her. So, she was getting him, getting me, and then *whooarr*, conjuring up this sort of energy and everything.

That night, I was tripping in her house and the guy she was cheating on me with came round, and he freaked out and he was throwing dustbins around or something. I'm upstairs, tripping – and like when I was with Cathal – I could hear these weird noises. This wasn't pleasant, though. I could hear these noises and I was thinking, 'Is that a bin? Is that people coming up?' and there was talking. Then the police arrived, because somebody had called them after he'd been throwing around the bins. There was a copper downstairs and I went up and locked myself in the toilet, and that was not very nice. I was quite paranoid in there, wondering what I was going to say or what was going to happen if the copper suddenly came up. I was looking out of the window and I thought, 'Is it the daytime, is it the night-time? Fuck . . .'

MARK: There was dope around at school, and Parliament Hill was the magic mushroom hill of London, really. I was never a massive imbiber, but there were a lot of kids who were and who would spend the summer afternoons there. There was a back door from William Ellis which led straight on to Parliament Hill, so in the summer, for lunch break, we'd literally just walk out the back and sit where the bandstand is there, or sit up on the hill, and a lot of people never made it back in the afternoon . . .

WOODY: Everyone smoked dope at my school, and that was about it, really. There was experimentation with stuff, but it was kind of very of the time. There was a lot of 'Try smoking this' – banana skins and different herbs. That was the funny side of it.

But my brother Nick first took acid when he was 11. He had a friend who lived in an equally bohemian household as we did, and he was given some acid. A little later on, when he was about twelve or thirteen, he took a second tab of acid that really did him. It was just one of those awful, awful things where he opened a door that never closed. He's got schizophrenia and it triggered his episodes.

Let's face it, you're growing, your brain is growing, everything is growing. I certainly wouldn't risk giving that drug to anyone, full stop. But at that age, bloody hell. Poor Nick, his episodes were exacerbated by anything. If someone stuck a joint in his face, he'd completely freak out. It would just set off all kinds of stuff. It was really, really, really worrying, seeing this boy change. He was an extrovert, he had loads of charisma, he was intelligent. Everyone loved Nick. He was just an amazing person. And then, over the years, he slowly withdrew and went into his shell, and couldn't cope with the world.

LEE: I weren't really into smoking dope. I really pegged out and got really sick one time with Chrissy Boy, and it turned me off it. I think that was a good thing. Possibly . . .

CHRIS: In those days, there was always a party on somewhere. One night, there was me and Barso and our mate John Jones, and this Greek kid, Dino, in the Duke. John Jones . . . he was terrible, and he was going 'Come on, we'll nick Mike's car.' Barso wasn't going to drive it anyway because he was drinking.

So, we nicked his car, and we went to this party in this nice house in Primrose Hill. You'd go to someone's house and you'd start looking in all the rooms. I looked under this bed and there was some fireworks. I thought, 'I wonder . . .' and I took a lit fag to them. Suddenly it was like it was *aargh*, as all the fireworks started going off. Someone called the fire brigade, so everybody got chucked out, and we skedaddled.

John Jones said, 'There's another party over in Golders Green.' So, we go to this party, and it was really crap. There was all these sort of hippies by a bonfire. Kind of stonerheads. We're in the garden and it was cold and I said, 'Tell you what we'll do, we'll go home, but we'll all chip in and fill the car up with petrol and put it back where we got it. Then Mike will think, "Ooh, what's happened?". So, we'd all got good intentions, y'know.

But these two stoned hippies started pushing each other around, and John Jones, always ready to antagonise, to accelerate anything was kind of encouraging them to fight: 'Go on, hit him. Hit him, man . . .' and we're kind of laughing. Then somebody said something to John that was a bit threatening so John head-butted this guy. The guy went down, and then suddenly, it was like a zombie film: there was all these hippie types shambling towards us, holding things, threateningly.

I thought, 'This is going to be a right old tear-up here. But there's three of us and it'll be alright.' Then, who comes running in? Barso. 'You nicked my fucking car . . .' We were going, 'Mike, Mike, we were going to fill it up . . .' But it was too late. So, me, John Jones and Dino had to do the walk of shame, because there was no buses or nothing: had to walk from Golders Green, for me, to Kentish Town. Then, from that day on, Mike stopped giving me a lift for a bit, and I thought, 'Fair enough.' I just swallowed it.

**SUGGS:** A lot of my teenage years were spent hanging about in Soho. Those clubs I used to go to that my mum used to work in, you'd get painters and writers, but then you would get builders and plumbers. There were a lot of people in Soho in those days either working or gravitating to somewhere where you had what you could call 'glamour'. With the licensing laws, the pubs shut at 3.30 in the afternoon and didn't open again until 5 o'clock. So, if you knew someone in Soho, you could get into these clubs and then they'd open again at eleven at night, until three in the morning. So, they were a big magnet for a lot of disparate and interesting people.

People like Francis Bacon and Lucian Freud were pointed out to me. It didn't mean anything to me. But George Melly I remember, because he used to play the Merlin's Cave pub, which was opposite the Merlin Street Baths. Some Sunday mornings, I'd go in and have a bath, and my mum would be singing in Merlin's Cave on Sunday afternoon.

Peter Chalk, my best mate Chalky's dad, was a site foreman, but he was a bright man. He was a Communist and he taught me to play chess and all these other things. But he was a piss artist and he spent all his time in the bookies. He was knocking about with my mum for a couple of years, and he gave me an indication that there was a bridge between the real rough side of life and the slightly more bohemian side of life . . . that they weren't mutually exclusive.

MARK: We used to sneak into Dingwalls in Camden on Saturday lunchtimes. This was the dark, dark, dark seventies Dingwalls, where you could sneak in pretty easily, because it was so pitch-black. They had a Saturday lunchtime jazz session with The Iggy Quail Trio. They were straight-ahead jazz, and they had a lot of good people who used to sit in with them. A lot of really good London jazzers used to come in on a Saturday and, really, I think they got paid in drink, pretty much. We could sneak in, and if we weren't making a fuss or anything, watch the band.

We used to go to Camden Lock a lot, because we were chasing girls. A lot of girls from Camden School for Girls used to work at Camden Lock on a Saturday, on the food stall there. So, we'd hang around the food stall and they'd give us tea and we might be lucky to get a burger or something, and when it got too cold, we would move inside and watch the band at Dingwalls. As we got a bit older and my mate Gary, in particular, had a bit more facial hair, he tried to buy a drink for us, with varying degrees of luck.

Camden at the time was a big Irish drinking place. The public toilets that are in the middle of Camden – still are to this day – that area used to be called Penguin Island. The folklore was that it was called Penguin Island because all the Irish dudes, to go to Mass on a Sunday, would wear a black suit and a white shirt and a black tie, and were, like, half-pissed from the night before. They'd be in the toilets getting ready to quickly nip into Mass and then wait for the pubs to open at midday and keep going. But Mass in-between, of course. You had to go to Mass for ten or fifteen minutes on a Sunday, just to clock in and do your religious time . . .

We also used to sneak into the Stapleton pub in Stroud Green a lot and watch whoever was on there. Again, bizarrely, they never, ever threw us out, and there was lots of us – ten of us maybe and all teens. We used to somehow get in and I think they must have used to turn a blind eye, and we'd sit in a corner, just listening to the music.

Sunday afternoons and Sunday evenings at the Roundhouse were a musical education as well. I know Woody was there a lot. You'd have these amazing bills, in the just pre-punk period. You'd have the Kursaal Flyers, you'd have Man, you might have Budgie.

The big one though was when I saw The Clash at the Round-house. It was September '76, only their second gig, and they were at the bottom of the bill. They were met with complete silence, because people didn't understand what they were doing . . . could not figure out what it was. Me and my mates were looking at one another, going, 'We don't know really what it is, but it looks brilliant.' Because they were dressed to the nines, and it was pure energy. Musically, it was all over the place, really, but you could just dig the energy. And you thought, 'Fucking hell: who is this? What are they doing? This is kind of pretty much what rock'n'roll is meant to be, isn't it?' These four blokes and they're banging away and they don't give a shit about what people are thinking.

CATHAL: People thought we were punks, because we had, like, flat tops and crops, and green, red, blue boots. But we weren't punks. The mood in the country then was really anti-punk. We experienced that when a few of us – me, Mike, John Hasler, Paul Catlin – all went on a camping holiday to Cornwall. It was a complete disaster. It was almost like a film, y'know. How to do it wrong . . .

First off, we pulled into our mate Kit's place in Hampstead, and John liberated a lump of hash. Then we drove down to Corn-wall and we ended up in this hotel pub. There was a small room in the back of the hotel, and we ended up there playing pool all night – not going into the hotel itself, just staying in this tiny room. It had a little window hatch, and we could get our beer, and we drank there till it was closing.

When we left, around 11 o'clock, we walked out into the main hall, and it was full of Cornish blokes. They all looked at us, and of course, we were all crops and baseball jackets and Levi's jeans high off the different coloured boots. Basically, a strong look. But they took us for punks, and as we walked out, about fifty of them started chasing us.

MIKE: Yeah, they thought we were punks, and we hated punks, so it was all very strange. All the locals came out in incredible force. First of all, we were walking up the hill, and they were all behind us. I can't remember if they were throwing stuff at us or whatever, but it was looking a bit hairy. Then we started running.

CATHAL: So, we're running along, and I'd taken this lovely old glass ashtray from the pub. We went past this house and through a window, I saw people in there watching TV. So, I threw the ashtray through the window, in the hope that they would call the police and alert them to the fact that there was something going on. Because we were running for our lives.

MIKE: We were thinking, 'These people will look out, ring the police, and we'll be saved by the local police force . . . who are obviously going to help us and not help these bloody yokels who are probably their kids and their brothers' kids.'

CATHAL: We ran into this car park, and it was a dead end. But it turned out to be a church car park. So, we climbed up on this small roof, and looked into the church.

MIKE: At this point, I was like Captain whatsisname in the *Enterprise* . . . Captain Kirk, *Star Trek*. I had a sort of sense of responsibility. I said, 'Quick, we'll hide in the church,' and I said to John Hasler, 'Break that window . . .'

*

CATHAL: So, we broke a window and got into the church hall. We opened up the attic, got in, and we were hiding in there.

MIKE: We had to keep really silent. I was saying, 'Nobody breathe a word,' and at a certain moment, I hear *ckkk*, and Cathal lights up a fag . . . I mean, if they'd found us, I don't know what they would have done. I felt convinced there was a great chance that we would have really got our heads kicked in. And he's sitting there, lighting a fag, risking that possibility on the need to have a fag. But anyway, then the coppers arrived, so we just stayed in there, which I suppose we'd done quite a few times, to avoid getting caught. The police were all looking around, and then in the end, everybody seemed to bugger off and we came out.

CATHAL: It took a while – like an hour and a half, two hours. We got out of there, got into the van. But when we got back to the camp site, we realise we'd only pitched in a cow field, and the cows had trodden the tent down and crapped over everything.

MIKE: It was comical. Our tent was completely gone flat and there was all cowshit on it. It's like the cows really didn't like somebody camping in their field. By this time, it's like, 2, 3 o'clock in the morning, on the outskirts of town somewhere, and our tent was flat, covered in cowshit. It was like 'Jesus, this is surreal.'

CATHAL: So, we're sitting in this van, and we're all spliffing, and the van is full of spliff smoke. Of course, next thing, there's a tap on the window: it's the police. Someone had been breaking into stately homes, and they thought that it was us.

*

MIKE: I don't know what we must have looked like, and they were chatting to us about a break-in at the church. We said, 'Ooh, what church? I don't know any church. Is there a church round here?'

It all seemed to go alright, and it was almost like they were about to go, and then the copper said, 'Let me see your hands.' We got all our paws out, and they were all scratches and dirt and everything. That seemed to tie it up for them. They said, 'Right, you lot are coming with us,' and so we all got nicked.

CATHAL: They pulled us in for questioning. And at that point, they searched the van. We'd been in a bookshop that day, and I'd seen a book, *Crime and Insanity*, that was 25p, but I stole it for a laugh.

Like an idiot, for a joke, I'd written in it: 'Stolen on holiday'. The policeman said, 'What about this, then?' I said, 'You've caught me red-handed. It's a fair cop,' and we all laughed. But they locked me in for the night and wouldn't let me go. One of them said, 'We've lost the key, sorry. You can't go with your mates.' They charged me, but, y'know, it was a small thing. But it was just stupid. Really stupid.

MIKE: The unfair thing was that when we'd been getting into the church, and I was like Captain Kirk, saying, 'Break that window,' and John Hasler broke the window, and we all went in . . . the coppers didn't care who'd said, 'Break the window' . . . they just cared who broke it. So, John Hasler had to go back some months later and I think he got fined. But it was typical – as far as we were concerned, it was just his affair, really. Nobody gave a flying fuck.

## CHAPTER 7

# CROUCH END INVADERS

**MIKE:** I was 18 in 1976, when we moved to Crouch End, farther out in north London. My mum had been wanting to move from Kentish Town for quite a long time. I think she was having financial difficulties. I kept saying I didn't want to move, but then occasionally I would get caught by the police doing something.

I mean, that was a recurring theme when we were young, that we would get caught by the police. We'd go to the police station and they'd ring your parents. In those days, to try and discourage you from doing them sort of things, they would call your parents, and they'd try to make a big scene. So, my mum kept getting called down to the police station, and she was a single mother, and that was a bit traumatic. I suppose it was humiliating, rather than anything else. But she found all that difficult, anyway.

She wanted to move out to Crouch End, I suppose to save a bit of money, and also to get me away from what she saw as negative influences. My brothers were sort of drawn to hippies. Well, Ben was hanging out with the hippies at school, and smoking dope.

So, it was me that kept getting into trouble, because I was hanging around with all these hoodlum mates, whereas my brothers were not; they were hanging out with good boys, middle class, which my mother saw herself as.

We moved to Park Avenue South, number 20. The very first inkling of having a band was when I was in Crouch End. We had big rooms there, because my mum bought a very big house . . . or it seemed big at the time. My brother Ben was serious into music and he bought himself a little baby grand piano, which he had in his room, and he had some amps because he played the guitar as well. I suppose all that stuff was there, waiting to be used, like Aladdin's cave, y'know. You wanted to rub the lamp, sort of thing. Having all the instruments around, it was like, 'Ooh, shall we have a go?'

CHRIS: When they moved to Crouch End, we had certain inside information that Barso's gas meter in Kentish Town had a dodgy lock, and him and his brothers were always nicking the money. So, me, John Jones and Paul Catlin went round there and did his gas meter. There was a right load of old foreign coins and washers in there, I'll tell you . . . Mike's brother Danny and him were really pissed off. Luckily, Danny saw the funny side of it, or he would've bashed me.

I bought my first guitar in 1976, off a tax rebate I got. I'd been working for the council as a gardener, and then Thommo said to me, 'I've seen a second-hand guitar in a shop in Pratt Street.' It was £20, a semi-acoustic with a tremolo arm. It changed my life.

Thommo said to me, 'Here, they're hiring painters and decorators at Camden Council.' So, I went into the council, and they were like, 'Yeah, you can start on Monday.' I go in the council

yard on the Monday, and they're going, 'Where's your whites?'
I'm like, '*Whites*?' I ran home and I got my dad's scabby old
white overalls, rotten old brushes, and went back, and, they were
like, 'Alright, you can start.'

They put me with this bloke who was younger than me, and
I just said, 'Look, I don't know anything about painting and
decorating . . . I ain't got a clue,' and he said, 'Oh, it's alright.'
The first thing we had to do was to paint a ceiling. I had to keep
looking at what he was doing. But I have to say that over the
course of the probably five months I worked as a painter and decorator, I got quite good at it: getting the old brush and slapping a
load of paint on the ceiling.

But this bloke I worked with was funny. He said once, 'I'll
tell you what . . . on this job, we'll water the paint down, and I'll
sell the paint.' And I'm painting this ceiling with this paint that
was like bloody milk. It totally ruined a great light-blue Adidas
T-shirt. And, of course, it all went terribly wrong for this bloke:
he gets seen at the bus stop with two tins of paint and we had to
paint it properly.

I was sort of happy doing that job. But then the guy who was
the foreman in charge, he didn't like me. Because he knew that
I was a chancer, really. He knew I didn't know jack shit. One day
this foreman comes in, and he says, 'I'm going to have to let you
go.' I thought, 'What does "let you go" mean? Let me go where?'
Then, I realised, 'Oh, I'm getting the sack.'

I'd never been to the dole office, and blimey, the one in Kentish
Town Road, in those days, it had a big Perspex thing that the
staff sat behind, because there was always people attacking them
and stuff. It was really violent. One time I saw a guy with one leg
in there, whacking his crutch on the Perspex. You'd go down the

dole office, and of course in those days, there was a lot of jobs – this job and that job – and I kept dodging the bullet.

I was married to Susan and we'd had our son, Matthew. Before we got married, I used to go round her house, watch the telly and say goodbye, then jump over the wall and sneak in her window and get right bang at it. She stopped taking the pill and got pregnant. I was 19. We got married at Marylebone Register Office.

I was so poor, man, and so I used to do a bit of ducking and diving. Go down Sainsbury's and, whoops, a leg of lamb's gone in the kid's pram. Only every now and then.

I was squatting in my old house, in the flat on the top floor. The whole block had been owned by the railway, but the council bought it, and they were doing the houses up. So, there was this whole street of empty houses, but the gas and water were still on. I could only afford a mattress. I had a mattress and a sort of offcut carpet, a little stereo. Didn't have a telly. But then we got this little council flat – after persistent hassling of the council, day after day – in a block called Penshurst, off Prince of Wales Road.

When I started playing guitar, all I could do at first was play one note – just hold my finger on a note – and listen and play along to songs. Then I went and bought this book by this guy called Mel Bay, and it was really good, because it had photos of the guy's fingers, rather than those dots, where you think, 'What finger goes where?' I had that Dr Feelgood live album, *Stupidity*, and I played along with that. So, I was on the dole and playing guitar all the time.

Lee really wanted to play sax, so he just used to practise and practise. It was incredible, really, the dedication he put into it.

\*

**LEE:** I started off on clarinet, but I could not play it for love nor money. The first chance I got, I traded it in for an old Boosey & Hawkes tenor sax down at Dingwalls. It was altogether odds and sods: bits of cotton and elastic bands on it and stuff. Only four or five keys worked on it, because it needed a good overhaul, and I just couldn't afford that. But you could get the notes you needed out of it for, like, 'Rock Around the Clock' or 'See You Later, Alligator'. You couldn't get 'Take Five' out of it, put it that way. Or 'Tequila'.

I was very drawn to the saxophone. Whenever I went to a gig, I'd stand in front of the sax player. At home, I'd play along to records . . . anything really, but especially fifties R&B: Fats Domino . . . Coasters stuff . . . which I tried to master, but it took a hell of a long time. I liked what Andy Mackay played in Roxy Music. He didn't do ten-minute solos or anything. He just played stuff that wasn't too jazzy, or too technical. He used a lot of staccato, which rubbed off on me. Nothing too fancy.

I was living in Luton at the time with my parents, but I ended up coming down with the saxophone in a bin liner and squatting at Chrissy Boy's. I was finding things really difficult. I was staying around various places. Sometimes I was living with my uncle in Denyer House in Highgate, which was OK, but I couldn't blow the sax too much round there. He'd be like, 'Get the fuck over the park and play that thing. Can you not play Nat King Cole?'

So, then I used to practise on a derelict industrial site backing off the Highgate Road with my old Boosey & Hawkes. I'd just wander over and have a blast by the big bonfires that normally went on from the wood being burnt there. It got pretty cold, and the bonfires kept us warm outdoors. I'd do, like, an hour there, just blowing away on the sax, into the flames.

Or I used to stay at my girlfriend Deb's. Her parents allowed it, provided there was no hanky panky, and I'd practise the sax there: stuff a sock down it, or I used to get a rubber doughnut dog-chew thing and wrap that in a T-shirt or something and push it down the bell to dampen the sound.

Up in Luton, sometimes it would get claustrophobic and I'd just make a bit of a packed lunch and take a cassette recorder into a field and just blow away. It was quite nice. You were looking out at all the bales of hay and the odd inquisitive cow. Soon got shot of those . . .

MIKE: I was into commercial art and cartoons, so I ended up going to Hornsey College of Art in Crouch End. But I didn't have a very good attitude, I suppose, and it wasn't really what I wanted it to be when I went to art school. It didn't seem to be about art: it was about theorising. My mother used to say that art was always looked down on in academic circles, and at that time, they were trying to make themselves more intellectual . . . to make out there's more than just being able to draw . . . it's not just, like, a technical skill. So, maybe they were emphasising that too much, I don't know.

They had this big room downstairs in the college with a grand piano in it. I don't know what they used it for, but there was never anyone in there. I always had this issue with being late. So, often I would come late, and then there would be that thought: 'Oh, there's no point in going now, because the class has already started. It would be better not to go at all, than to come in late again.' I used to go and play the piano instead.

By then, we also had more than one piano in the house, because my brothers both used to play. I've got one memory of trying to learn 'Sad Lisa' by Cat Stevens, which had a very nice piano part. I tried slowing the record player down to 33 from 45, really trying to hear every note so I could play it properly. As it changed key it was complicated, but I kept going at it

My brother Ben was studying music at that time and he went to America. He was hands-all-over-the-place, really fast, which I never was able to get to, past a certain level, in syncopated style. He was into modern jazz particularly. He used to play in a band in a pub down by the Oval, and it was all instrumentals. So, it was a funny thing, again, the difference between us brothers. I used to go down there and I thought it was alright and I occasionally liked some of the things they were playing. But when I started a band, the last thing I would have done was some experimental jazz thing.

CHRIS: There's Mike, who's the youngest brother, then there's Danny, and there's Ben, who's the oldest. Danny was in Bazooka Joe, and he was quite a hard nut. Out of all the three brothers, you didn't want to get in a fight with him. Ben was really musical and had long hair, though he wasn't really a hippie. Because we rehearsed in their mum's house, and I was using Ben's amp, he used to encourage me on guitar. But Mike really helped me learn guitar. He'd go 'C7 . . . look, that note's a 7th . . .' But a lot of the stuff we were doing then was so basic, it was C, F and G. If you don't know that, you might as well blooming go home. We just did that classic thing of learning all these songs that we liked. John Hasler became the drummer and so he would bring his drum kit along.

MIKE: Chris was learning guitar by me saying, 'Press that one, that one and that one, and then you've got a chord there.' We were playing 'Rock Around the Clock' and things like 'Crippled With Nerves', which was an old Kilburn and the High-Roads song. We did 'It's Too Late' by Carole King, and that was the first time I guess when it sounded like, 'Wow, we're actually making music.' That was a bit of a buzz, for everybody, that we were actually all playing different things and it was making a whole.

CHRIS: I bought another guitar which was a sort of Fender Telecaster copy. It cost, like, thirteen quid or something. I changed the price tag in the shop. I didn't get that much off it with the different tag, really.

Then, that other semi-acoustic guitar I had, I ended up smashing it up. Mike was a good mate, because he still used to come in his van and pick me up. We used to rehearse three times a week, and it wasn't going down well with my wife, even though it wasn't like I was going out and getting pissed or anything. But, one time, I was outside, leaving for rehearsals, and I looked up at our flat and she was hanging my other guitar, the one that I wasn't taking with me, out of the window. Now, I can go from nought to zero: I can get angry quick.

So, I thought, 'Fuck this' and I went back inside . . . and I had this really nice old spin-round chair with wheels on that I'd got off a skip. So, I just got this guitar and went *bang* – smashed the guitar to bits and smashed the chair to bits and went to rehearse.

But I had a friend on the council called Brian Pierce, and he knew a bit about electronics and guitars. I went round his house and we made this composite guitar from the two guitars – took bits from the one I'd smashed up, like, the pick-ups were better and stuff like that. So, I made this guitar and then I made a case.

I knew a bloke, Dave Webster, who had this little carpentry shop in Kentish Town Road, and he showed me how to make a guitar case. I used to get the bus up to Crouch End, with my guitar in this case, and it weighed a ton.

LEE: I had my old Boosey & Hawkes sax, and then I got a much better one, a Selmer Mark VI. An old pal of mine – who I was starting to go down the wrong road with again – was at the Sundown one night, this soul disco place that used to be opposite Centrepoint. He came out with a couple of friends and made his way up Hampstead Road to the Fender Sound House shop, where he got up on a friend's shoulders, and slid out these Venetian-type windows they had. Then, he climbed in and handed out some instruments.

One of them he went to hand out was a Selmer Mark VI. But his friends had drew the attention of a policeman who was slowly approaching. My mate was in the shop window and had nowhere to go – it was lit so brightly, as they are, and with the shiny tinsel that makes it all the more inviting to come in and buy an instrument. So, he just stood there side-on, like a mannequin, with this sax in his mouth, in a dummy pose, and the policeman didn't notice him. Luckily, they were looking more the other way.

So, I bought the sax off of them and I was still playing it when we came to make the first album. Another fellow I knew had turned up and spoke to Debbie.

'Uh, is Thommo about?'

'No, he's out,' she said, 'doing his gardening,' or whatever it was I was doing.

'We've got something that might be of interest ... it's a new saxophone.'

They all wanted to get rid of it quick, and I was the obvious choice, and she got the money together to pay for it, off some local fellow. She paid £100 for it, and I still haven't paid her back . . .

So, I'd got myself a proper sax and I think we got better as a band pretty quick. Mike was classically trained – he knew a chord or two, and it was like he had six fingers on each hand. He wrote some discordant tune thing, which I really liked. To me it was nutty, it was mad, it was very fairground. Kilburn and the High-Roads-sounding. It was kind of plinkety plonk, and that really attracted me.

**CATHAL:** That Kilburns influence can't be underestimated. Lee came up to us one day in Southend Green with a copy of the 'Rough Kids' single. He said, 'You've got to hear this track, "Billy Bentley",' that was on the B-side. It was an amazing moment. It just seemed to be our thing straight away, what we loved.

Mike, Lee and Si used to pilfer eight-track tape cartridges, from Woolworths in Kilburn High Road. They could fiddle with the racks and slide them out. Then, they'd go in and exchange them for albums. Polaroids became our big thing. We were flamboyant and dressed to be visible. So, there were lots of these photos of everyone throwing shapes. Weekends would be, like, meet in the pub, do Polaroids.

I left school when I walked out in the middle of a caning: 'Listen, I'm not having this. I'm off.' Within a few days, I had a job in Eastbourne Terrace in Paddington, being a time analysis clerk for this oil-rig company, CJB. Dad had got me this suit from Burton's, off the peg, gave me a few words to use in the interview – y'know, heat exchange, metallurgy, vendor prints, just some relevant words. And I think just because I could say that I'd lived in Iraq and Iran and Dad was in the oil game and all that, I got the job. I was making great money. I was earning probably more than my teacher, six days after I left school.

It was sweet revenge, 'cause in a maths exam just before I'd left – and being crap at maths – I just sat reading a book. There really was no point bothering trying to answer any of the questions. The teacher, Mr Keenan, came up to me and whispered in my ear, 'I can't wait for you to fuck off.' Truth is, neither could I.

MARK: I first picked up the bass at school. One of my mates was Gid London, whose parents had bought him a guitar. Gid was very keen to be in a band and he said to me, 'Come on, can you get a bass?' Then another mate of ours, Will Gosling, became the drummer. But I thought, 'Jesus Christ, how am I going to get a bass?' So, my nan – God bless her – she said, 'I'll buy it for you as a birthday present.' So, I bought a bass and an amp from Woolworths. I think the bass was thirty quid – quite a lot of money – and the amp was about the same, and that's how I first started playing.

At first, I was no good at all. Gid taught me some things and we played a lot of blues, because it was three chords and easy. But then I just got really into it. I used to try and play along to records: put the needle on the record, play a section, try and get what the bass player was playing, very slowly. Take the needle off, practise it a bit, put the needle back on. The old trick used to be that if you had a single, you'd slow it down to 33 ⅓ rpm to hear it slower, to try and pick notes out.

We were called Ratz and we used to rehearse in Will's house in Hampstead, in the basement, when his mum and dad were away. It was funny, because we had an early affirmation about how great it was to be in a band: one time when we were rehearsing in Will's basement, we heard a knock on the door. We opened up the door, and these two girls walked in and said, 'We're having a party this evening, do you want to come along to our party?' We went, 'Yeah, yeah, sure,' trying to be cool. But I'd never really spoken to many girls before that. Then when they shut the door, we were like, 'Yesss . . . this is it . . . this is being in a band. Girls come round and go, "Do you want to come to our party?"'

**WOODY:** I only gravitated towards drums because I couldn't bloody play an instrument. I tried piano, I tried violin . . . oh, God, that was an awful, squeaky mess. I was just trying to play along with my brother Nick, somehow. So, I bashed a piano stool that we had with a pair of sticks for a while. But it was alright, really, because it was the seventies, so that very dull, thuddy sound actually sounded like most of the records that we were listening to at the time.

I did eventually get a drum kit. We had a mate in Parliament Hill and he had an old snare drum, a rattly old thing, and a few bits and pieces knocking about which he gave me, to kind of get a kit together. But it wasn't proper. So, my godmother, Clemence Watt, bless her soul, cobbled together some money to buy me my first, Ajax drum kit. I was a coin collector, and I managed to sell some half-sovereigns to buy some cymbals. They were the cheapest, nastiest cymbals around. But I loved them, because they were *cymbals*, and it was all just brilliant.

Nick and I started playing in our house. I mean, God, the neighbours on one side wanted to kill us. They used to knock on the door, like, steam coming out of their ears, just red and apoplectic with rage. But we carried on. I built a little amp for Nick, using the amp from a TV, and attached tiny little speakers.

Even though I was at Haverstock Hill School and Mark was at William Ellis, kids at the schools did intermingle and go to the same parties. All the musicians from the schools generally got together round friends' houses and we used to jam a lot. Bands were made up, and drummers and bass players and guitarists came and went. There was a lot of mixing up of bands. There seemed to be a different group every week.

There were loads of bands, and it was all connecting at parties, basically. Whoever had drum kits and amps set up at their places around Hampstead and Highgate and Colindale and Hendon – a north London thing, basically – you used to meet. I met Mark as a bass player at our mate Laurie's house. He was really nice . . . quiet. I mean, he was not the greatest of bass players when I first met him, but the one thing that I really admire about Mark is he does everything correctly. It's all very precise and it's all about technique. When he learns something, he learns properly. He doesn't rush things.

Steel Erection was me and Nick's first band, with some mates at school. Back in the late sixties, when the Westway was being built, we'd seen a sign saying, 'Beware – steel erection'. We just thought it was hysterical, being wee kids. So, in Steel Erection, we did The Doobie Brothers' 'Long Train Running', The Animals' 'The House of the Rising Sun', the Stones' 'Jumpin' Jack Flash' . . . y'know, all the classic school band songs. We used to have gigs at our house in Stratford Villas – have a party, set up the gear and then we'd play. We played at school a few times, and then we got a gig at the Enterprise pub, opposite the Roundhouse, when I was fifteen or sixteen.

A few year later, when I met Suggs, and his mates Chalky and Toks, I think it was Toks who said, 'Oh, I remember a gig you

did.' I went, 'Yeah?' He said, 'Yeah, we came and smashed it up.'
I went, 'Oh, yeah, it was you, was it?' Steel Erection did a gig
we'd set up in some hall, and it was all the nicer, kind of gentle,
posh kids from Haverstock Hill School in the audience. But these
rougher kids turned up and smashed up the gig. My dad was fling-
ing his camera around and taking a few of them out. It did get a
bit nasty. Toks thought it was a right laugh: it was quite traumatic
for me. But my dad dealt with it . . . told them all to fuck off.

SUGGS: When I started calling myself Suggs, I was looking for a
graffiti tag more than a nickname. It was partly that I was bored
of being called Haggis and Fleabitten Jock Bastard and all that.

What happened was my mum had an encyclopaedia of jazz
musicians. Me and Chalky were sitting one afternoon, looking
for a tag for me: 'Graham McPherson . . . that's going to use
up far too much spray paint, and it's going to be pretty obvious
who it is, isn't it?' So, I put a pin in the encyclopaedia of jazz
musicians, and it stuck in the letter 'e' of the word Peter, and
I thought, 'Well, that's no fucking good, is it?' But then I saw his
second name, which was Suggs. And it was like, 'Drugs? Thugs?'
I thought, 'That sounds good.' I was about thirteen or fourteen
when I went into school and said to Mr Thomas – the one teacher
who liked me – 'I'm just going be called Suggs from now on.'

Another big moment was when I'd got into some juvenile
affray up by Southend Green – a fight with my mate Tommy
Mallory – and we both got arrested. I had to go to Highbury
Magistrates' Juvenile Court, with my mum. She was having a
fag out of the window and she could see the back of Highbury
overground station where, in great big letters, it said 'SUGGS'.

'That's a bit weird, isn't it?' she said. 'Isn't that that stupid name they call you?'

'No, mum, no,' I went. 'That's somebody else entirely . . .'

Funnily enough, spraying your name up was a form of communication. Later, when I started drinking and going in the Hope & Anchor, the guys there were all called things like Toks – who became my mate – and Dixie and all that. Just skinheady types from round there. They'd go, 'Oh, are you that Suggs bloke?', because they'd seen your name around. That in itself was a kind of status. Of course, that's what all graffiti is . . . it's just trying to create a kind of status for yourself. People would go, 'Fuck me, that's Mr B and that's Kix and that's Suggs.' You'd overhear someone going, 'There's Dixie.' 'What, *the* Dixie?' Because he'd been spraying his name all round town.

All that stuff gave you status and confidence. A couple of times we went down the West End on speed, a load of us, and I had this idea that we could actually take over the West End . . . We were going to go in some strip club and take it over. That lasted about twenty minutes, until we got our arses kicked.

In May '76, when I was 15, I went to my first gig, The Who playing at Charlton FC's ground. Me, Chalky, and a load of us went down there, and the wall around the ground was quite low. We were trying to put our hands over, and there's security people banging it on the other side with spanners and iron bars and fuck knows what. We started going round the wall, till we got to a bit where they weren't, and then we dived in and found ourselves head-first, down in the urinals, because they were actually against the wall. I just about got to my feet and all the bouncers came bursting in, and these great big geezers who were fans of Alex

Harvey, who happened to be supporting The Who, went, 'He's with us . . . fucking leave him alone.'

Then, seeing the outrageousness of Alex Harvey . . . you can't not be hit by that as a teenager. He was properly Scottish, but he was funny, he was charming, and theatrical, and he brought things like Jacques Brel to our firmament. 'Next!', and all that lyricism and poetry. Somebody, and I don't know who, coined the phrase 'comic malevolence'. Now that is a fucking great phrase, because that describes Alex Harvey and Ian Dury and some aspects of us. I mean, we weren't quite as malevolent as Alex Harvey, on the outside. But we were really . . .

MARK: Around '76, '77, you used to see The Clash wandering around in Camden. I worked for a bit as a screen printer at a shop in Camden Lock, to earn some money and get a portfolio together for art college.

The Clash were rehearsing there, and you'd see them walking up and down, and they'd look great, really striking. I'd seen them play a few times by this point, as well, so I was really into them. One time, I even plucked up the courage to go into their place, Rehearsal Rehearsals. That was really scary. You could hear the band playing sometimes, in the back of the market called the Stables. There were some steps that led up to this door, and we knew that that was where they went in, so we'd sometimes hang around.

We'd hear them and think: 'Shall we ring the door?' 'No . . .' But we knew that they had two women there who made all their clothes for them, and one day we plucked up the courage to go in. 'Hi, are you selling any of the clothes?' We were really shy, and they had everything: they were making those Clash trousers, and they had all the shirts and the famous Westway Riot T-shirt that they were screen-printing there. We didn't buy anything that time, but I went back on my own, and I bought one of those Westway T-shirts.

**WOODY:** Dr Feelgood were always on at the Roundhouse, and I saw a really early version of The Stranglers there, in '76. Jean-Jacques Burnel was having a go at the crowd because he was tuning his bass. He said, 'We do like to be in tune, y'know.' It was like, 'Be patient.' I liked that. They were punks but they were good bloody musicians.

**CHRIS:** As we started rehearsing more round Mike's house, it was usually Mike and Lee that would suggest songs for us to play. Mike was very committed to it. I was kind of serious about it, but he did things like he went and bought a reel-to-reel tape recorder, spent a lot of money. And he did these great little recordings. He did Stevie Wonder's 'For Once in My Life', and he played the piano, but he did a little guitar solo. Because he could look at a guitar and see where the notes were. I couldn't see what the notes were. If someone went, 'Play an A note,' I'd be, like, 'Er?'

We were sitting round Mike's one night, and it was late, and we were having cups of tea and fags and talking, and saying all these possible band names. Mike said, 'The Invaders?' I was like 'Oh, yeah, yeah . . .' I just thought of the science-fiction TV series from the sixties, where they used to say, 'Only one man has seen them.' So, I thought The Invaders was a great name.

**MIKE:** We were almost in an alternative reality, or I was. That was the appeal of the shoplifting trips we used to go on. We used to go to Biba a lot, in Kensington. That was a bit of a fashion thing, because they used to have these kind of spy Mackintosh coats there.

Biba was in Barkers, the department store, and you went round the side and you could go up to Biba in the top. It was all very dark in there, and they were very lackadaisical. A lot of people used to go down there stealing clothes. A lot of different kids in our sort of gangs. They didn't have their security well sorted out there, and then it's like, once you've got a hole in the thing, these little terrors start turning up.

One time I got chased by a policeman, in Kensington, after I went after one of these Mackintosh coats from Biba. Getting caught, or nearly getting caught, was a regular thing. Every now and then, a man would go down. That used to be the big moment, when you were leaving the shop: your hair's standing up . . . is somebody going to suddenly jump out? And somebody did when we came out of Barkers in South Kensington this time. He said, 'Oi, you didn't pay for that.' So, then, suddenly I'm running full speed down the street and there's a guy chasing you. You're a bit outside the norm of society at that moment. Everybody else is following the rules and they've got their shopping bags and everything, and you're some character who didn't want to pay.

But this guy was as fanatical as anything. I ran down to the Tube. I mean, I was pretty young – I was only 18 – so I thought, 'I'll be able to outrun him.' But he was not giving up. I ran into the Tube station, over the old barriers and all that, and down the stairs. I thought, 'I've got to have lost him,' but there he was. So, I went down the stairs, I came back up again, and he's still behind me, and it was like, 'How am I going to lose him?' And then I thought, 'I know . . . I bet he won't dare go off the end of the platform.' So, down I went. By then, I was all spitting up, y'know, gooey spit and everything. I went to the end of the platform and I ran off the end, down the line, and he stopped. It wasn't underground, it was the open-air bit, and I managed to climb up a wall somewhere. I found a little laundrette and sat in there and waited for the heat to die down, for a couple of hours.

Maybe I started to think around then that we were going too far with the nicking. One time, when we were in Camden Lock, and some guy comes along in a boat, and he says, 'Do you want to have a ride on the boat?' He takes us down the canal a little bit in the boat, and what does Lee do? He goes downstairs in the cabin and he nicks the bloke's wallet out of his jacket. The bloke's being so kind to us, friendly and everything, and then he gets that thrown in his face.

But the big thing that happened when I was 18 was I ended up in prison. That was pretty stupid. Me and a mate were on a Tube train one time, and we found a load of these long, neon light bulbs, and we were just smashing them. We were just playing, in some ways, making a bit of a mess. But there was some bloke walking along, a member of the public, and he was making snooty noises, expressing his dislike about what we were doing.

We started walking behind him, and I was provoking him a bit, I suppose. I was putting my foot under his jacket or something, which was pretty harmless, but I don't know if he would have known that. I was a bit cocky, I suppose: 'Oh, don't like it, do we?' Anyway, the police got called and we got chased and caught and taken to the police station. Then they said it was, like, grievous bodily harm or something. They said it was a serious, sort of violent crime. It wasn't really, but maybe that was a debatable thing, whether it was or not. I mean, nobody got beaten up.

But then, when it came to court – because we'd been stopped by the police a lot of times – the judge decided he was going to make an example of us. We were in the cells in King's Cross, where they used to have a court house, and people there were talking about the judge: 'He's a difficult judge' . . . 'He's not a difficult judge.' But we wasn't really listening to it. And our case came up and we got taken out into the court.

*Knock, knock, knock.* They were all talking away. Then the judge said, 'Remand without bail.' *Tonk.* And I heard it, and thought, 'Hold on . . . what's that mean?' We were taken back downstairs and then, five minutes later, we were in a van and off to Wormwood Scrubs, because we were 18. So, all our childish shenanigans when we were younger were starting to look a bit less childish, 'cause we were now men. The judge was obviously looking at us and thinking, 'These are going to be wrong 'uns.' So, he thought, 'I'll short, sharp shock them.' He would give us a little bit of a taste of where it leads to, sort of thing, and so we ended up in the proper prison, totally unexpected.

We were in there about three weeks, and it was pretty horrible. I had some unpleasant experiences. Most of the time, we were in the cells. I was sharing with a couple of black guys, and one of them was sort of friendly. We were chatting, and it was funny how separate people are. He was saying to me, 'Is it true that white people turn on the hot water before the cold water when they run a bath?' I thought, 'What the fuck's he on about?' But it was that idea of, 'Ooh, you're a white man, I've never really met one of them before.' Then there was this other guy, doing all these karate chops in the cell, and I thought, 'Fucking hell, I don't want to mess with him.'

I didn't see my mate that much. Every now and then, I saw him in the corridor. In the morning, the door opened and everyone got out and you had to go and empty your piss bucket in this big piss fountain thing in the corridor, and it stunk like anything. A lot of the 18-year-old kids didn't mind it in there, they thought it was fine. But I really didn't like not being able to do what you wanted to do, and having another human being saying 'No.' I found that very difficult.

One time, we were in circuit training, a small group of prisoners, about ten or fifteen of us. There was this right sadistic prison guard bodybuilder, and he had us going around the circuit: lift up this medicine ball, pick up the chair, six press-ups, on to this one, that one, that one. We're going round and round and round this tiny little claustrophobic gym, and he's going, 'Two minutes left . . . one minute left. The first one who drops out, he's going to stay behind and we're going to do some serious training. Just the two of us.' And I was totally petrified of staying with this fucking guy. God knows what he was going to get up to, locked in the middle of Wormwood Scrubs. So, I just pushed myself and pushed myself. You were never quite sure how serious they were – whether they were slightly pissing around with you or not. But I didn't want to be the one to find out . . .

In the prison, I wrote a lot of letters to my girlfriend. It makes you want home sweet home. After that, when I got out, I went into probation, with some guy in Highgate. It was the first time anyone had really talked to me, I suppose. Because I never had a dad . . . I only had my mum, and she was always busy doing things, like mums do. But not really discussing stuff the fact that I had, like, six hundred albums or something in my bedroom. I didn't have any money, so I don't know what she thought. She never said anything to me, so I don't know if she ever thought, 'Where the fuck did all these albums come from?'

So, I'd never really had anyone to talk to, until I went to probation. I mean, it's all a bit clichéd, really – I'm a bit of a sad fuck, I guess . . . But, I mean, there was all these really tough kids who would just brush this stuff off. I don't know really whether that was any better, because some of them ended up probably not in a good place. Anyway, this guy's talking to me and I'm talking about my situation, and I start thinking about it. He's helping me to self-reflect a little bit, and I realised that I was taking it too far.

But, like I said, we were getting older.

CHAPTER 8

# SHAVED HEADS AND
# DEMOB SUITS

**LEE:** We turned up at a Bazooka Joe gig at the Hampstead Town Hall, and these rock'n'roller bikers that were there picked on Si Birdsall. Si had very long, blond hair and he was a good-looking lad, but baby-faced. He got separated from our crowd. We probably ran up the stairs to bunk in or something: 'We can't hang about, come on, Si, keep up,' and he got caught. He got chained across the head, and his hair just turned red, caked in blood. We're going, 'Who the fuck's done that to you?' and he's saying, 'Those blokes down there.' Fucking big bikers, y'know. He did get a bashing.

**CATHAL:** Danny Barson was the singer in Bazooka Joe, and they were all rockers. Their set used to end with them singing 'Somebody's Gonna Get Their Head Kicked in Tonite' and there was a right tense atmosphere in the crowd. It definitely felt like it would kick off. I don't think we were particularly aggressive. I think we just stood out, being skins, and it annoyed the rockers.

LEE: Si landed up getting his head shaved. I think he had to have some stitches and they shaved parts to get the stitches in. We were like, 'Fuck' – it really suited him. So, me and Cathal and John Hasler all got our heads shaved.

CATHAL: He'd been chained on the head, so in sympathy, we all had a crop, at the old Greek barber's on Pratt Street in Camden.

MIKE: I certainly didn't shave my head in sympathy for him. Simon was Cathal's best mate, so he's probably thinking, 'Oh, we're all doing it in sympathy.' That sounds a bit weird to me.

LEE: I had a bet in The Holly Bush with Hasler. I said, 'Oi, go and get your hair shaved and I'll pay for it.' I mean, it was only 50p. I still haven't paid him, and I do regret that . . .

I used to give Chris and Mike haircuts with those little plastic clipper gizmos from Woolworths: it was a bone colour and it had a razor blade in each end. I got pretty tasty at it, and I wanted to become a hairdresser. I ended up going to Vidal Sassoon's night school that he put on for students. I done an evening or two there, but, yeah, I didn't go after a while.

CHRIS: Apart from Bazooka Joe, another band that used to play Hampstead Town Hall a lot was Split Rivitt, who were kind of quite competent. They used to mainly do covers, and they had a bit of money behind them. One time, me and Mike went to see them, and when they'd gone off, we said, 'Let's go and nick a couple of microphones.' We got up on the stage, pretending we were roadies, and then, *whissh*, nicked a couple of mikes.

SUGGS: That whole skinheady style was our thing. I mean, I was dressing like that from when I was about fourteen. It was just a coincidence that Cathal and Mike and Lee were a bit like that. Mike had a little bit more of a Teddy Boy thing going on. But it was all just about finding these funny old retro styles and the music attached to them and all this other stuff.

Teddy Boys at that time were like old blokes to us, because we were kids. But they were bizarre times: running round the King's Road, and we were like proto-skinheads. We'd be chasing the punks one way and we'd be chasing the Teddy Boys the other way.

You'd just agree to meet at a Tube station: 'Apparently this is where the Teddy Boys hang out.'

'Do they? Well, let's all see how many of them there are before we get carried away, eh?'

Then, suddenly you'd think, 'Fucking hell, there's not that many of them. Fuck it, let's go for it.' But then you'd come unstuck sometimes when it'd turn out there'd be a lot more of them than you.

I mean, I wasn't a great fighter by any means, and really hurting people didn't turn me on. It was much more the thrill of the charge and the noise and the *wheee* and winning, basically. Scattering them. Actually kicking someone in the head . . . I didn't really like it. You'd see people who were properly psychopathic, who actually liked the sight of blood, and got turned on by it. I had no interest in that, not at all. But, y'know, bowling in somewhere with all your mates and scaring off the enemy . . . it was exciting. I don't know what it was. I think it's why people join the army or something – to fight the enemy and have all that camaraderie. Then afterwards, to go, 'We all survived.'

It was a thrill, going en masse down to see Chelsea on a Saturday. My mate described it perfectly: 'You wake up nervous and you go to fucking bed nervous.' When I say it was a thrill, it was a terrifying thrill, because you could just bump into anyone, anywhere. Y'know, get on a Tube train and it's suddenly full of West Ham fans, and you could get kicked all over the place.

Millwall fans were the worst. One time, going to the old Den at Millwall, with Chalky, he had the great foresight to go, 'Let's not go in the away end. Let's go in the Millwall end. Hide your scarf.' Anyway, we just saw the Chelsea fans being sort of annihilated in the away end.

Terrific excitement, though, going down the Tube and you'd hear a roar coming round the corner, and you didn't know who it was. We went to Charlton once and went in their end. You'd hope that someone was going to start singing Chelsea songs and at the same time you'd hope that there'd be enough of you not to get beaten up. There was enough of us, so much so that some of them got bored and set fire to the stand. By the time I left, the ground was on fire. Outside, through the smoke, we were greeted by a phalanx of mounted policemen. Some clever fucker realised that if you scattered marbles on the ground, the horses went flying, especially if they had a dart or two in their arses. Then, there'd be a volley of Coca-Cola cans from the upturned hot-dog stall, knocking the coppers off their bucking horses. It was like Agincourt.

We were the generation that were just rebelling against everything. One of the greatest days I had in that context was when the one teacher I liked said to me, 'There's this picket thing going on at Grunwick Film Processing Lab in Dollis Hill, where the Indian women workers have got no rights. If you like throwing bricks at policemen, come with me.' We went down there at six in the morning, and then whatsisname turns up from the NUM ... old shredded wheat barnet ... Arthur Scargill. This was before any secondary picketing bans. Suddenly it was like, 'Fucking hell, the Old Bill have been scattered. This is brilliant. Throwing bricks at the Old Bill!' But, it was for a cause, and it was a buzz. At last! Rebel *with* a cause ...

CATHAL: Around this time, Si Birdsall had allowed me to get a room in his place. Lee wanted the room, but I got it. I was very grateful.

The Birdsalls were a really cool family. The father, Derek, was uber-cool. He was a self-made man and a top graphic artist. He did all these really cool book covers for Penguin; he worked with the photographer Harri Peccinotti on the Pirelli Calendar and he did a seminal book called *Notes on Book Design*. I said to him one time, 'I suppose art's about going against the grain.' He went, 'Yeah, but first you have to know which way the grain goes.' He's a real Zen master, old Derek Birdsall.

Their house on Compton Terrace in Islington was a really cool place. A big old Victorian house. Beautiful place. Dark brown cork tiles in the bathroom, and two massive speakers as well. I'd never seen speakers in a bathroom. Their house was a big part of our sort of thing at that time. Me and Lee spent a lot of time there. Si was always playing a lot of Motown, Kilburns, Roxy and Stevie Wonder. The house was over the road from the Hope and Anchor pub, so we'd go over there. I can't count how many bands we saw there.

This was around the same time as John Hasler got me a bass guitar through his friend, this Polish kid Marek, for four quid. We used to go round to Marek's in West Hampstead and listen to Wishbone Ash, Genesis and Be-Bop Deluxe and we'd all be stoned, crashed out on the carpet. It was John's idea that I learn to play the bass, really. I had no affinity. I mean, I knew E-A-D from the guitar. My cousin Pat had showed me those three chords on the guitar – and coincidentally, it was Chrissy Boy's dad who had taught Pat. Anyway I thought, 'Fucking hell, I'll try it.' This bass came with the strings, which was lucky, because I wouldn't have known how to put them on.

Mike was very helpful. He put stickers on all the frets to show me what to play. I could just about manage 'The Girl from Ipanema' and 'It's Too Late', 'I'm Walkin'' and 'Just My Imagination'. There was lots of people in our little gang who didn't make the effort to join the band. But I knew I wanted to be in it.

I met Suggs around then, but it wasn't a big meet or anything. Him, Chalky and Toks suddenly arrived in one of the pubs in Hampstead. Maybe they were there before and I hadn't noticed them. It was a time of coming together.

**SUGGS:** I bumped into Cathal outside of my mum's flat when I'd moved with her out of Cavendish Mansions into a beautiful new council flat above Maple's the carpet shop at the end of Tottenham Court Road.

He was bowling along with his blond cropped hair and this lovely Prince of Wales suit. And I thought I looked pretty sharp in this sheepskin coat that I'd nicked from the bannister at a party in Hampstead the night before. He looked me up and down and went, 'Ah, yeah, but it's a bird's one, innit?' I went, 'What do you mean?' He went, 'Look, it's got tit shapes and it buttons up the wrong way.' Crushed! Crushed! 'It's a bird's one!' Slightly crushed.

But as we were chatting, he said, 'I'm playing bass in this band called The Invaders who're doing Kilburns covers, Motown and reggae.'

MIKE: The first Invaders gig [June 30, 1977] was in Si Birdsall's garden in Compton Terrace. It was a bit of a disaster. We were supposed to play upstairs, and then Birdsall stuck us in the back garden. I don't know if it was his dad or something, but somebody said we couldn't play in the house. It would have been great, in the house, with everybody. It would have been a real party.

LEE: Mike got quite upset: 'What the fuck are we doing out in the garden?' There was loads of big rooms, and Mike thought we'd been fucked over because we'd been relegated to standing out there in cat shit.

CHRIS: It was Si Birdsall's birthday party and I'd said, 'Oh, we can play there.' But on the day, I rang him up and I went, 'What's with that noise in the background?' He said, 'Oh, they're moving the piano into the garden.'

CATHAL: Yeah . . . carrying the fucking piano down the stairs. It was fucking hard. It was an upright, and eventually we got it down in the garden. It was a nightmare. But there was a feeling: it was our thing, and it was very exciting. I can't even remember if I played that gig. I don't even know.

*

LEE: I remember Cathal was sitting on the wall in the garden, he wasn't in the band. He was sitting with Birdsall, Catlin, Jonesy, and three or four other blokes. As I was playing, I was thinking, 'If that wall collapses, someone's going to really get hurt . . .' Because it was an old nine-inch brick wall, and you could tell it was bowed and it was about to go. One push and that'd have been it.

John Hasler drummed at that gig. The front man was this guy Dikran Tulaine, who was the brother of Araxi, Mike Barson's girlfriend at the time. Dikran looked great and he wanted to be an actor, but he certainly wasn't a front man, I thought. But he was all we had. You had to make do with what you had. He did one gig and that was it. He didn't do another one . . .

MIKE: I don't know if we even rehearsed with him. He turned up and he said he was going to be able to do it. He had a bit of paper with the lyrics on, but it was dark and he couldn't read the lyrics. It was just a shambles . . . diabolical.

But I was playing the piano and all these girls were hanging around, like, 'Ooh, I didn't know you could play the piano so well.' I obviously enjoyed getting some special attention.

LEE: Fortunately, it didn't rain, as we were playing these rock'n'roll numbers, a complete mish-mash, out in the garden.

CHRIS: We did 'It's Too Late', we did The Temptations' 'Just My Imagination (Running Away with Me)'. Every now and then, there'd be someone being sick in a bush, or someone shagging.

*

MIKE: That first gig might have been better than I remember. Because maybe we got some notoriety from it, among our peers.

SUGGS: I was there. I'm 16, and finally I'm being allowed into parties at these lovely houses, and there was a gig in the garden. It was just a load of mates, making a bit of music. It seemed alright.

John Hasler comes up to me in the garden after and says, 'It looks like the singer's leaving.' And, I suppose I was pretty charismatic. I was getting to that sort of point where Suggs was somebody round there . . . people knew who Suggs was. I'm not saying necessarily the girls, but, possibly, I had some charm.

LEE: Suggs must have listened to us playing and gone, 'Fuck me. If it's that bad, I can do that . . . Gizza job' type of thing.

SUGGS: Suddenly I was gravitating towards these people, and this sort of gang was formulating, almost out of the ether, like magic. Like when you see a magnet under iron filings, and we were just all drawn together. As I look back, I see their faces coming out of the gloom towards me. The faces just became clearer and clearer to me: 'He's good, and he's good . . .'

CATHAL: After that, I'd rehearse with them sometimes round Mike's mum's house, with John Hasler covering the drums with stuff to try and make them quieter. Chris was always trying to say, 'Quieten it down, quieten it down.' Or it would be Mike, saying, 'My mum . . . the noise . . .' It was thrashy, and Mike was trying to get some kind of cohesiveness going. But I can't remember anything other than fumbling, and Mike trying to tell me how to play stuff. I mean, I wasn't a bass player, although I was the bass player. I'm enthusiastically lazy. I do love the bass, but I wasn't serious.

I wasn't in them for that long playing the bass. We must have started rehearsing somewhere else . . . I can't remember . . . but one night Mike gave me a lift home. He used to charge you petrol money, and he dropped me off at Highgate, instead of driving me over to Muswell Hill and then letting me out and driving down to Crouch End. He went, 'Fuck that, see ya,' and drove straight down to Crouch End, and I had to walk home. I thought, 'Oh, fuck this . . .' And my heart wasn't in the bass. In fact, the reason he probably dropped me off was I wasn't that good a bass player. He probably just couldn't say it. So, I was out the band.

MIKE: I suppose we both had a bit of an ego, and he wanted a lift home and I didn't want to feel like a doormat. I didn't get much money, and in my mind, it was like, 'Who's paying for the petrol? Why should I help you?'

But I felt like I was realistic about what needed to be done. And we're not going to start a band by being really half-hearted, which most of them may have been. They would have thought, 'Ooh, that bird fancies me if I'm in a band,' and that was about as far as it went. I was a bit more on the practicalities: 'If we're going to do a gig, we've got to have all this equipment and we've got to do this and that and the other.' Chris was a bit like that as well: practical planning, sort of thing.

Y'know, if you want to learn something, there's a way to do it. And it's maybe not very pleasant, but you've got to get your head down and do it. If you want to learn that song, you play it

20 times. It might not be fun – well, there'll be a bit of fun in it – but that's the way you learn it.

**SUGGS:** I'd never really sung. I'd been out with my mum when she sang, but certainly, there was no notion that I was going to sing at all. Football matches, really, was the only time I sang with any kind of lust, or in public.

But, apparently, one night I'd come out of the cinema after seeing *American Graffiti* again and I was singing 'See You Later, Alligator'. John Hasler heard me and he goes, 'D'you fancy singing in the band?' It was just one of those bizarre things.

**CHRIS:** The first time I saw Suggs, I'd got off the bus in Crouch End with this bloody heavy guitar case. I was walking down the hill towards Mike's mum's house, and I saw these two kind of like lairy skinhead types. I thought, 'You young whippersnappers! I was a skinhead back in '69 . . .' I got to Mike's house, and then these geezers I'd seen, who were Suggs and his mate, turned up. So, we got Suggs to sing a few songs, and thought, 'Oh, great . . . he seems good . . . he's big, he's charismatic.'

**SUGGS:** I turned up with a bottle of vodka and they asked me to sing 'See You Later, Alligator' and a Fats Domino song which I didn't know very well, 'I'm Walkin''. I mean, who would hire anyone who could sing 'See You Later, Alligator'? Unless they were a fucking wedding band.

But we were already getting on, and it was almost like it was more important who you were than what you could do. Mike and Chris had this drive that we could actually make it professional, whatever that word means. But, y'know, for me, it was just great hanging out with these guys, and having something to do other than run around the streets nicking fags or smashing phone boxes. It was just something to do. It started off just having a bit of fun in Mike's bedroom with a few instruments that had been acquired from various gigs . . .

MIKE: I can't even remember Suggs coming down. I guess I must have thought he was alright.

SUGGS: I've got a vague memory of Mike actually writing my name out, the way I used to do it for graffiti, and going, 'I think you could do it better than that.' Mike was that sort of person. You were thinking, 'Why would you bother to even think about what graffiti I'm doing?' But that's creativity, and that's how you get a band. If you all just sit about going, 'That's alright,' then it don't get nowhere.

I could draw quite well and I had aspirations to be an artist. My mum knew someone from Soho who had an advertising agency, and I wanted to do commercial art. So, I went to see this guy – just turned up with a load of rolled-up drawings I'd done – and he goes, 'But have you been to art college?' I most obviously had not, and I didn't have the qualifications to go to art college, anyway. Plus, the band was already kind of underway.

You had two choices – the criminal activity and all that, or maybe being a bit more creative. Lee and Mike and Chris just had a little more creative nous or something. But it was always a very thin line between that and going the wrong way completely. I know that's a right old cliché, but really it was true with us. You had a choice between a bit of criminal activity and maybe some sort of job on a building site, or trying to get out of that with whatever creativity you had at your disposal.

So many of our mates wanted to be in a band: walking down the road with a saxophone . . . never played a note in your fucking life. Jack Kerouac book in your back pocket and a beret. But that wasn't going to do it. That just ended up with heroin in some crappy basement in Finsbury Park.

You had certain friends who always had a tenner in their pocket, regardless of what happened. But obviously that's the foolishness of youth, and that goes on for so long, and then at a certain point, you do have to concentrate. You do have to put in some work.

Lee, I suppose, was the conduit between us and the real criminality. A bit of stealing stuff from shops was nothing compared to what he'd been through. Quite early on, Lee sometimes used to say, 'You make me a bit nervous, Suggs.' I used to think, 'Because you make me fucking nervous . . . I don't know what the fuck you're going to do next . . .'

Mike just seemed very focused on this idea that we could do it, musically. His older brothers, Ben and Dan, had kind of got somewhere musically. It hadn't even occurred to me, or I don't think many of us, that you actually could make it.

It was a strange sort of dichotomy – because even saying these kind of words is a bit uncool – but, I mean, we were so cool. The one thing I would say is that all the band were famous before I met them, certainly round my way, and I felt I'd kind of reached a certain fame. By the time I'd got to 16, everybody knew me and my mates around our patch of north London. So, just being in a band and playing in a few pubs was going to be enough for me . . . y'know, birds turning up. But Mike was going, 'No, we can take this further.'

You had a lot of rich personalities in the band already. Lee had his little scene and Mike was the leader of his little scene and

Chris and him were quite close. But I was certainly quite a loner sort of person. I had my own little thing. So, it brought together quite powerful people. Really strong personalities, so it was never gonna be easy.

**CHRIS:** Our second gig – the first one with Suggs singing – was in late '77. We played in Hampstead Flower Hall at Hampstead Market. It was the birthday party for a girl called Evelyn that Mike had gone to school with. She was a lovely, pretty girl. I went round her house, and she said, 'But can you all play?' I was going, 'Yeah, yeah, we're really good.' But we had got kind of alright.

At the gig, there were loads of flowers there and people were chucking them around, like hippies. And there was Teds and punks there – not a lot of Teds, but I suppose the idea of any culture like that is you've got to be a bit threatening. We started with 'See You Later, Alligator', so they were all like, 'Ah, this is our kind of thing . . . these cats are gone . . .' and then I think we might have done that old rock'n'roll song, 'Feel So Fine'. We did a couple of songs that maybe appeased them, then I think we did 'Swan Lake'.

**MIKE:** That was pretty good, that gig. We did Stevie Wonder, 'For Once in My Life' – it may have been a reggae version, or maybe not – and maybe we did that 'Concrete and Clay' song. Anyway, yeah, it was not bad. We were beginning to have our own sort of thing going on, so it was almost like a proper gig.

**LEE:** We were now moving in reggae songs, because the rock'n'roll ones were easy. The music tastes were changing, or reggae numbers seemed to go down better.

\*

SUGGS: It just happened that ska and those old rock'n'roll tunes were, like, 12-bar blues type things. But we were playing a mixture of whatever we could play, basically.

CHRIS: Back then, there were these things called a Party Seven, which were giant tins of beer, and one of the Teds threw one at the stage. It flew through the air and it hit John Hasler on the head.

LEE: It was fucking half-full, and just caught him proper, and split his head open.

SUGGS: He went flying backwards off the drum stool. Mike's older brother Danny, who of course was in Bazooka Joe, jumped up and they started playing 'Jailhouse Rock'. Then, all the Teddy Boys, they started getting into it.

CHRIS: John Hasler just carried on, with this little bit of blood trickling down his head, and we survived to fight another day. I'd cut my finger somehow, so my guitar had all blood on it. Y'know, quite punk. So, we just thought we were the bees' knees.

LEE: At the end, I got a handful of petals and gave them to John. He left with a load of fucking rose petals on his head.

CHRIS: Around then, we used to go to second-hand shops to get our clothes. We'd get all these old suits, because we kind of liked them, and we didn't have any money. We'd go to bloody Oxfam.

SUGGS: I got these great cricket trousers in Oxfam. You'd go in the cubicle, take the clothes that you liked, put them on under what you were wearing and walk out, in the days when they weren't counting how many layers you had on.

**CHRIS:** There was a shop in Camden Town by Mornington Crescent called Alfred Kemp's. The sign there said, 'We can fit anybody', and it was a sort of upmarket second-hand shop.

**CATHAL:** We couldn't afford proper suits, so it was demob stuff, post-war kind of shit, really. I got a couple of great suits out of Kemp's. A lovely deep-blue pinstripe with wide collars, and a sweet grey one. Demob suits were made hard-wearing.

With the demob suits, you had to wear braces, 'cause the waists almost came up to your chest. One time I got a load of money out of a pool table in The Yorkshire Grey pub on Charlotte Street – the coin slot was broken. But I got so many 10p pieces that, even with the braces, the trousers were down around my knees. It was hilarious: walking out, trying to keep the trousers up.

**SUGGS:** Alfred Kemp's was my favourite place. In there, it was just bizarre – all these geezers with sort of comb-overs and waist-coats and really white shirts with tape measures round their necks. It was second-hand stuff, but it was like you were walking in Harrods, the way you were treated in there: 'Hello, sir,' and all that. Mr Kemp used to sit at the door, and he could judge your size within three hundred metres, and he could judge the value of a pile of second-hand clothing just by looking at it.

It was the one place you never stole from, because he knew everyone up the high street, and just one shout out of the door and you'd be rugby-tackled to the floor. It was a bit pricier than every-where else, but that's where you'd get things like Crombies. I got this fantastic grey Crombie there – with a black velvet collar and a beautiful claret lining – for a fiver, which was half a week's wages.

A lot of the Irish workers, builders, would have a suit made. It would be ready on a Friday, so they'd go out on Friday night and have that for the whole weekend, and then wear it on the building site on the Monday morning. The old labourers used to wear suits. Not necessarily the jackets, but they'd wear the same suit they wore at the weekend, and then take it to Alfred Kemp's on Friday and then get their new suit. So, you were buying suits that had only got a week's wear and tear, albeit on a building site. You were getting these really well-made suits.

MARK: The other place we used to go to was Laurence Corner, on Hampstead Road. It was literally army surplus – stuff that they must have bought off, I don't know, the Ministry of Defence or something. There was RAF uniforms, army uniforms, navy uniforms. I had a really lovely, very short RAF jacket that I got from there, like a bomber jacket. I had that taken in a bit, to make it look a bit more seventies, a bit more stylish. Just as punk came in, we bought shirts from there and did a lot of shirt dyeing. After seeing The Clash, we did a lot of spray painting and drip painting on shirts.

SUGGS: Laurence Corner was like the Harrods of army surplus gear. I came across it because of the whole straight trousers thing – you're coming out of Wrangler bags or whatever they were, and the boot-boy sort of look, and then you're looking for straight trousers, of which there were very few. But they had amazing khaki army trousers in there. You were buying good gear that was very, very cheap, well-made and fit for purpose. If you wanted to be running round the terraces or being chased up the road, they were very sturdy trousers.

Then, you'd have a laugh, and of course someone would come out with a tank commander's helmet or something. You'd go down to some club, dressed as a complete lunatic wearing an East German military uniform. One time we all got sailors' outfits with the great big white baggy trousers. It was two or three floors, just packed full of amazing stuff. Sometimes you'd get them double-breasted dinner jackets that the naval officers used to wear. Burrowing through the stock, you'd turn up with a dinner jacket, and those black trousers with the shiny stripe, and those wet-look shoes that the navy used to wear. Suddenly you were into the Bryan Ferry thing.

CATHAL: I bought a fucking awful able-bodied seaman top from Laurence Corner. You'd get air-force greatcoats and shit for nothing. A&A's on Chapel Street had the creepers. I got a green suede pair with a pointed toe. Well cool.

MIKE: I was never mad on Laurence Corner. Maybe just I went down there and couldn't find anything.

At that time, we were wearing creepers, and then you had sort of turn-ups with Dr Martens. But you could have turn-ups with creepers, as well. So, it was a bit of a mixture, I guess, of all those things, and some people would be wearing braces.

There were certain sorts of turn-ups that cut it – they had to be very thin. Then we took it a bit further and we wanted to have even higher Dr Marten boots than the ones in the shops. If you had an old pair, you got where the laces came up, and you'd cut off that bit and stick them on top of the other pair. So, you'd have, like, super-high Dr Martens. If you put that extra bit on the inside, you didn't notice it too much.

CATHAL: Then, we used to go down to Flip in Covent Garden to buy all the Americana.

SUGGS: We liked that Americana stuff – the bowling shirts, and then those bomber jackets with the leather sleeves. And those MA-1 jackets for American pilots, they became all the go. Then there was also the button-down shirts . . . all the Brooks Brothers shirts and American Ivy League kind of stuff.

So, it was just about finding things. But it was also about turning up in something that you knew your mates didn't have. You'd turn up in a really nice pair of pleated American trousers, and you wouldn't be able to go to the normal shop and buy these things. Everything that you could find in these old places was a badge of honour.

CATHAL: There was a shop called Ben Nevis on Royal College Street where you'd get your Harringtons.

LEE: Was that what it was called? I didn't know that. I tried to nick a Harrington jacket from there. It was outside the shop, on a hanger. I knew that I couldn't afford this dark-green Harrington – it was probably thirty bob [£1.50] or something, or two quid. So, I remember going in and trying ones on: different sizes, colours. I tried the small one, because I knew it was a small one outside, 'cause I'd looked at the label. Devious . . . 'Can I try it on? Oh, very nice: I'll pop back later. What time do you close?' Then, leaving, I grabbed the arm of it and pulled it, and I got several metres down the road and then got pulled back, because it was tied with some nylon string. So, they were savvy to us little urchins.

I did eventually get it. I took some scissors with me . . .

Then I bought a bottle-green one. It was sort of shiny material and the whole tartan all the way down inside. When you turned it inside-out, it was almost like a reversible jacket. It was quality, and it was paid for this time. So, it felt better on.

I used to wear a blue sheepskin coat, which was my mum's. It was warm, it was too small for her, and I liked it, because it was petrol blue. I used to walk about with a bottle of Listerine in one pocket, probably a *Penthouse* or *Parade* in the other.

There was adverts on the Tube at the time, inside the trains, bits of board they'd slide in. There was one with a pair of pillar box-red lips with a tongue running along this beautiful set of teeth, and two flames coming out the edge of the lips, and it said: 'Stay fresh all day with Listerine'. I'd take them and use a scalpel to cut out just the lips and the flames and put rows of them on my wall. Anyway, I was hooked on Listerine. That was my drink of choice. Used to do pints of it a week . . .

SUGGS: I was living at the end of Tottenham Court Road, so I used to go in The Roxy, which was the big punk club. I thought, 'This is fucking brilliant.' Chalky didn't think too much of it: 'All this fucking racket.' But Don Letts was playing reggae records in-between the bands, and we were already kind of getting into reggae. It was that famous thing that there weren't very many punk records to play, so Don Letts was playing reggae records. I took Lee and Cathal and Si down, and they lasted about five minutes. They said, 'That's a right load of old bollocks,' and fucked off . . .

Me more than them, I liked the energy. They all thought it was just musically shit. I wasn't really sure . . . I just thought the energy was good. But it wasn't music that I was bang into. I mean, I did buy the first Clash record, 'White Riot'. So yeah, I did kind of like it. But it wasn't the best music I'd ever heard.

**MIKE:** Suggs was into punk. He was going down to these punk clubs. But, yeah, for the rest of us, that was a bit of a no-no. That was frowned upon, punk. I don't know, maybe we were very conservative, mentally. I didn't like the spitting, for sure. Nobody liked the spitting. That just seemed like, 'What's that about?' And I thought the music was not much cop. So, I didn't like the screaming, either.

There were some things I liked about it. I liked the sort of 'We don't give a shit and it doesn't matter. It's not about proficiency in playing.' That was the main thing in punk for me – that anybody can do it and you don't have to be great musicians, which is right. Because everybody just does one little thing, and all together, it makes a whole. So, it's not about how many notes and how fast you can play. It's about what sounds good. So, I thought that was very refreshing, that part of it.

We were skinheads at the time . . . we had Dr Martens, turn-ups, and that's a very conservative type of look in a way. Y'know, it's like the mods and the rockers – the mods were very sort of conservative, and I suppose punks were a bit more like the rockers, really. So, I didn't count myself as a punk, no.

**SUGGS:** Punk's underway and every now and again there'd be a band that we thought we should go and have a look at, like The Stranglers at The Music Machine in Camden.

Lee took me up the fire escape round the back: 'You don't have to pay.' I'm saying, 'It's 50p to get in,' and he's going, '50p? Fuck that.' So, we climb up this fire escape. There's a hole in the dome on the roof, and Lee lights a match and drops it through to see how far down it went. It's, like, a fourteen-foot drop, pigeons all flying about. So, we jump down, and it leads out into the VIP bar. We're covered in pigeon shit and fuck knows what. So, we got chased out of the VIP bar and down the stairs.

Then we get down into the main venue and see a few of our mates. But then these Finchley boys who followed The Stranglers around were also there, and they were another enemy tribe. They were very possessive about their band, as a lot of them crowds were in them days. So, I'm like, 'For fuck's sakes . . . ' The next thing, we're being chased back up the stairs. I was at the top of the stairs, and there was about six of them coming towards me. I kicked the first one, and like a stack of dominoes, they all went back down. Chalky got kicked up the bollocks, and I think he got a hernia, actually. Happy days . . .

MARK: There were punch-ups at gigs and stuff. But I think people coexisted, because they kept to their own groups. If they were Teds, they stuck with Teds, if they were rockabillies, they stuck with rockabillies.

But, with punk, there were some miraculous transformations from '75 to '77. There were so many people that just changed everything about themselves. And it was literally, 'Are you a punk, then, now?' 'Yeah, I am.' And they had cut all their hair off, and they didn't wear flares any more, and they had really tight jeans on and spiky hair.

It was a massive musical shift, as well. From a playing point of view, you felt obliged to put more energy into stuff. You felt obliged to maybe play a bit faster, maybe a bit louder.

WOODY: In '77, I worked in a studio in Covent Garden, printing photographs. My dad got me the job. I was a runner, as well, so I was running up and down stairs all day long. Anyway, it was when The Roxy first opened, and Don Letts came in. He was taking photographs at The Roxy, and he got this studio to print them, and I was the assistant printer. So, I was there, printing these pictures of these absolutely bizarre people like Siouxsie Sioux that Don had taken pictures of.

It was just a really happening scene. I think the Sex Pistols showed up the industry for what it was and used and abused it – quite rightly – but changed the perception. My mum still lived in Maida Vale and I used to go to her place on the weekend. And there were punk bands coming out of Maida Vale, like Chelsea. Sid and Nancy used to hang out round there as well, so you used to see them walking down the street.

CATHAL: I wasn't into punk. Me and Lee went to see The Damned at the Hope & Anchor, came out and I got bottled. It just caught me on the side of my head. It was about ten smoothies who thought we were punks. But we weren't, y'know? Lee picked up one of those metal advertising signs outside a newsagent's and walloped a guy with it. He went down. Stopped in his tracks.

LEE: This feller's got the first punch in and done Cathal. It caught him off guard. Cathal's hit the floor, and I've just immediately gone running after these fellers. But, no one was hit with anything. I ran after this one feller, and I'm pretty quick, and then it all dispersed. We were running after them and we didn't catch up. Maybe that was for the best. It's possible they could have had knives on them.

SUGGS: In King's Cross, there were loads of squats where the punks lived. I went to one squat where it was, like, The Slits in the basement, half of the Sex Pistols. We were all downstairs playing drums and fuck knows what when The Slits came home. There was this barrage of beer cans down the stairs, and they chased us out the back door.

But, at the time, you only had punk really. That was the only new thing that was happening. When I say 'only', I mean, obviously it was the most amazing thing. But if you didn't want to go just into that slipstream, then the only other thing to do was find some obscure music that no one else was interested in any more.

So, for us, it was ska. You're the only ones that know and it's your little club.

LEE: I started going around London buying ska and reggae singles. It was mainly Willesden, because their main pressing place, where the tracks all came in from Jamaica, was in that area. The only outlets they had were in black areas, like Harlesden, Willesden, Brixton. So, you'd have to go there, and check out the shops. Because you'd go to your local record shop: 'Who? What? Ah, Trojan, we'll have to order it. It might take a week or two.' 'I can't wait that long. A week? That's torture . . .'

SUGGS: Lee was definitely more into it than I was. He was a bigger collector of it than I was. But I just started getting into it.

I was round his and Deb's one time – the morning when I wrote 'Baggy Trousers' lying on his floor, funnily enough. And they'd gone out, and I was skint, and there was two biscuit tins on a shelf. I opened one of them, and it was full of all Lee's rare Blue Beat records, and then the next one was full of 2p pieces. So, I took 12 pence – I didn't steal any of his records – and I still owe him that 12 pence . . . I'd already got twenty, thirty Blue Beat records; he probably had a hundred. But I saw that he had a lot more records than me and I started really getting into collecting those records.

It was looking for something different. There was this whole thing where at the time some of our more modern Teddy Boy friends were going back into, like, rockabilly, then they were going back into bluegrass. And so, our friends that were into reggae were going back into ska. There was a stall, in Soho, down by Archer Street, that sold Blue Beat singles and they were, like, 10 pence each. So, I was just buying every one I could. It was just fucking brilliant. Prince Buster was a revelation – a bit like that comic malevolence thing again – and his songs had humour and they had some sort of reality, like 'Al Capone'. It had a bit of edge, as well as being funny.

Then I came across this song of his, 'Madness', and I bought that single. A few of my punk mates had started this clothes shop, Boy, in the King's Road. I played it to them in there, and they were going, 'What the fuck's this? It sounds like the fucking Glenn Miller Orchestra,' because it's got that brass and all that.

But I was going, 'Can't you hear? The energy in that . . . ?'

## CHAPTER 9

# DOWN IN THE DENTIST'S BASEMENT

**LEE:** Early '78, I was in and out the band. There's spots I missed out. I kept wandering off like the Scarlet Pimpernel or something . . . Halley's Comet . . . 'cause I'd have a row with Mike.

**SUGGS:** Lee kept leaving. He kept going back to Luton. Mike was getting more serious, and the feeling was that Lee wasn't. I think he was, but he was still learning how to play. The feeling from Mike was that he was messing around a bit.

**MIKE:** Everybody kept effing off. It was hard. Maybe none of them really believed there was much point to it. Or maybe people around them were saying, 'What are you doing wasting your time?' and stuff like that. People would drop in and out. There was a period when Lee stopped turning up.

And in those days, I never questioned my opinions, y'know? I always thought I was right. At the same time, I was quite realistic, and maybe he wasn't so realistic. But also, I wasn't very appreciative, because I was just seeing: 'This is what we need to do. You've got to play these notes, not those notes that are wrong. You don't play a different song when we're playing this song.' So, if he thought that was bossy, I don't know . . . but maybe it was necessary.

I suppose I wasn't thinking about his life: how it was for him when he had to go back up and down to Luton. I wasn't thinking about his family life and what was actually happening; how would it be, having a dad who's in prison all the time. Everything was just accepted as it was. But at the same time, you're thinking, 'He's gone to Luton?! Is he going to move to Luton and you'll never see him again?' He might have done.

CHRIS: Lee kept going in and out, and a friend of mine's sister – this girl called Lucinda Oestreicher – could play sax. So, she came and played with us with at our next gig at City & East London College. It turned out to be the only gig she played with us. We'd got this other guy called Gavin Rodgers on bass who was the brother of Kerstin, Mike's girlfriend at the time. By then, we were starting to get quite good.

There was some guy there at this gig that Suggs knew, some scary kind of hooligan, called Binnsy, because he had these big jam-jar glasses. He was stood at the side of the stage as we were playing, and just looked shit, and I was like, 'Look . . .', trying to tell him to get off. He was going, 'You just do your stupid music and don't threaten me . . .' I was like, 'Alright . . . anything you say, Binnsy.'

*

**LEE:** For some reason I joined this guy Dave Banks's band. They were called Gilt Edge. It was very soul boy. Bruce Springsteen meets Bob Dylan type of stuff. It was great to practise along to, but I pined for my boys. I did several rehearsals then went scampering back to this lot.

**CHRIS:** In early '78, we played at the Nightingale pub in Crouch End, near Mike's mum's. Lee was back in the band and Debbie had bought him a microphone stand and she also had a T-shirt saying, 'I Go Out With The Sax Player'. He'd bought big WEM speakers, so we had our own kind of sound system.

**SUGGS:** It strikes me as the first professional gig. Chris had got hold of this WEM Copicat echo machine, and I was using it on the vocals. It was just a piece of tape that went round, and literally just played your voice round and round. I was suddenly like Elvis Presley meets Lee Perry . . . uptown top fucking Crouch End. There was an alley at the back of the Nightingale pub and this woman leaned out of her window opposite and banged on the pub window with a broomstick and told us to pack it up.

**CHRIS:** We played in this pub, and it was good, and we thought, 'This could be a regular.' But then it was kind of like, 'Sorry, but the neighbours complained about the noise.' Lee left the mike stand behind, and we had to go back and get it, and it woke the guvnor up with just his underpants on. So, we didn't go back there.

**SUGGS:** There was this girl called Kate O'Leary who used to live just round there. She was one of our biggest fans – or mine, anyway – and she was trying to start a petition to get us back to play there again. She must have got four signatures . . .

Anyway, this was just before I got thrown out the band for going to see Chelsea rather than going to Mike's to rehearse. I find out that I've been sacked from the band by looking at an advert in *Melody Maker* that says, 'Semi-professional north London band require professionally minded singer', and it's Mike Barson's phone number. So, I ring him up in a posh accent, and I go, 'Just enquiring about the job of singer in your band . . . out of interest, what's happened to the old one?' Mike says, 'We had to let him go. He had a bad attitude problem. He was always down the football.' I go, 'You fucking bastard,' and he goes, 'Is that you, Suggs?'

**MIKE:** Certain people were half-in, half-out, like I was saying before: Lee being one of them and Suggs being one of them. If you want to be in a band, you can't be in a band when you're not there. We all turn up for a rehearsal and Suggs don't come, and you ain't got a band. Nothing's going to happen. So, if you don't come, y'know, you've got to move on. But, I mean, I wasn't objecting to him. It was his behaviour.

It was never like the band was a really solid thing. It was always half falling apart, but there's chaos and then there's too much chaos, and they were edging into that sort of area.

**LEE:** You can't do much without your main man. If you ain't got a singer, it's difficult. All the cogs were in the place except Suggs wasn't there, gone to football. He was torn between singing in someone's sweaty, smelly bedroom for a couple of hours on a Saturday afternoon, or going to football and singing with a couple of thousand people around him. So, he was kicked out, and it was touch and go at that point, about whether it was going to carry on.

CHRIS: Suggs didn't come, and then Mike went, 'I'm not playing with him anymore.' It was kind of like Mike's ball, his thing, because we rehearsed in his house, and he had the van. So, if he said he didn't want to do it, it's not like we could carry on doing it. I thought, 'Well, I'll just carry on,' because I enjoyed what we were doing.

Mike said one day, "'Ere, we were doing something the other day and John Hasler started singing and he was really good and I think he should be the singer.' I was like, 'Christ, no.' So, John Hasler became the singer.

We did a rehearsal, John Hasler's singing, and it was dire. I think Gavin Rodgers just walked out. I think he even knocked his bass over, going, 'This is shit.' And he was right, it kind of was shit. And that was it: never seen him again.

Then, John Hasler goes, 'I know a drummer. Gary Dovey.' But now we didn't have a bass player.

MARK: Gary Dovey was a friend of mine at school, and he was the connection to John Hasler, who was two years older than me at school, and then to Mike, Chris and Lee. John said, 'Do you want to come down and rehearse?' Someone had a studio set up in a basement on Essex Road. And I walked in and thought, 'God, this looks professional.'

CHRIS: That local band Split Rivitt whose microphones we nicked; they had a really nice rehearsal room. So, the first time Mark meets us, he gets in the back of Mike's van with all lawnmowers in – because Mike was doing a bit of gardening by then – and goes to this really swish rehearsal place. We did Kilburn and the High-Roads' 'The Roadette Song', and I did the solo, flipped the old pick-up on the guitar, and he thought, 'Cor, I'm really in a cool band here.'

MARK: I could play OK at that point. They taught me some old reggae tunes, which I didn't really know how to play. And they also taught me 'Mistakes', as well, which was one of the first songs that was written by the band. John Hasler had written the lyrics, and Mike had put a reggae organ beat to it.

MIKE: In those days, reggae . . . not a lot of people could play it. I was thinking, 'He can't really play it, but anyway, he's not a bad bass player, so off we go.' It was good in some ways, that he wasn't able to play it properly, 'cause it sounded a bit different. And we were pretty desperate. I mean, I wouldn't say we would take anyone, but we could barely play and we'd managed to get up from nothing.

MARK: There was a bit of nervousness on both sides, and trying to suss one another out, y'know. And I made a real effort. I dressed in a button-down shirt and a jacket, and I must have looked quite good, because Chris said, 'Oh, you looked quite professional.' I didn't really know some of the songs and I thought, 'Oh, maybe that's going to count against me.' But I picked them up quite quick, I think. I came home with a huge blister on my finger. Then, they got in touch with me to say, 'Do you want to come down to another rehearsal?'

CHRIS: Mark was still at school, and he said, 'Oh, the end of term concert – I can get us on.'

\*

MARK: As I was leaving school, a few of us put on a gig at William Ellis. We only got the chance to play it because this punk band, The Stains, dropped out. There were three bands playing for this thing called the Summer Bop, and I screen-printed posters for it, and The Stains were still on the poster. Woody's brother Nick was in one of the bands as their lead guitarist. The bands totally reflected the mixture of people that were around – hippies, punks, rockabillies and then that weird mixture that was The Invaders. We managed to scrape in at the bottom of the bill, and we were pretty ragged, pretty terrible. But we were interesting, if nothing else.

I was really nervous. I think we all were. But Chris started to do the Chuck Berry duckwalk across the stage, which went down very, very well. I think I joined him at one point, and then we did the Feelgoods' thing of walking backwards and forwards, because we'd all seen Dr Feelgood at that point. There was a lot of people there, and it was one of those gigs locally where everyone claims to have been there. But I'm not sure if many of them were.

CHRIS: John Hasler was singing, and he looked the part. He had this sort of Homburg hat and he came out and, all theatrically, he put it at the front of the stage. The audience was, like, miles away, but someone come and threw money in the hat.

LEE: That was me. I was back out of the band at that point, so I chucked two bob in the hat and started heckling: 'Where's the sax player? You need a sax player. You sound great, but you need a sax player.' I was heckling to get me old job back.

*

**MARK:** Chris was like, 'Pay no attention to him . . . don't let him put you off . . .' or something like that: 'Pay no attention to that sax player in the audience . . .'

**SUGGS:** I was there, standing at the back of the hall. It was like a scene from *American Graffiti*. By the end, there's all these birds down the front, screaming, and at that moment in time, I thought, 'I should be up there, not down here.' As I say, some of our mates were becoming more famous for, y'know, impropriety. But I thought that this was my way out, and it was just about to leave the fucking station. Nothing was happening in my life at that time. So, time was running out.

**WOODY:** It was amazing to see The Invaders at the William Ellis dance. However, I also experienced seeing my brother turn his back on the audience – he was in another band, and he couldn't cope with the gig, and had a complete freak-out. It was just awful to watch.

But The Invaders were the best band on the night and I was absolutely glued to them. I was really frustrated because I wasn't playing with anyone at the time and I just thought this band was absolutely fantastic. I hadn't heard anything like it, really. And it was all just on the edge of falling to bits, but that was what made it so good.

They played 'Mistakes' that night and it was the band's own song. It wasn't a cover or anything, and it just sounded great. I was standing there thinking, 'I'm a better drummer than Gary Dovey . . .' I was feeling frustration at not hearing the tracks the way I thought they should be played.

**MIKE:** The next gig was in this place called The 3Cs Club, which was like a youth club. We were doing 'The House of the Rising

Sun' in reggae style, and John Hasler sang it at the wrong tempo. We were playing half-time and he was double-time. It irritated the fuck out of me.

SUGGS: John Hasler was leaping about, doing 'The House of the Rising Sun' in a Laurence Corner boiler suit. I'm watching them, thinking, 'I could definitely do better than that.'

We were still friends, there wasn't any animosity. But it was starting to become obvious that something real was happening, and I was becoming increasingly aware of the fact that I was outside what was happening.

MIKE: There was a punk sort of contingent there and they were spitting at us, and I didn't like it. We came offstage and I'm going, 'Fucking cunts ... fucking spitting at us ...' John Hasler and Gary Dovey were running around the gym, running in circles with excitement. I was thinking, 'Hm, that's not a good sign. You two are a bit too much into the punk thing.' That was a cross against John Hasler's career potential; that was a note in my book that maybe somebody else would be better.

MARK: Mike drove everyone on. He's got a very dogged personality. We might have fallen by the wayside, but he kept it going and rolling along. He deserves a hell of a lot of credit for that because he was quite determined about rehearsing and pushing the band and making us do stuff. Lee would mysteriously appear from Luton at some of the rehearsals. He'd come and blow his sax, and then we might not see him for a little bit.

\*

**SUGGS:** Then John Hasler went off on holiday, and they had a couple of gigs. I was the only one who knew the words to the songs, and, much to the surprise of nobody more than me, I was back. I mean, talk about a turning point in your life.

**CHRIS:** Suggs came back and sung, and you could see he was better than John Hasler, so Hasler became the manager.

**SUGGS:** We were rehearsing in this church hall, near Crouch End, and it was £2.50 a week. Lee was in charge of collecting the subs, and about two months in, the vicar walked in and said, 'You're sounding great, by the way, lads.' Y'know, with his teeth hanging out to dry, rubbing his knees: 'Looking great, sounding great, guys. Is there any chance I might see some of the . . . how can I put it . . . money?' We all looked at Lee. Lee looked sheepish, and we had to leave. But, nicking from a vicar, that was a sign of pretty much past, present and future.

**LEE:** Yeah, I mean, I don't remember this at all! They pin it on me . . . fucking joke! I don't remember no dog collars coming up to me for money. I do not recall that. But, if the truth be told, if anyone's going to wander off with the dosh, it'll be me. I mean, who would trust me with their 50p? But, what a load of bollocks. It's myth. A fucking myth.

Myself and Cathal tried working together as window cleaners around then. We were absolutely shit. We were cleaning windows around the Finchley area, and it paid well. It was quite a big Jewish community round there, and they weren't afraid of giving you the odd tip – a quid for a set of windows. But I couldn't get the putty out . . . no good to me – I much preferred the Venetian ones . . .

We weren't ones for sitting on corners, begging. We'd go out and get out and do a bit of work. Cathal was pretty good at motivating us. I had the vehicle, he had the sponges and the tools, and we'd go out. I don't know how long that lasted, but it certainly paid for the odd beer or two. We were entrepreneurs.

**CATHAL:** Yeah, me and Lee window cleaning, that was hilarious. Six pounds, inside and out. We weren't very good, but it got us a bit of cash and we had nothing else to do. I tried to go on the dole and I was so disgusted by the paltry amount that they offered, I thought, 'Fuck this.' I went to three different places to get £4.30 or something in the end, and I just thought, 'Forget it.'

We weren't window cleaners for long. It was a complete disaster. The winter of the dustmen strike, it was all snow and ice everywhere. We thought we might make a few quid collecting people's rubbish, but no one wanted to pay us, 'cause they just threw the rubbish out onto the streets. So, we just ended up on this really steep road by St James Church in Muswell Hill, skidding down the ice in Lee's Morris van. Thommo is a bit of a daredevil.

**WOODY:** I left school and I didn't really know what to do. I'd gone for a CSE in art, and I got a Grade 1, some really ridiculously high mark, because I was able to bring all my creativity to it. I loved surrealism, and I used to really mess with reality – distorting things and making them a little bit weird. I'd make faces from clouds and trees and rivers, so close-up, you would be kind of wrapped up in this strange world, and when you looked at it from a distance, it was a head, a face, and bodies. Kind of really mad art. I used to be completely absorbed in it. That was my way of cutting off from the world.

Everyone at school said that I needed to go to art college, and I just thought the life of an artist was, well, just abject poverty, really. My careers officer said, 'What do you want to be?' and I said, 'Well, I either want to be a rock star or maybe an artist.' He just looked at me and said, 'No, seriously, what do you want to do?'

So, then I wanted to work in a music shop, and I went round all the ones in the West End. The managers in every one of them said that I wasn't old enough and I didn't have enough experience, so that was really devastating. At the unemployment centre, near Maida Vale, where my mum was living, they came up with a job for me at Whiteleys, as an apprentice to a sign-writer in a department store.

I went in, and the head of the department was an amazing free-hand sign-writer. He said, 'I can teach you how to do this. But in the meantime, we've got these machines where you set type.' You had these racks and racks of different type sets, made of metal, and you laid them out. I lasted nine months. Used to walk from Warwick Avenue and started at eight-thirty in the morning, clocked in and then clocked out at four-thirty. Just after I started working there, I went to Blanks music store in Kilburn and bought myself a massive Premier drum kit, and all that job did was pay off the hire purchase.

CHRIS: Mike knew this girl Fiona Russell who lived in Finchley Road, and her dad was a dentist. He had this big house, and this kind of house next door, and she said it had a basement that we could use to rehearse. We swept it up and cleared everything, and there was some sort of carpet in there, and a really low ceiling. It was great.

That place was the making of the band, y'know. Having somewhere you could go to whenever you wanted, to write and rehearse. There was this little back room, which was scary, and it had thousands of impressions of teeth in it. They weren't real teeth: they were just doing impressions of teeth . . .

MIKE: It was horrible in there, but it was a great opportunity to have somewhere to rehearse. We left the gear in there and just had a key. That was quite instrumental: they were pretty crucial sort of rehearsals. We were regularly rehearsing, maybe two days a week or something. I mean, my memories are of the rehearsing more than the teeth.

SUGGS: Having it! Amongst the plaster casts of north London gnashers! All chattering away in the background. We knew we were getting somewhere . . .

We could set up our gear and Mike kept his organ and some stuff down there. My mike was plugged into Chris' guitar amp, so it was very hard to get any quality out of my voice. But we had a reel-to-reel tape recorder to record ourselves with, and you could hear the beginnings of us getting better.

MARK: We rehearsed a lot. We were quite dedicated. I was always amazed by our dedication to rehearsing early on.

That basement was where Lee and Gary Dovey had a punch-up. Well, not really a punch-up . . . a scuffle.

LEE: It was a scuffle. I'd been bloody on the drink, out the packet, when I should've been at rehearsals. I've never been any good with drink. I act the clown, but also sometimes I get aggressive . . . as you do with a fucking drink.

I'd been to The Railway in West Hampstead, that had The Pink-Eye Club, and they had strippers on in there. I'd been on the Pernod and blackcurrants, then landed up going to the rehearsal. Gary Dovey was nice enough, but we were trying to play the Kilburns' 'Rough Kids', and he kept on getting it wrong.

MARK: Gary kept getting some drum fill wrong or something, and Lee just had enough and jumped over the drum kit.

LEE: I ended up lunging at him. Bloody stupid, really. He was a bit of a big lump, an' all. He must have thought, 'Who is this little midget – this fucking garden gnome! – with his pink boots and his green hat, attacking me?' I took a swing at him, but then he just grabbed my hands and I stopped, and I thought, 'Oh, fuck.' And I retreated very quick.

MARK: Gary threw down the sticks and stormed out, never to play again.

LEE: Finger-pointing was going on. The band said, 'What the fuck? Sort yourself out. Fucking calm down. Go for a walk.' I walked out, just left. I don't know why I did it really. All these things are going on in your head at that age. It was probably something that pissed me off, and I took it out on the drummer. But it was all drink-related.

MIKE: I suppose I quite liked it, because Lee was sort of standing up for the band, standing up for me, I think. I mean, I didn't really connect with Gary. Because it's not just musical; it's also about things that you all like together, like him with that punk thing of his that I wasn't into.

**WOODY:** My girlfriend at the time said that Gary had left The Invaders. So, I rang up Mark, because I'd been told by someone that Mark had mentioned me as a possible drummer for the band.

**MARK:** He said, 'Are you looking for a drummer?' and it took me by such surprise. I just went, 'No,' and there was silence on the other end of the phone. I think he was totally freaked out and crestfallen by the fact that I'd so obviously just said 'No.' Then I realised what I'd done, and I went, 'Oh yeah, yeah, we are.'

**WOODY:** Mark went, 'Er, no, but, come along anyway. We're holding auditions.'

**MARK:** I know this'll go down in history, that I said no. But I didn't mean it like that. I was very surprised that he'd rung me up. It wasn't my call really. It was Mike's call.

**WOODY:** Mark came with Mike Barson to pick me up, in Mike's Morris 1000 van. Mike didn't say a thing to me. He just grunted 'Alright?' at me and that was it. Mark was all like, 'It's OK, Woody, don't worry. He might be a bit gruff, but he's alright really.' Mike's a really imposing figure, so I was really nervous. We piled the kit into the back of the van, I squeezed in the back and Mark sat in the front. Anyway, we arrived at Finchley Road, below the dentist's, got out and piled the kit into what I can only describe as a cellar.

It was a really, really bizarre place with no lights in it at all until you opened the door. And then whoever walked through was just this silhouetted figure. Chris didn't even acknowledge me either, just kind of nodded and grunted as well. It was really a weird atmosphere.

I'd heard all these rumours about the sax player beating up Gary Dovey. Then I remembered Lee from Haverstock. As I said, he used to appear occasionally and then kinda disappear over the shed roof. He was kind of a notorious chap in Haverstock School.

Then, of course, Suggs was this other imposing figure that had been kicked out of the band because he went to watch Chelsea. And I was a Chelsea fan, so I knew what the Shed end at Chelsea was like. I thought, 'Oh my God, what have I got myself into? This is just another world.' And when he did finally arrive, he was flanked by two equally imposing-looking skinheads, all in the clobber. Looking very good. But they were silhouetted against the door and you didn't see their faces until they came in. It was all really interesting. It was just that kind of atmosphere where you didn't know what was gonna happen.

MARK: Woody still looked very early seventies: woolly hat, long hair, greatcoat. He turned up as one of the Mahavishnu Orchestra, and he had a huge drum kit, all in banana yellow. I looked at the tom-toms and went, 'Fucking hell, most of these have got to go.' Because, I mean, having been to see The Clash at that point, they just that tiny drum kit.

SUGGS: Woody had this drum kit with sort of 44 tom-toms which – as the drum rolls got more concise – slowly, one by one, got thrown away.

*

MARK: He'd listened to a lot of the same music as me, so I think the reggae thing was a bit new to him, like it was to me. But I'd learnt as we'd rehearsed, how to play those old records, how to play in that style.

WOODY: We played some of their songs – one called 'Sunshine Voice', which John Hasler had written; maybe 'Mistakes', 'Believe Me'. It was very, very basic stuff. And it was alright.

MIKE: Yeah, he was a proper drummer. He could more or less hold down a beat through the whole song, and up until then, when other people had been drumming, it'd been amateur hour. So, Woody gave us a very solid base, I guess. If the drums and the bass are really locked in and playing at the right tempo all the way through, then it makes it sound more like a goer.

WOODY: We arranged for me to come back another week. But Mike was still going, 'Well, I've got this advert for a drummer in the paper . . .' He kept on going on about it. So, I really didn't feel at all secure. I didn't know if I'd got the job or not. We went back in the next week, and then I kept on going, really. I never really heard that I was officially in the band. Maybe I'm still not . . .

SUGGS: Mike had this song called 'Grey Day', which was really not going anywhere. Then, suddenly it started to. Tunes that we were messing around with were starting to become more cohesive. We were using the WEM Copicat echo on that early version of 'Grey Day', and it sounded a bit Roxy Music. In that basement, things started to become feasible.

*

**WOODY:** They were a bit stand-offish. They weren't easy to get to know. But you soon realised that there was a loyalty there. It was like a family, and you saw it very early on, at early gigs. They'd be like, 'Oi, mate, he's with us. Don't fuck with him.' There was a protection, a bubble. As soon as I joined the band, it all kind of clicked. It felt good to me.

**MIKE:** Me and Lee both had Morris 1000 vans that we'd use to travel to gigs.

**CHRIS:** I thought, 'This is it . . . we've really made it. We've got two vans . . .'

**LEE:** Mine was yellow, Mike's was white. When we drove to gigs, Woody would be in the back with the gear, 'cause he was the lightest. Barson drove, I drove. Probably Suggs in with Mike, and Chris in with myself, and the other two, Woody and Mark, relegated: 'Get in the back.'

**SUGGS:** They were ex-GPO vans, and they were practical to start with. Lee had his little plastering business, which I got a bit involved in. Well, I worked for him and barely lasted a day. My apprenticeship involved nicking a bucket and a trowel from Woolworths. Lee's saying to the customer, 'Yeah, we've done loads of this. Don't worry about it.' Then he's saying to them about me, 'He's a bit slow, but he's a good kid.' There was more plaster on my head than there was anywhere else.

Then Chris said, 'What about painting and decorating?' and again, my apprenticeship involved nicking a pair of overalls and a bucket from Woolworths. And then Mike had a little gardening business. My apprenticeship involved nicking a bucket and a pair of gloves from Woolworths. I was always the muggy mate . . .

But happy days, man, driving around in them vans, feet up on the old dashboard, the windows all steaming up and all that. We'd stop at Apex Corner for a breakfast break that would last until about eleven.

We got this job planting six pine trees outside this mansion block in St John's Wood. Do you realise how big a fucking hole you have to dig for the root ball of a fucking tree? Big. So, I took the executive decision just to saw the fucking roots off, get a couple of bricks, just jam the fucking trees in. Three weeks later, I went past on my scooter to see them all fucking bent sideways, brown, and dead. I think that was my last real gardening gig.

The trouble with the vans if you were using them as a mode of transport on a night out was that you only had two seats in the front. So, there'd always be a big fight over who had to sit in the back, because inevitably it would be full of petrol cans and stink, or paint pots. Not the most aphrodisiacal smell when you're going into a boozer, trying to pull a bird with your band and all that. You'd see the sort of parting of the seas when we walked in: it was like that little kid from Peanuts with the flies round his head. 'What the fuck?' The waft of petrol and turps.

**LEE:** The vans were extremely reliable. The only problem with them was the design – the rainwater would hit the wheels, go along the front wings and they'd bubble up. But more so, under where your feet were, by the pedals, that would rot.

We had some great times in them vans. Once, I drove from London to Great Yarmouth to see relatives, and I took my mum in the back. I threw a mattress in for her to be comfortable. My sister was in the other corner, and my cousin was in the front. We all took off in this Morris 1000, and the accelerator cable went on it. So, I got me mum to take her stockings off, and we somehow tied it around the accelerator. The last 30 miles were a bit hairy. But a pair of me mum's stockings saved the day . . .

CHRIS: Around then, the music we were playing started changing a lot. Simultaneously, we started writing our own songs and we dropped all the rock'n'roll ones; started doing our own stuff and old ska stuff. Suggs and Lee definitely got us into the ska stuff. I knew 'Al Capone', but I didn't really know 'One Step Beyond'. It was Suggs that went, 'Look, I've got this thing we could do. "Madness" by Prince Buster.' We all thought, 'Yeah.'

LEE: I wrote 'The Prince' as my tribute to the King of Ska, Prince Buster. It wasn't difficult to write at all. I had the melody in my head, but I wasn't able to get it out. So, I hummed it to Mike, and the band as a whole. Mark picked it up, he got a rhythm going, and then Woody came in on the drums. It was done in the time it took a kettle to boil.

CHRIS: Lee wrote 'The Prince', and I thought, 'That's it . . . Lee can write all the songs . . . ', even though it was a right old flipping cobbled-together Prince Buster bit of this and a bit of that. Then Mike wrote 'My Girl'.

MIKE: I don't know if I ever spoke to my girlfriend about writing it. But, with the music, there was this theory going around that white people couldn't play reggae; that you had to be a black man to play reggae. I think it was more about rock bands. You'd get a rock band saying, 'Let's do a reggae bit,' and they didn't bother their arses to really listen to how it was, and so they just played it a bit half-heartedly.

But Elvis Costello's 'Watching the Detectives' was out then on the radio, and that was great. It was a bit different, the way they were playing. But the drums and bass and the guitar and that organ sound, just the whole thing, sounded brilliant to me. That was a big inspiration. There's a minor and a major chord in the beginning of 'Watching the Detectives', so I started with those minor and major chords and then I just carried on from there and made up 'My Girl'. It came together quite easy.

CHRIS: I used to go home and play the guitar. I was still living in that council flat, and one time Suggs came round. I had a little amp in my son's bedroom and me and Suggs wrote 'In the Middle of the Night'. I was like, 'Oh, it's not that hard, is it?' So, I got more inspired.

SUGGS: He was decorating the bedroom for his firstborn child when we wrote 'In the Middle of the Night'. We were sitting on a couple of tea chests with all the staples sticking out and the tin foil on the top. If you weren't careful, when you sat on it, it cut your arse on the tin foil.

The lyrics went back to Mr Bianchi, who ran the newsagent's opposite Cavendish Mansions in Clerkenwell, because, as I said, I found all this underwear in his basement. I didn't know at that time that he'd bought damaged goods from a ship. And there were stories in the papers at that time about knicker thieves.

Every other week, there'd be somebody caught nicking knickers off a washing line. So, I had this vision that it was him, and I wrote it about that. Although it wasn't him, and I don't wish to disturb his ghost.

Half the songs were written on the top deck of the bus. Sometimes I'd wait for Chris on a bus from Kentish Town to Camden. Me and him would talk a lot on the bus about what the band were doing and where we were going. Chris was funny, just funny. Always taking the piss. I'd get a half fare, and the conductor could see I wasn't 14. Then Chris would be going, 'Well, he's having a half a fag, can't he pay half a fare? Is that alright?'

**CHRIS:** Suggs was six feet tall, tin of lager and a fag, saying 'Half to Muswell Hill, please . . .'

**MARK:** I got us another gig, at the shop I was working in, in Camden Lock. They used to have a summer party for the people who had shops there. I was doing this sort of screen-printing stuff in this shop called Blind Alley. By then, the band felt like it was really taking shape.

**CHRIS:** We'd got offered Blind Alley and John Hasler was away in France, so I rang Suggs and asked him if he could sing. I knew he still liked the band, because he'd been to all the gigs. Mike reluctantly agreed. The place was rammed, and we were getting pretty good. Thommo was in the audience shouting 'Where's the sax player?' Mike sung 'My Girl', which he'd just written.

**SUGGS:** Mike chucking me out of the band gave me a great kick up the arse, for sure. I'd had two singing jobs on a Saturday – 'You're going home in a fucking ambulance!', or 'Buster, he sold the heat . . .' And I'd been thinking, 'Which one do you want?'

MARK: The next gig, in November '78, at Acklam Hall in Ladbroke Grove, over in west London – that was a baptism by fire. We were playing with The Tribesmen, who were a pretty heavy reggae band. And because it was in west London, it was a little bit out of our area, since we were a north London band, really. But we had a lot of home support that had come over to see us from Hampstead and Camden and all that. It felt like it was a biggish gig for us, y'know, supporting a proper band and everything.

SUGGS: It was that whole thing about going under the Westway, where Acklam Hall was. Very little street lighting. It was an exotic place – a bit scary and dangerous – and definitely not where we would hang about normally. So, it was a big deal for us. I mean, that whole reggae thing was much more prevalent in west London than it was where we were, apart from Finsbury Park.

In those days, the skinheady stuff aside, just going to someone else's area with a load of your mates was taken as a kind of threat of some sort. People would prepare for you to come, and give you a sort of welcoming committee. And because there was six of us in the band, and at least three or four of our mates working with the band, and then say another five, you've got nearly twenty people straight away. Someone across the road sees twenty people going in the local pub on their way to the venue and, immediately, it starts getting around that there's this gang from north London are coming to try and take over. There was an element of that in the Acklam Hall on the night.

\*

**CATHAL:** Even though I wasn't in the band, I was still going to see them all the time. Me and Si Birdsall used to hire a van on Liverpool Road, tell 'em we were just using it locally, and we'd follow the band. We had this sort of Praetorian guard, this gang, the Totts and Whets, and they'd be in the back. Because it was a bit like going into bandit country. There'd be a mattress in the back and lots of spliff. When we got to the Acklam Hall gig, we'd all dropped some speed and the night was on.

**WOODY:** The Totts and Whets could definitely look after themselves, and they'd all converged on this gig. I mean, it did look intimidating. They were on my side, and I still kind of went, 'Ooh, fucking hell . . .'

**LEE:** There was an air of, 'Something's gonna kick off . . . other cats piss in this area . . .' This was another cat's area you were venturing into. We got there, and it was a big hall, nice sound system, nice music playing, a few black dudes dotted about. But the main audience was, I'd say, sort of eighty per cent white skinheads.

**SUGGS:** There was this funny frisson between the danger and, then, people like Mick Jones from The Clash who were there. Cool cats that we kind of liked had turned up to see us.

**CHRIS:** Glen Matlock who'd been in the Pistols was there.

**LEE:** Clive Langer from Deaf School – another band that influenced us – had turned up, and we wanted to try and put on a good show. It was very edgy, but we got on with it. There was a bit of intimidation going on from the locals. But it was like, 'You ain't intimidating us . . .'

CHRIS: Cathal was there, but he was in the audience. Him and Si Birdsall would dance in the audience, like, really mad dancing. Then, Cathal and Chalky used to do this thing: they'd dance like a bullfighter and a bull . . . keep going towards each other and then head-butt each other. In the end, they had to pack it up, because they were getting scar tissue on their heads.

There was this old guy in front of us as were playing, and he was going, 'Whurr, whurr.' He was a really pissed old guy, but he was really funny. After, I went, 'Did anyone see that old geezer?' and Woody went, 'That's my dad.'

WOODY: My dad had come rolling in, completely plastered, and he threw a fiver onstage at me: 'Dan! Dan!' He rolled it up and chucked it and Cathal immediately put his foot on it. Cathal seemed really dodgy. He scared the life out of me, because of his demeanour. But to his credit, he picked the fiver up and he gave it to me after the gig.

CHRIS: I went in the toilet, as you do, and there was this skin-heady bloke there, and he had a strange-shaped head. I thought he was Hammerhead Al who Suggs knew. I said, 'You a mate of Suggsy's?', and he's like, 'Wot wot, you wot? Who the fuck's he?' I thought, 'Ooh God, there's gonna be a fight.' I ran out and I went, 'Cathal, where's Brendan? Quick, quick.' 'Cause him and his brother Brendan were ones for the old fisticuffs at the time. Then these other skinheads came in . . .

*

CATHAL: There was a fight. I mean, it was just fisticuffs and shit. It wasn't serious, really. I mean, people do stupid things when they drink. And it's all that, 'I'm not going to back down . . .' Then a load of other people turned up outside.

CHRIS: It got a bit flipping hostile outside, and we decided to make a swift exit. We got all the gear in the vans and we had to push one of them and it backfired. Chalky got left behind, but he blended in with the local skinheads. Later he told me these guys thought we had a shotgun. They heard this bang, and they were going, 'Oi, they've got a shooter.'

MIKE: They weren't the brightest.

LEE: We had to make a hasty escape. It was quite touch and go whether we'd get our tyres slashed or whatever.

MARK: I went for a drink round the corner. So, I missed the lot.

CATHAL: The band fucked off and left me and Si, our girl-friends and my brother Brendan. My brother climbed over the back fence behind the venue to get help. Someone in the hall had called the police, 'cause there was a crowd of these west London guys outside who were gonna do us. As the police were keeping the crowd at bay, we got out sharpish and, at the end of the road, there was Brendan waiting for us with a taxi. We all piled in and got away. It was a close one.

But, I dunno, at the same time, everyone was buzzing. It was like being in a film. We'd all been to see *Mean Streets* and *Rebel*

*Without a Cause* and *American Graffiti* and it felt like all that kind of stuff.

SUGGS: I escaped with this girl that night – which was unusual – after we'd had this fight with these Ladbroke Grove skins. Everyone got in the vans: I didn't. I'd stuck right with this bird, and I ended up in Golborne Road, after giving these skins the slip. Anyway, so I'm in her flat, in the morning, and I open the curtains, and I look out and there's a stall outside in the Golborne market and who's standing there? Half the Ladbroke Grove skinheads, right outside the front door. She's going, 'Do you want to go out for a coffee?' and I'm saying, 'D'you know what? Not just yet . . .' Because I looked out and saw Chrissy Harwood, the leader of the Ladbroke Grove skins, and a lot of his mates, hanging about outside the fruit and veg stall that his family ran, directly opposite the front door of this flat. I'm going, 'Coffee? Nah, I'm alright thanks.' I knew they'd spot me straight away. This was still when you didn't see a lot of people about with short hair and straight trousers. Four fucking hours later, I was still in her flat . . .

CATHAL: There was a real mix at the gigs then – punks and Teds and skins and mods . . . the last tribes. It seemed to be the last burst of that sort of obsessional identity stuff. It was quite an edgy vibe. But I think loads of bands had that vibe at their gigs. The Sex Pistols had that vibe. Even fucking Bill Haley had that vibe once. That's something that goes with a burgeoning scene, I suppose, and that explosion. It was just exciting, really.

WOODY: I was considering whether being in the band was something I really wanted to do. I was 17 when I first joined the band

and then I was going to the rehearsal room and we did a couple of gigs here and there. But my best friend was moving to Ireland and I was honestly thinking of going with him. Just to lead a completely different life . . . a kind of alternative, hippie lifestyle. I didn't know what I was going to do with my life. I'd left school with no O levels or anything and I just happened to be in this band. And I actually questioned whether I really wanted to do it or not.

I was a drummer in this kind of mad, wacky band, but I didn't know whether it was me. I really didn't: I was really struggling with my own identity at the time. I kind of felt separate from the band. I felt like a fish out of water, really – stylistically, clothing-wise, culturally, the whole thing. There weren't many things that I could identify with when it came to the individuals in the band, apart from the schools we went to and the area we grew up in.

I got a bit down, and I went to a rehearsal, thinking, 'I'm going to tell them how I feel and I'm really seriously thinking that maybe this isn't happening, and I want to move on.' But, that day, somehow, everyone opened up and they all talked quite openly about how each one of them had the same fears and doubts about the future. So, the irony was that then I was thinking, 'Bloody hell, I can really identify with them,' because each one of them was going, 'I'm just really not sure this is happening. Where are we going with this? Are we good enough? Is it really what we want to do?' It was like, 'Hang on, that was my line . . . I was supposed to say that . . .'

And then, from that moment, you realised that they were vulnerable human beings. They're just exactly the same as anyone else, and they all had their fears and doubts and loves and pain and suffering. They all had a persona of cocky geezers and hard men and what have you. But really, every one of them had a soft underbelly.

SUGGS: There'd been all this violence at Acklam Hall and then we got asked to do a gig at Middlesex Polytechnic. I said, 'Come on guys. Let's hold this together, for fuck's sakes. This is it . . . This could lead to a whole string of nice middle-class university gigs.'

Next thing, on the night, the toilets have been smashed to pieces. There's water squirting in all directions, toilet doors hanging off . . .

CHRIS: What happened was one of our mates at the gig for some reason unbeknownst to anyone but him, trashed the toilets of this uni.

SUGGS: I think he'd had a row with his girlfriend.

CHRIS: So, they thought, 'Right,' and they got us off the stage. It was hilarious though – they were coming and picking us up by the waist and carrying us off . . . these student union security guys who were a bit drippy. So, as they did it, Chalky and Toks were picking us up and carrying us back on.

But yeah, we didn't get asked back.

SUGGS: Twenty years later, in 1998, I went to the Cup Final, and Chelsea were playing Middlesbrough. I went with a load of my mates, including these guys Alfie and Jimmy. I'd hired an open-top double-decker bus to get us there, which wasn't easy, because they don't like taking football fans to football matches, for obvious reasons. The driver said to us, 'I'll have to remind you, of course … no booze on the bus.' Alfie and Jimmy are loading on the jerry cans of orange squash, and off we go.

So, we get to the game, and unfortunately, when we get off the bus, there's a slight altercation with some coppers up ahead, and Jimmy gets involved and gets nicked.

The beginning of the next season, I go up to the pub and I see Alf. I go, 'Fuck, what happened to Jimmy?' He said, 'Oh, he's going to court next week.' I said, 'Oh, fuck, maybe I can do something? Maybe I'll give him a character reference? I mean, everybody knows me. That can't hurt, can it?'

So, there I am on the balcony of Court No. 2 at the Old Bailey, with Jimmy's nervous son. And before the judge sums up, he's reading out the character references.

He says, 'Oh, yes, is this the same Graham McPherson who is also known as Suggs from the pop group, Madness?'

I'm like that, to his son, 'Don't you worry about a thing, mate.' And I says to the judge, 'Yes.'

Then the judge goes, 'The same pop group Madness that played at Middlesex Polytechnic in 1978, when I was head of the student union, yes? And in an act of wanton, drunken thuggery, smashed up our new toilet department?'

I'm thinking 'Middlesex Poly? Oh, for fuck's sake, I know where this is going … shit …'

Jimmy got six months.

## CHAPTER 10

# THEY CALL IT MADNESS

**MARK:** Late autumn of '78, winter of '79, we did a lot of work together – just rehearsing and trying to push the songs along . . . trying to get better. Our first gig of '79 was on New Year's Day. A stupid day to play a gig, I suppose. It was at the London Film-Makers' Co-op, which was quite a groovy place, in Gloucester Avenue in Primrose Hill. We went on pretty early, and the head-liners were Shane MacGowan's band, The Nips. The first band on were called The Millwall Chainsaws. But it was a pretty terrible thing, because there was no one there, really, from my memory. There was snow on the ground outside and it was freezing cold.

**LEE:** My fingers froze on the buttons of the saxophone. The venue was just like a puddle-strewn, cobwebbed warehouse: paint cracking up everywhere, with a couple of sound boxes put in. There were quite a few people there, but I just wanted to get back home in the warm . . .

\*

CHRIS: There was about fifty people there. It wasn't bad. The Millwall Chainsaws were almost like a joke band. They must have thought, 'What's the hardest name you can have?' On the night, they said, 'We'll go on before you.' We thought, 'Well, that's good . . . it's put us up the bill.' But then they came out, and they were like, 'You cunts' at the audience. They were dreadful.

SUGGS: They were dressed as surgeons with masks on and blood all over them. Basically, it was a lot of chaos and crazy, eclectic kind of energy.

MARK: One day not long after that, Chris or Mike came into the rehearsal, saying, 'There's another band called The Invaders.' Everyone was like, 'What?! What are they doing?' 'Well, they've got proper gigs . . . What're we going to do?' We couldn't believe it. The other Invaders were a bit, like, power pop or heavy metal or something. So, either Mike or Chris said, 'We'll call ourselves the north London Invaders,' which was a bit of a mouthful.

CHRIS: Jimmy Pursey of Sham 69 had signed a band called The Invaders to his record label. So, for a while, we were the north London Invaders, and then, it really was like, 'We've got to think of a new name.'

SUGGS: Suddenly, there was this other band called The Invaders, who had a deal, and so for us there was a certain sadness that we'd spent a lot of time building up some kind of reputation using that name, and now we were going to have to change it.

At this point, we were just starting to get the feeling there might be some sort of living in the band. Even if it maybe wasn't a career, it was certainly fifty quid every Friday night, and that's not bad. We weren't even thinking about success, but just being recognised, which was, of course, a real joy. 'Oh, you're that bloke out of The Invaders?' 'That's me, girls . . .' And now someone was taking that away, just as we were slowly climbing up the ladder of recognition.

We did one gig as Morris and the Minors, at The Music Machine in Camden, supporting Sore Throat. I wasn't mad on being Morris, and the others weren't too keen on being the Minors, neither. It was like, 'What are we? A fucking Morris dancing troupe?' Mike goes, 'I just thought it sounded funny because of the transport we use.' Thank God we weren't The Hillman Imps, or The Ford Fiestas . . .

**MIKE:** Nobody liked Morris and the Minors as a name. Especially Suggs, I guess understandably. He thought, 'So I'm fucking *Morris*? I don't want to be Morris.' I was just thinking I liked the vans . . .

**LEE:** Trust Mike to come up with that. Y'know, fantastic car but not a name for a band, surely.

**WOODY:** It was either that or The Big Dippers.

**LEE:** The Big Dippers, The Soft Shoe Shufflers . . . The Soft Shoe Shufflers sounded a little bit forties, a little bit black American. The Big Dippers, I liked that, because it had that fairground feel to it, and dippers, as well, could mean dipping, y'know, dipping pockets . . . hoisting.

**WOODY:** We were in that little dentist's basement rehearsal place, all standing round a light bulb in the middle of the room, with the set list. I said, 'Why don't we call ourselves one of the names of the songs in the set? We've got loads of songs here.' And Chrissy Boy, really sarcastically, went, 'What . . . yeah . . . like Madness?' and everyone went, 'That's really good!' And Chris went, 'No, I'm only mucking about! I didn't mean it!'

**CHRIS:** I went, 'Oh, yeah, Madness, huh huh,' as a joke, and they went, 'Yeah!'

**LEE:** Immediately it was like, 'Nice one . . . yeah.' Everyone was definitely on the same page there.

**MIKE:** It just sort of stuck. Everybody liked it.

**MARK:** But, after that, Chris always said, 'Ah, I regret it. I don't know why I said that . . .'

**CHRIS:** And there you are. So, I own the name, really . . . We were billed as Morris and the Minors but, in our minds, we were Madness. It was actually the first show with all seven of us. We blew Sore Throat off the stage and they never offered us gigs again.

**LEE:** We did nick that show. It was a very fast, energetic gig. There was a lot of sulphate and blues about at the time. We was all sulphated out a bit, and it was a very manic gig. Y'know, 'One Step Beyond' played at 78 rpm, type thing. That was the first time I noticed, 'Hold on, we're getting a bit of a lively crowd here . . .'

*

**CHRIS:** The Music Machine was the first gig where Cathal got up onstage, doing his dancing. He was just totally on one, and there was that kind of thought: 'Y'know, he's quite good . . .'

**LEE:** He put that edge into the band. Weird dance moves, very starched. How he danced, it was very animated and static at the same time.

**CATHAL:** The feeling was . . . just to be nutty. We're nutty: that was it, really. The dance was a bit of martial arts, a bit of the old skinhead braces-pulling. Moving the head like a Trojan. It felt like a quirky Ealing comedy mixed with British lunacy. I was insecure, massively insecure, and just trying to be in the band. Honestly, I was walking on air, and just happy to be involved. I was like, 'Can I stay on stage a bit longer?'

**WOODY:** My mum by this time was the floor manager at *Top of the Pops*. She knew all the record company pluggers and A&R men. So, she would say to us, 'Oh, they're interested in the band . . .' But the general questions to my mum were, 'Are they going to be Morris and the Minors? What's happening with them?' And then the decision was made to be called Madness, and my mum conveyed this to pretty much all the pluggers and A&R men, and the overriding consensus was, 'Oh, what a shame that they've chosen Madness as their name. They've blown it. Oh dear . . . never mind.'

**MIKE:** We played in the Windsor Castle pub in Maida Vale and that was a bit difficult. We got there and the guy denied that we were booked: 'You're not on . . . there's no band tonight.' We set up the gear anyway, and the only people there was my mum and a couple of her friends and my brother. Generally, we had a crowd, and that gig we didn't. Maybe 'cause it was a bit out of our neighbourhood.

SUGGS: Seeing and then playing gigs downstairs in the Hope & Anchor in Islington was the real opening for us. That pub was the real crux of the biscuit.

John Eichler who ran the Hope & Anchor was just a great guy. I mean, we were all underage when we first went in there: 16, 17. We were this little gang of skinheady types, but we would never be horrible unnecessarily. And he took some shine to us. He was a pretty scary character, so we would listen to what he said.

We would go down there, just to see whoever was playing. I mean, fuck me, are you going to stay indoors with your mum and watch Bruce Forsyth on the telly, or are you going to go down the pub? If that night's gig hadn't sold out and there maybe was only forty or fifty people there, John'd say, 'Alright, you can go down for nothing. At least it'll make it look like they've got a bit of a following.' So, we got to see a lot of great bands down there. I certainly wasn't looking at it then like some sort of education, but I think it must have had a big impact. All those bands we saw come and go, you'd think, 'That's fucking good . . . What's that geezer doing? That's kind of interesting.' So, we were just immersed in music. The other great thing was Johnny let us put our own records on the jukebox. So, it was our jukebox in there, and we'd just play our own music. Whatever bands came through town, they were in our place. It was very much *our* place – probably about twenty or more of us and our friends, pretty much in there every night. If you had no money, you'd have one pint of beer and then you'd have to do a bit of minesweeping for the leftover drinks . . .

MARK: At the time, you had to bring a PA into the Hope & Anchor if you played a gig. So, it was forty-five quid for the PA. The first time we played there, we didn't make the money back on the door – we'd only made forty quid – and John Eichler gave us an extra fiver to pay the PA off. He was really sweet, and he said, 'Here you go . . .' Don't forget as well that the gigs were, like, 50 pence to get into.

LEE: My wife Debbie was on the door a few times when we played there, and Toks, who'd become our roadie. They'd be on the door, charging people to get in, which was good, to keep it in-house. I mean, people you could trust and all that. It was nice to be able to keep it in the family.

CATHAL: The Hope & Anchor reminded me of The Cavern, a bit. I wasn't in the band then, but it was at The Hope and Anchor that Lee said, 'Look, I want you to come on and introduce us.'

It felt like a gang doing their thing. It felt fresh, dangerous. The crowd was a mix of punks, Teds, all kinds of people, loads of friends . . . So, there was lots of different tribes, which was kind of exciting. We had an energy. We were doing our thing, and it felt strong. There was something powerful about knowing that you were doing something different.

We were deadly serious about it. We were serious about being funny, if you know what I mean. We really meant it, and everyone was giving their all at every gig. I mean, at the same time, things went wrong on stage, and there could be real anger, or frustration, because everyone was really serious about it.

WOODY: We wanted a residency somewhere, 'cause the Hope & Anchor was actually quite a difficult gig to get hold of. So, we looked for a pub of our own.

MARK: A friend of mine I'd known from school, a guy called Indra, was a piano player. He had a band who were a bit like Weather Report or something, and he told me, 'We went to this pub in Camden Town, The Dublin Castle, and got a gig. You should go down there and see if you can get a gig.'

Me and Mike and Chris went in and we saw Arlo, the guvnor, and just said, 'We heard you're doing gigs here now.' He said, 'What do you play? Do you play a bit of country? A bit of jazz?' We went, 'Yeah, yeah . . . we play jazz, we play country . . . we play all that,' thinking that this would hopefully sweeten him up. And he said, 'OK, yeah, fine.'

CHRIS: Our first gig at The Dublin Castle was with Mark's mate's band, who were called ABC, funnily enough. Not *that* ABC. We'd got quite a following, and I think as soon as Arlo saw how much beer was getting sold, he was like, 'Alright, you can play here on your own.' So, that became our kind of residency.

It was just a rough-looking old pub. You went in, and there was a room at the back – not that big, and it had this tiny stage. Mike used to have his piano sort of off the stage, on beer crates or something. But anyway, I just felt, 'Yeah . . . this is it.'

*

WOODY: It wasn't at all designed for us: we spilled over the edge of the stage. Just me setting up my drum kit took up most of it, so people kind of balanced precariously on the edge of the stage. It was a real tight squeeze, but we did pack the place out.

MIKE: We started to build a crowd up there, and because we had a residency, somewhere regular to play, that really helped us to develop.

MARK: It was that great tipping point for a band, where you're doing these gigs and you've got all your mates there, and it's everyone local and everyone you know. Then suddenly, there are people you don't know there, and the next week there are more people you don't know there. That's the point where you realise, 'Ooh, hold on a minute, they've obviously heard about the group from somewhere . . .' That tells you, 'We must be onto something here.' As it started to really take off, the gigs were packed and really sweaty and people were jumping around.

SUGGS: Playing week-in week-out at The Dublin Castle . . . you didn't realise until later how fucking formatively marvellous that was. Because without that, the rest of it could just so easily have become an abstract concept of 'I could've been . . . I was definitely nearly gonna do it . . . I was definitely gonna get out of this shit.' But you didn't.

CHRIS: The band, they all used to do a bit of speed, and it's funny, because someone like Cathal, he didn't need it! I mean, it kind of ramped him up, so it was great, actually. He just never used to stop dancing. It was fantastic.

*

**CATHAL:** I didn't really do that much booze. I was always a stoner. But then there was a guy down The Dublin Castle who sold three blues for a pound . . . that started me moving! I was so insecure and uptight and sunglasses were my psychic barrier. I couldn't look the audience in the face. I used to flicker my eyes behind the glasses, to kind of create a strobe to put me in the zone, to go into a trance. The music really did send me, and I was doing things which I never would have done offstage. I let myself physically get lost in the music. Not out of body, but out of character. I became this kind of character that went wild to the music.

**SUGGS:** Yeah, speed was the thing. You got your money's worth. It was blues and black bombers . . . I don't remember snorting anything, This guy at the Hope & Anchor had these things called Tombstones, and they were just slimming pills. They were made out of chalk and you had to take 14 of them, and it was just getting the fucking things down . . . But of course, by the time you'd swallowed the fucking things, the night was over. They'd start kicking in about six in the morning, just when you got home: 'Oh no!' And then the comedown . . .

I suppose I was a little bit wary of drugs because of my dad being a heroin addict. These little, funnily enough, middle-class characters used to walk in the pub with no shoes or socks on and I'd think, 'Oh, yeah, right: that's how you end up looking.' So, the fact that my dad was what he was, it wasn't that difficult to stay away from it.

**LEE:** For myself, personally, it was blues, speed and alcohol. Those gigs at the Hope & Anchor, you used to get mainly sulphate.

**WOODY:** We charged 50p on the door at The Dublin Castle. I think the PA cost us fifty pounds, and after one gig, we did so well, we decided to split profits and we all got a fiver each. Barso or Bedders or somebody gave me a fiver, and it was like, 'Bloody hell . . . amazing.' We were starting to be able to pay ourselves a wage from it.

**CHRIS:** *Melody Maker* reviewed us there and suddenly you were a bit more popular, so there was a lot more people coming. Barso went, 'Alright, we'll charge them a pound.' Being a socialist, I went, 'Mike, y'know, you can't just double what you charge people . . .' There was a big argument about it, but we agreed to make it 75p to get in.

**SUGGS:** I was 18 when I first met my wife, Anne, who was Bette Bright and in Deaf School and all that. Then eventually I was living with her above Swanky Modes, the designer shop on the corner of Royal College Street and Camden Road.

**LEE:** Some of Anne's crowd, who we called the Swanky Modes set, started coming along to our gigs. The Dublin Castle was where it picked up all round. It was like, 'Who are these lot? Where have these people come from?' and it was just word of mouth. A bit of a buzz is created, and before you know it, people are clamouring to get through the door.

Also, this feller, Keith Wainwright, the hairdresser who had his Smile salon down in Kensington, he was quite fond of the band. He wasn't pushy or anything, but he'd just advise you on, say, how you should hold yourself and present yourself. He was giving advice, positive advice, which he didn't have to. But he was always, like, 'Lee, tell you what you should maybe do . . . when you hold your sax, do this or that.' He was more into the visual than the music, Keith, but he was a very nice chap.

MARK: As we went along, more influences were feeding into what we were doing. Not just musical influences, but from films and TV comedy shows.

If there was a big comedy show on, everyone watched it, because there was only BBC1, BBC2 and ITV. So, for us it was Tommy Cooper and Morecambe and Wise, obviously. I loved Dave Allen. Just a man, just sitting in a chair, drinking whisky and having a fag and telling long, long stories. I was always intrigued by that, how one person could just sit there in a chair and really hold your attention.

Then, there was *Steptoe and Son*, which the BBC showed again and again. Everyone loved the pathos of it. Maybe at the time, we didn't know exactly what that was, but it was that thing of this guy being stuck on his own with his dad, and he couldn't leave him. I think, again, that had a huge impression on everyone. Not only the programme, but the music – the theme tune, with the skulls rhythm and the wah-wah-wah brass. We liked that sort of slightly comedic kind of tune.

SUGGS: For some peculiar reason, we all watched Max Wall in Beckett's *Krapp's Last Tape* when it was on *Play for Today*. I suppose it was a bit like what they now call a watercooler moment.

'Spool . . . spool . . . spool . . . spool,' and he's just talking into a tape recorder and playing it back to himself. We were all into Max Wall. His thing was unmitigated comic malevolence. He was crazy, angry, but he could dance like a madman, and be just fully entertaining. So, it was that sort of stuff we were into, and Les Dawson playing the piano out of tune, or Tommy Cooper doing his stuff. I think also, with all these things, there was a fragility. You can see that sweat on the top lip that we all know is what's really required for a great performance. When it's all perfect and polished, it ain't quite as great as when you see your Alex Harveys, your Ian Durys, your Tommy Coopers. The people that we loved, there was an element of like it could all go wrong.

LEE: One particular Tommy Cooper gag I loved was when he was on a big stage – it weren't his usual curtains with a little table in front of him; it was him with an orchestra, suited and booted, strings, brass and that. They were all in the background, and in front, there was a big screen with moons and stars on it. He pops his head out of one side, and the board's wobbling and that, and then he's behind it doing whatever he's doing and he pops his head out the opposite side. Then at the other end, his boots appear, like the sawing-the-lady-in-half trick. It's obvious what's happening, but what done me was the orchestra: that they can see what's going on behind the screen, and they're falling off their chairs laughing. I thought, 'I like that, yeah.'

And, of course, there was Max Wall. There was one sketch he did where he spent three or four minutes just pulling his arms towards a piano. First of all, he's looking for the stool: 'Ver is the schtool?' and then he walks round the back of the piano, 'Ah!', and there's the stool. He sits on it and it's too far away from the piano. But instead of moving the seat to this piano, he stretches his arms, and he stretches his arms.

In the band, I was never trying to be 'cool'. I was the opposite. I was fighting against that shit. It was just that British underdog type thing. We always go for the underdog or the fool; the feller that trips up. We went through a phase of tripping up on purpose: 'Right, as we walk in this room, trip up . . .' 'OK,' and then everyone would do it. It was about just not being perfect, and hopefully, getting a laugh. I like it when things cock up. You picked a few tips up from watching comedians. Certainly, with Tommy Cooper, you'd watch it again and again.

CATHAL: We'd watch a videotape of a Tommy Cooper show to the end, rewind it, start it again and still laugh as much.

Chris would tell jokes in the van, and we got to know the jokes so well, he could just tell the punchline and we'd start laughing. Really, we were somewhere between, like, a male *St Trinian's* and a *Carry On* film. There was a lovely innocence to the whole thing.

MIKE: Lee especially was never like, 'That's not hip . . . I shouldn't like that.' Y'know, he just liked what he liked. And so that genuineness opened up more possibilities for the band to be into different stuff. But we were all cut from the same wood, to an extent. We had the same sort of taste and the same appreciations.

CHRIS: Something that unified all the band was *Monty Python*. Going right back, as a kid, I didn't have a telly when that was on. But I knew this other kid, Phillip Douglas, and his family were quite posh. One night I was round his and he said, 'Oh, we're going to watch *Monty Python's Flying Circus*.' I thought, 'What's that? It sounds like some old thing from the war, y'know, a Flying Circus . . . "We're going to go and get the Jerries." ' I watched it, and I was like, 'Oh, my God.' It was such a big thing. You'd go to school and everyone would be reciting bits of the script, or writing 'Spam, spam, spam' on the blackboard.

SUGGS: With those influences coming into the band, it was all about being wholehearted when you were doing it. Mike said, 'If we're going to fuck about, let's not fuck about. If we're going to dress up and make clowns of ourselves, let's be fucking serious.'

## CHAPTER 11

# DON'T WATCH THAT . . .
# WATCH THIS

**SUGGS:** May '79, we had such a bit of luck, when The Specials turned up to play The Hope and Anchor. I'd seen a double-page spread about them in *Melody Maker*, and just thought, 'Fuck me . . .' From what I read, I realised they were using the same basic building blocks of the music that we were into.

So, I was there that night at the Hope & Anchor and they came bowling in, and it was just like, 'Fucking hell, there they are, and they're from where? Coventry, for fuck's sakes.' I mean, of all the places I thought we might have a connection with, it wasn't Coventry.

They were brilliant. We were just so shocked. We didn't know whether to feel jealous or vindicated that we were onto something after all. They were more professional than us. Neville Staple's blowing holes in the ceiling with his starting pistol, and they're going bananas.

At this point, Cathal's got his Chas Smash thing starting to happen a bit, with that dancing. But I'm still pretty static, and the rest of us are pretty static. I mean, we were still sort of Ian Dury and what we'd seen from him, which is a lot of colourful characters, but not necessarily leaping about in the way that The Specials were. That definitely informed the way we started to perform.

**CATHAL:** I think I came up with the name Chas Smash, or it might have been John Hasler sent me a postcard calling me Chas Smash. Anyway, I always thought it was good if a pseudonym was based on your initials, and I was busy developing this persona.

**SUGGS:** I got chatting to Jerry Dammers after the Specials gig and he had nowhere to stay. In those days, the best chance you had of finding somewhere decent to stay after a gig was pulling a bird. And with them teeth . . . He ended up staying with me at my mum's flat in Gower Street. That night he said, 'I'm going to start a record label.' I was going, 'Jerry, that's fucking great. But, is it not a smidge optimistic when you've just played to 35 people in a pub basement?' He said, 'No, I'm going to create an English Motown.' He opened his briefcase to reveal a mouldy orange and a copy of *Melody Maker*. He said, 'Do you want to sign to our label?' I said, 'You haven't even got a fucking pencil, Jerry, what are you talking about?'

**MARK:** I'd seen The Specials, as The Coventry Automatics, on a bill with The Clash. I'd thought, 'These lot are interesting,' because it was pretty much literally a reggae and punk mix: it was reggae being really played really fast. The Coventry Automatics looked a lot different from how The Specials did finally. They were a real rag-tag mixture. Terry Hall looked a bit Jim Morrison-y, with a flowing shirt. Roddy Radiation looked a bit punky. Some looked a bit punky and some looked a bit sixties. But you could tell that they were a real mixture of different people from different bands who'd actually all come together up there. It was only in a relatively short space of time from that when Suggs saw them at the Hope & Anchor, and by then they were in the sixties mohair suits, and they had the black-and-white check thing going.

MIKE: It was in West Hampstead, at The Moonlight club, that I saw The Specials for the first time. They were incredible – they all had suits on, and I guess it was premeditated, but they were all jumping around when they were playing, so there was a great energy. That was the thing that I guess we learnt, and when we started playing with them, we were all jumping around. That was what you did at that time, and it got the audience going. If you didn't jump around, you'd better hang up your clogs . . .

I guess we owed quite a debt in that period to The Specials, because they'd been working up a name and they were in the papers and everything. So, then, we could quite easily step up straight into that world, because we became associated with them. Jerry was very socialist-minded and he was very into equality, so he really gave us an opportunity. We were lucky sods.

MARK: The first show we played with The Specials, they offered us a gig with them at The Nashville in West Kensington. But we'd already been booked to play at The Dublin Castle the same night. So, we decided we'd make a dash between the two and play both gigs. We had the Morris 1000 vans, and we loaded up all the gear and got down to The Nashville.

*

SUGGS: We turned up and there was a queue round the block. Now we realised, 'Something's happening. This isn't just two hundred disparate mates who've turned up. This is a scene.' There was a queue right round the block. All these black and white kids dressed to the nines, looking the part. Jerry Dammers told me he'd seen a car screech up outside and it was Johnny Rotten, on his way to somewhere else. He jumped out and he was looking at them all, and he went up to this little kid and he went, 'Are you for real?' This kid went, 'Yes, we fucking are!'

But then it was that moment of walking in The Nashville and it was like, 'Fucking hell, this isn't just us messing about in The Duke of Hamilton with what trousers we're wearing. This is something happening . . . this is really fucking happening.'

The whole thing tied up all those bits and bobs that we liked: ska music, reggae music, dancing, the energy of punk but not tearing your clothes up. All this started to come together, and suddenly it was like a cohesive thing. It was really exciting, even though it was this weird dichotomy of vintage nostalgia and something new. Black and white kids were making music together and hanging about together, in a way possibly you might have had in some of the gay discos. But I hadn't seen it pretty much anywhere else.

Also, those clothes were an effort to find, so suddenly you were thinking, 'Look, these lot have all made that effort.' All those button-down shirts, Crombies and Harringtons, you didn't go down to Marks and Sparks to buy this gear. You had to find this gear, and to find the band and find the gig.

LEE: It was a larger than usual crowd that night at The Nashville. I went outside just to check it out, and it wasn't at that stage where you was going to get pulled right, left and centre. I mean, I just looked like a punter, but I was getting a little bit of the butterflies there. So, I said to the butterflies, 'Oh, this is looking good.'

**WOODY:** What was amazing was walking into the venue and seeing all these blokes from The Specials in two-tone suits and pork pie hats and thinking, 'Bloody hell, they're just like us.' It was really weird that they came from Coventry, we came from London, and there'd been absolutely no communication what-soever, until Suggs met them at the Hope & Anchor. I have to say, though, we were a bit more eclectic when it came to our style. They were a bit more uniformed, in the sense that they all looked like rudeboys and had nice suits and hats. But they looked the business.

**MARK:** The Nashville was kind of an amazing place. You'd try to avoid the toilets, because they was just so bad. It was a big Victorian pub, with a back room with this amazing curved glass as you came in. It was literally a stage, a bar and a big open space, and then the terrible toilets and the terrible dressing rooms. We had this famous picture taken with The Specials at the sound-check on the stage at The Nashville. We look so young, and we're still in jackets and hats and stuff. So, it was all evolving.

**WOODY:** It was a great gig. We used to kick off with the theme from *Hawaii Five-0*, which was a good laugh. The place was dripping with condensation. It was just unbelievable. We were all speeding out of our heads.

The Specials did make me think about my drumming, because their drummer Brad – John Bradbury – was really authentic. But then I also came to the conclusion at a very early stage that

Madness were unique in the sense that we had our own sound, and The Specials were desperate to sound like the original records. I thought that was very admirable of them, but it was something that I didn't think that we could do, and I kind of railed against it a bit. Because the band were always going, 'Oh, do the dropbeat and do this and do that,' and it was, 'Well, you know what? I feel comfortable playing it the way I hear it. I can't play that stuff, so I'll just do what I do.'

There was an absolute fundamental difference between ourselves and what became the 2 Tone bands and that was the fact that they were constantly looking for that authentic, original sound. Ours was not a recreation of the original music. Ours was purely influenced by the original music.

But it was just amazing, because two bands had come together with the same kind of crowd, the same vision, the same eclectic mix of music that we liked. So, that night, we played, and then The Specials played, and then we couldn't get our gear out. We were really late, because The Nashville had all these restrictions there: 'You can't leave until the other band's come off.' We were going, 'Well, we need to get out now.' Anyway, we made it out of there and raced across town to The Dublin Castle.

MARK: All our friends were waiting there, going, 'Where have you been?' And then we set up and did another gig.

These were times, at those gigs, when Chris would sing 'Bed & Breakfast Man' and give the guitar to Suggs, who'd play with one finger, going *blink-bling-bling-bling*. Mike would sing 'My Girl', and Lee would sing 'Razor Blade Alley'. They'd sing their own songs, basically.

\*

**CHRIS:** Bedders had told me that people were calling John Hasler 'the bed and breakfast man', 'cause he'd turn up at your house, eat everything, kip on the sofa and then leave the next day. So, I started writing a song called that. Mike added some extra lyrics and the music.

**SUGGS:** Clive Langer, who ended up producing us, came down to see us rehearsing in the dentist's basement. We all loved Deaf School: that drama-fucking-theatre thing was right up our street. Clive was Mike's older brother Ben's mate, and we all liked Mike's older brothers, Ben and Danny. Another adjunct to our whole thing was the Hampstead hippie crowd. There was a correlation between the boot-boys and . . . they weren't wanky hippies; they were like tough hippies. Not that they wanted to fight or any of that, but they had a bit of go in them. Clive had a bit of go in him, for sure.

But he walked in the door and he had six cans of Heineken, like some sort of offering. We're going, 'What's that supposed to be? Six fucking cans of Heineken? Whoo, having it with the lads? Fuck off!' Then, it just went very well, very quickly. After we got over the try and impress us with your six cans of warm Heineken bit, we started to talk about music, and it just made sense . . . everything he said, from the word go.

We were doing 'My Girl' and he said to Woody, 'Right, forget all those drum rolls' – and that was the end of them tom-toms. 'Just go *boum-boum-boum*, and Bedders, you simplify the bass part.' It didn't suddenly become something else entirely, because it was always a great song. But he started to focus us on what we were good at and what made us different from other people. That was something that Clive had a really big hand in.

He had a clear vision. He was just trying to get us closer and closer to what people now call the sound of Madness. To stop us meandering, basically. He just wanted it to have more punch and he added it.

MARK: Clive's influence was definitely there in the verse parts of 'My Girl', to get that sort of jumpy rhythm. It is kind of two songs in a way, because you've got this quite hard and staccato verse and then you break into this flowing chorus. It's got that tension and release.

CHRIS: We didn't know what a producer was. What Clive had was a bit of knowledge: 'I know this studio that you can go to,' which turned out to be Pathway. We went there and it was a tiny little place, but it seemed incredibly flash. Upstairs, they had an Elvis Costello disc on the wall and it was like, 'Oh, my God, he recorded that first album of his here.'

MARK: Yeah, it was tiny, but it had a reputation because it was where Elvis Costello had recorded *My Aim is True*. Dire Straits' 'Sultans of Swing' was recorded there, and then a lot of really good pub rock bands that we'd seen around the circuit all recorded there. So, it was the place go to.

It was a really thin building – you couldn't really call it a house – on Grosvenor Avenue, close to Stoke Newington. The studio and control room were on the ground floor, then these rickety old stairs led to the office up top. The studio had that old-fashioned aerated board with the holes in on the walls, so it was very fifties.

*

**LEE:** It was just down a cobbled street back alley. Unassuming, nothing flash, nothing big: just an oversized garage with a couple of speakers in and soundproofed rooms. It was very rough and ready.

**WOODY:** What was supposed to be the first session at Pathway was disastrous for me, because I got lost. It was just terrible. The band really still take the piss out of me for not being able to find the place.

I was following the two Morris vans on my motorbike, because I'd thought, 'Why should I squeeze in that fucking van, on top of the gear, again?' I kept my eye on the vans all the time, but then at one point there was a queue of traffic and they turned off at a junction. So, I turned off, and then they were just gone. They just disappeared, and I went, 'Fuck!'

I didn't even have the address of the place – all I knew was that it was 'Pathway Studios'. So, I was asking everyone, and then people were going, 'Oh, I think I know it, mate, it's down here.' And I never found it.

**CHRIS:** We got there, and we were thinking, 'Where is he, where is he?'

**LEE:** We missed the first session because Woody got lost. That was like, 'Jesus Christ . . .'

**MIKE:** I just couldn't get it in my head that he'd got lost, y'know? No mobile phones in those days, nothing. So, he got lost on the way there: unbelievable.

\*

**SUGGS:** Pathway was one of them places . . . I still don't know where it was. It was down some alley off the back arse of Stoke Newington, and once we'd lost him, we'd lost him. So, that day's recording went out the window.

**CHRIS:** Clive said, 'Look, we'll just pay the studio guy some of the money.' We'd saved all this money up and it was a bit sickening.

So, Clive went to see Rob Dickins at Warner Bros Music Publishing. He said, 'Can you put up some money for a demo?' and we got three hundred quid. Rob Dickins was pretty canny, because he said, 'I'll give you the money, but I want the publishing.' I don't think he knew much about us. But he had faith in Clive.

**WOODY:** It was about a month later that we went to Pathway and recorded 'Madness', 'My Girl' and 'The Prince'. To this day, Clive Langer says that actually he's glad the session was delayed, because he believes that we'd gotten better in that short period of time.

**CHRIS:** Pathway had a tiny little eight-track machine, but a good mixing desk and microphones. And they had this upright piano that was quite good because it had that sort of pub sound. Clive got us in there, and because it was only eight-track, we had to do it live.

**MARK:** We all stood up and played. They had screens, so they screened off the kit and then there was a little cubicle for the bass, a little cubicle for the guitar, and a little cubicle for the singing.

But we broke the mixing desk – one of the VU meters. The engineer was getting up the sound, he said, 'Oh, what do you want the bass to sound like?' and we all said, 'We want it reggaeish.' As he turned up the low-end tone control on the bass, I hit a really big note and it went pop and actually broke the glass on the VU meter! And I went, 'Oh, sorry!' and he went, 'It's alright, don't worry about it.' But that stayed there for years: they never fixed it. Every time I went back there to do various things, the meter was still broken.

**LEE:** It was an experience, that first time putting those headphones on. Going from playing live to that was just a completely different ball game. I was thinking, 'Oh, I quite like this . . .' Warm, comfortable, kettle on the brew and it was very quick.

**MIKE:** It was amazing to hear what it sounded like, because up until then, we'd just had cassette recordings in the rehearsal room. I was playing the piano and thinking the whole band sounded really authentic. It was all just coming together, really.

**MARK:** We got that reggaeish, dubbish effect on 'The Prince' with the Roland Space Echo, and for the 'gow!' on the guitar. We'd obviously wanted to make it sound like a Prince Buster song. The groove was very good. It really rumbled along.

**MIKE:** I was singing 'My Girl' at that point and I don't know whether Clive already had that idea to get Suggs to sing it later.

It didn't sound great with me singing . . . I don't know if I've got a very good voice. Clive was saying, 'Try and sing it like this,' sort of, 'This is not good enough.' But with hindsight, I don't know if it was just a game on his part, that he was manipulating me to think, 'Oh, I haven't quite got it,' and then 'Stand down for Suggs' kind of thing. But if I listen to that vocal on that recording now, it certainly doesn't make you think, 'Oh, what a wasted opportunity . . .' or anything like that.

**SUGGS:** I didn't think it was so bad myself. I think Mike's not a bad singer. But, after, Clive was saying 'Y'know, to have a cohesive band, you've got to have the lead singer singing the songs.' I knew I could sing 'My Girl' good – and I'm not saying I could sing it any better – but I really liked the song.

That Pathway session, though, suddenly I realised, for the first time in my life, that I had to take things seriously. Up to that point, I'd taken nothing seriously. We were going over and over the songs, and it was like, 'For fuck's sakes, come on, Clive.' It got to sort of one in the morning, and I was thinking, 'How many more times have we got to do these songs?' Then when I heard them back at the end, I thought, 'Fuck! That's why you sometimes have to take things seriously.' And as it was, 'The Prince', 'My Girl' and 'Madness' came out pretty good.

**LEE:** It was money well spent.

**CHRIS:** And there you have it: we had the three songs that started us off.

**SUGGS:** We're still playing those first three songs. They're still the foundation of any live gig we do.

**WOODY:** Somehow one of the next gigs we got was supporting The Pretenders at the Lyceum, which was the biggest gig we'd done up till then. This was Madness in our very earliest stage, doing a gig with a huge band, and we blew them offstage, because the majority of the crowd had come for us.

**CATHAL:** When we came on, Lee wheeled me on in a big old fridge cardboard box, and I leapt out and started the intro to 'One Step Beyond'.

**MARK:** We played really well that night. We came on and we were all energy and went for it, and it went really, really well.

**WOODY:** I was like a rabbit in the headlights, because I wasn't used to big gigs. I was nervous as fuck and I had this kind of tunnel vision of 'Whoo', trying to get through it. The whole place was rocking for us. Massive cheers, and the crowd heaving and jumping up and down.

The Pretenders came on and half the crowd left . . . By the time they got on, it was not the same crowd and they were restrained – not like it had been for us – a completely different vibe, like a different gig. It was really not a good gig for The Pretenders. It was a fucking great gig for us.

**CATHAL:** We really pissed them off, and then we danced across the stage as The Pretenders were playing, which they really didn't like.

**MIKE:** We were of the opinion that we blew them off stage, which we often felt like. Whenever we were supporting people, we always felt like we'd got a secret weapon: they ain't going to know what's happened. They were probably down in the dressing room . . . didn't know anything. But we were feeling like we were blowing them offstage.

**SUGGS:** At the time, we said we blew them off, but that's just the sort of thing you say, isn't it? I think Chrissie Hynde's had the hump ever since. Because we probably didn't.

The other thing that happened that night was afterwards we were all there, and someone's nicked the till out of the upstairs bar and got caught halfway down the stairs. Then I had a tin of spray paint, and I wrote, 'Nut, nut, nutty . . .' all down the corridor. John Curd, the promoter, whose company was called Straight Music, he was another real character. And he rang me in the morning, and he said, 'Look, never mind the till, but that fucking spray paint . . . you've got to come back here and scrub it off the wall now.' I had to go back and scrub the wall with sugar soap.

Anyway, around then Jerry Dammers rings me up and goes, 'I've done it! I've started a record label. It's called 2 Tone.' Thank fuck we'd recorded 'The Prince', because we'd decided that the version of 'My Girl' with Mike singing wasn't ready to put out.

**CHRIS:** John Curd was this big swarthy bloke, with shoulder-length hair. After we did the Pretenders gig, there was a tour called March of the Mods and they were playing at the Lyceum. John said we'd be second from the top of the bill, below Secret Affair. When we got there, the tour manager said no, you're going to go first. So we told John Curd, and he went and bashed the guy on the head with a torch, and knocked him out. So we ended up second from the top. Result.

\*

**MARK:** 'The Prince' was the obvious A-side, backed by 'Madness'. We just gave Jerry the Pathway tape and said, 'What do you think?' and he said, 'Yeah, it should be the single.'

**CHRIS:** It was great because 2 Tone was the happening label.

**SUGGS:** Getting our hands on the actual singles was such a great moment. John Hasler was our manager by then and we were meeting outside Archway Tube, to go to a gig, and he just turned up with a box of them. It was that brilliant thing of fresh records, fresh vinyl, with our name on it and the black-and-white 2 Tone label. Really, really was exciting.

**WOODY:** John Hasler handed our first single out to us all, and it was the most amazing feeling – actually to have a record of your own that you'd made.

**LEE:** It was like, 'Wow, I've arrived!' type thing.

**CATHAL:** I've got a photo somewhere of John wearing one of those orange bollard things on his head, with a copy of the single.

**CHRIS:** John Hasler was squatting in King's Cross, and we'd been saving the band money up, and he had it hidden there behind this loose brick. Probably with all the cement missing around it, so you could obviously see . . . Anyway, some guy supposedly nicked the money.

**LEE:** We talking about it in the van, going to or coming from rehearsals, and there was a plot being hatched about kidnapping this feller and taking him to a cashpoint with his card. I was thinking, 'No, come on . . .' But I think, yeah, Cathal, Mike, they weren't having it. They weren't having some probably down-and-out hippie doing our money on a load of drugs or whatever. But I kept me distance from that. It was, like, two hundred and fifty quid or something. Is it worth getting involved there? I know that they weren't going to let it go, and rightly so. I just didn't want to get involved in it.

**SUGGS:** It was farcial, like *Carry On a Kidnapping* or *The Lavender Hill Mob*!

**MIKE:** It was a fucker, y'know, he nicked our money. I mean, it was a very enjoyable experience, although I don't even know if we ever got the money back, because it went wrong at the end.

It did look maybe a bit aggressive and a bit serious that you've actually kidnapped this bloke. I mean, I didn't feel like it was. Mainly because he'd actually nicked this money off of us, so I felt very righteous and that we had every right to get that money back. We felt we were only going to get it back by taking things into our own hands.

We found out where this bloke lived and we went up there. We somehow got him in the car and he stayed with us all night. He had the money in the bank. We said, 'You're going to the bank in the morning,' and he was saying, 'Yeah, yeah, yeah, alright.' I mean, obviously, he'd nicked the money, so he had to.

Except in the morning the bank manager wasn't having it. This dodgy geezer was saying, 'I want to get some money out of the bank,' and he didn't have his passport or something, so the bank didn't let him. I mean, it was all a bit iffy. The police

**Mike:** My brother Dan (centre) with his band Bazooka Joe and his girlfriend Kelly (his left), of the Lillets; Willy Wurlitzer (white tie), who wrote 'Rockin' In A Flat'; Danny Kleinman, who now designs the Bond movie title sequences, kneeling. This was before Adam Ant joined as their bass player.

**Mike:** A poster I drew for them for a gig in Hampstead Town Hall. They changed the knife for a comb for fear of inciting the already aggressive Teddy Boy contingent.

**Mike:** Bazooka Joe off duty at the Stapleton Arms, with a pair of sycophantic fans, c.1974.

**Mike:** My brother Dan playing some Rock 'n' Roll in the hall at Park Avenue South.

**Mike:** The pub – Cathal looking cool on the pinball; Suggs, Chris and Mark on the pool table.

**Lee:** Up in Luton, I'd sometimes go into a field with a packed lunch, and blow away. There was the odd inquisitive cow. Soon got shot of those.

**Lee:** Myself, Cathal and Rockin' Billy Whizz, c.1977.

**Lee:** Tokins and Kix attempt the Swan Lake Kiss.

**Mark:** Suggs used to draw/write out the set lists. This one was taped to the bass. He'd shout, 'Slap that bass, Louie', during 'Madness'. He drew that in.

**Mark:** Curtains drawn to create more atmosphere at The Nightingale in Crouch End. A very early pub gig.

**Lee:** Bathing in the glory of my Morris van with holiday stickers from Cornwall expedition.

**Mike:** Giving it the big one on the road to nowhere!

**Mark:** The Acklam Hall gig was one of our first 'proper' gigs, which became a baptism by fire. I, of course, missed the punch-up, because I was in a pub around the corner.

**Cathal:** When we got to the gig, we all dropped some speed and the night was on.

**Lee:** There was an air of, 'Something's gonna kick off'.

**Chris:** It all got a bit flipping hostile outside, and we decided to make a swift exit.

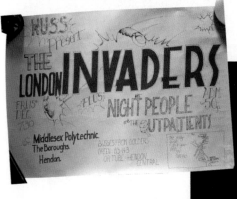

**Suggs:** There'd been all this violence at Acklam Hall, then we got asked to do a gig at Middlesex Polytechnic. I thought this could lead to a whole string of middle-class university gigs.

**Mark:** It didn't.

**Suggs**: Seeing then playing gigs downstairs at the Hope & Anchor in Islington was the real opening for us. That pub was the crux of the biscuit.

**Mark**: You had to bring a PA into the Hope & Anchor, cost: forty-five quid. The first time we played there, we made forty. John, the pub landlord, gave us the extra fiver. Bless him.

Publicity shot for the 2 Tone Tour.

**Woody:** We were now signed to Stiff, but we were still asked to do the 2 Tone tour with The Specials and The Selector.

**Chris:** 2 Tone tour starts. Brighton, October 19th, 1979. Chalkie Davies somehow managed to get all the bands in one place at the same time.

US Tour 1979.

**Woody:** When we got to LA, it was all sunshine and palm trees. I thought 'Fucking hell, this is amazing.'

**Mark:** In LA we stayed at the Tropicana Motel. The black swimming pool personified its seediness. But we had so many great times around that pool.

**Mike:** One minute we're in a basement in Finchley Rd and the next... 'There we were in New York. Who wudda guessed it?'

got involved, and then it was in the hands of the courts . . . just like, you'd see the money two years down the road, or something.

But it was a very satisfying thing that from a totally hopeless situation, we went to a situation where we almost got our money back again.

**CATHAL:** One of the other things about then was that Lee was always disappearing. The saying, 'Where's Lee?' is something that I must have heard . . . God knows . . . I can't even begin to think how many times. 'Where's Lee? Where's Lee?'

**SUGGS:** Yeah, absolutely. I wrote a song called 'Where's Lee?' that I've got somewhere.

But I understand him always wandering off, to a certain extent. I mean, I've got no problem with just floating off into the ether, on my own. People go, 'How can you do that, just ending up in some weird situation?' But you get some sort of buzz out of just being somewhere where you don't know where you are, you don't know who these people are, and it all can go horribly wrong. I think the idea that everything's regulated, or in some way predestined, is boring sometimes.

But Lee, for sure, every time . . . 'Where's Lee?' 'It doesn't matter, man, he's gone, he's gone. No point in looking for him.' I mean, we did try and look out for each other when we were out. But then there was just no point with Lee.

I think he just likes the thrill. One time I didn't have the keys for my house, and he climbed right up the drainpipe to the top floor. Just because he doesn't mind. He likes the danger.

*

LEE: I don't know what it is. Y'know, I never use the front door: I always use the side or the back door. I always go in where I should be coming out, or vice versa.

Gents' toilets, ladies' toilets . . . it's the ladies' all along for me. You're guaranteed a dry, warm seat and a toilet roll. The amount of times the screams have gone off in the downstairs of The Dublin Castle in the ladies' toilets. I'm finished, and then girls come in, and I'm waiting for everyone to leave. In the end, I'm just like, 'Oh, fuck it,' and step out. 'Waaaah!' 'Alright, calm down!'

I just don't do the conventional. I don't know what it is. Just can't put my finger on it.

MIKE: In that period, there was some guy appeared in The Dublin Castle saying he'd come from up north somewhere, and he'd heard that we were releasing a single on 2 Tone. That was strange, because he'd been hearing about it up in Manchester or wherever he came from. So, you got the feeling that it was getting bigger and bigger and it was spreading round the country.

That was obviously due to The Specials. They'd been doing a lot of touring, so we suddenly came in with the suits on and we were part of the bandwagon. That was through Jerry being so open and taking us straight in. Same time, he wanted to start a sort of Tamla Motown, didn't he? So, that obviously fitted with his aims, as well.

SUGGS: I didn't feel any rivalry with The Specials so much. I know Mike did, because he had this more professional attitude. To me, every step was a privilege and a joy, just to be hanging around with these people. A lot of our mates and their mates from the Midlands came down and we started to get to know each other.

There was a whole mutual scene going on. The Specials became this sort of beacon of all that scene, and for me, I was just happy to be there.

CHRIS: The look of the band started coming together. I mean, I think I still had longish hair and I used to wear bowling shirts, because I was slightly soul boy. I had these big baggy Oxford bags, a dogtooth pair, and I got my wife's sewing machine, and took them in myself to make them into pegs. Oxford bags were officially out of fashion in my world. My wife also had this long, kind of Mackintosh coat type thing, and I was wearing that. It was like cross-dressing.

WOODY: The band sort of styled me. It was like, 'Get your 'air cut.' Somewhere in the archives are pictures of the band and I'm wearing a pair of dungarees and Kickers, and I think I've got a woolly hat on. I did look just out of place, really.

Then, amazingly, we got the chance to do a photo session for the *NME* and Bedders and I went out together and we went round all the charity shops. In an Oxfam shop, I found a suit that bloody fitted me: I couldn't believe it. It was a two-tone or, I think, three-tone suit. But it fitted absolutely perfectly. I mean, for me, I'm slight; I'm small, and to find anything that isn't huge is a bloody miracle. So, it was meant to be. But good old Bedders came with me, and said, 'Blimey, that's good.' And of course, as soon as I got into it, it was absolutely bang on. But I used that suit for all of the gigs. It was all I had . . .

CHRIS: The first airplay we had was, of course, John Peel. He played 'The Prince' and the next night he played the B-side,

'Madness'. It was fantastic hearing it on the radio. A few months later, we did a John Peel session and I sung 'Bed & Breakfast Man'. We never met the great man, sadly.

I was working at the GPO, by Mount Pleasant, when 'The Prince' came out. Because it was the GPO, you could make free local phone calls, and there was this thing called the Capital Radio Hit Line, where it was like a record request line, and the more people called in, the more chance you had of getting a record played. So, I got all of them working there ringing it every flipping ten minutes. And 'Madness' got played on Capital, I reckon, because they were all ringing them up going, 'Can you play "Madness"?' – the B-side not the A-side.

**WOODY:** Hearing 'The Prince' on the radio was amazing. Fucking hell. But it sounded like no other record on the radio, and it was like, 'Oh, God, is this good enough, really? It's a bit weird . . .' Because it didn't have that kind of high-fidelity sound: it was all a bit echoey, and a quite unique sound. And yet it was really good. At the same time, you thought, 'Ooh, is it any good? I don't know . . . is it any good?'

**LEE:** I was painting someone's cast-iron bed, down Haverstock way, when I heard it on the radio. I was doing a bit of private for some Asian lady after someone had put my name forward as a fantastic decorator – fools! I heard it being played and I was getting the old goose-pimples. I don't think it mattered to us whether it charted or not. It was on the radio, so that was good enough. But then, of course, it chipped away, chipped away . . .

CHAPTER 12

# IF IT AIN'T STIFF . . .

CATHAL: The success of 'The Prince' was meteoric, I suppose, and it captured the zeitgeist. It was that magical moment where it was a movement, instantly. But to be honest, I was more concerned that Revolver Records in Islington didn't have it in the reggae section. I was pissed off with them. The guy said it was, like, novelty and I was really offended.

SUGGS: Suddenly, because we'd only done a one-single deal with 2 Tone, we were in a situation where all the record companies were coming after us, which was a very unusual position to be in. It was pretty much me and Mike went to do the rounds of meetings. We'd have these incredibly expensive lunches, sitting under palm trees in atriums of enormous tower blocks, with blokes with cigars . . . It was all just a blur, a surreal blur.

MIKE: They were all taking us to lunch and we were trying to max out what we were getting out of it. I'd always choose the most expensive thing on the menu. Some of them you felt were simply doing their job: 'Oh, another latest thing . . . better make an appointment.' There was this buzz going around town and all these record bods would be ringing up. But they didn't even really know why they were asking us out.

For us, it was like, 'Bloody hell, we're in a big posh restaurant having a big posh nosh-up.' But you just definitely felt they didn't know who we were: 'What was your name again? What was the name of the band?' It was like that. And they were probably just going back to the office and thinking, 'Oh, I've done my bit . . . I've invited that latest thing around . . .'

SUGGS: You'd get a geezer saying to his secretary, 'Celia, would you go and buy these guys' record? I need to hear this . . .' So, y'know what I mean: you're talking to people who haven't even heard the fucking record. All they know is that this 2 Tone thing is apparently a phenomenon they need to get a bit of. Me and Mike were just very wary, going to see all these people that were bullshitters.

CHRIS: It was ridiculous. We went to see Chrysalis and the guy asked his secretary to go and get the Madness single. 2 Tone was a subsidiary of Chrysalis, so you couldn't take these people seriously.

MIKE: Obviously, it made a buzz, so it was good for us. But I don't know how we would have chosen one of those faceless record companies from another.

WOODY: I mean, we are very, very cynical people, believe me. And we'd met some wankers of the highest degree in the music industry. They paid for the drinks, and that was as far as it was going to go. We were like, 'Yeah, yeah, yeah, sure, mate, of course,' and behind their backs, we were like, 'No fucking way.' Because they didn't have a clue. We'd go in and we'd introduce Chalky as the lead singer, and they'd got, 'Ooh, nice to meet you, I've seen all your gigs and you're fantastic.'

SUGGS: When we were starting to look at deals, they bandied the word 'perpetuity' around. I went to a phone box and rang my mum and asked her, 'What's "perpetuity", Mum?' She went, 'It's a fuck of a long time.'

MARK: Elton John's label Rocket Records put an offer in, which was quite sweet, really. He still holds it against us that we didn't take it: 'You didn't sign to my bloody record label!' But, in general, with the major record companies, we were a bit like, 'Oh, who are these fucking people?' Obviously that was a hangover of the punk thing, as well, to be a bit distrustful and a bit, like, 'What do they know?'

CHRIS: People at Stiff Records had seen us and, because some of them were a bit more muso, they thought we were just some rough flipping Ian Dury knock-offs. Maybe they were right.

SUGGS: But Dave Robinson, the boss at Stiff, he was interested in the band for one reason or another. He hadn't had a chance to see us, and so he booked us to play at his wedding reception. I don't think his missus was too pleased: 'What, you really don't know any Hot Chocolate numbers?' We're just leaping about, off our heads on sulphate.

*

**LEE:** Dave brought the mountain to Muhammad or whatever. Or, actually, to The Clarendon Ballroom in Hammersmith. Elvis Costello and all the Stiff acts were there, and it was a very joyous occasion.

**SUGGS:** We started a conga around the dance floor, and we got Elvis Costello and Nick Lowe involved.

**WOODY:** It was just us being ourselves and larking around and playing the songs. Cathal and Suggs were very into getting out and interacting with the audience and getting people to dance: 'Don't be shy.'

**CATHAL:** I got out into the audience, doing my 'I'm the nutty geezer in the band' thing, and dragged Costello forwards to have a dance. Ian Dury refused, but I managed to pull Elvis into it.

**CHRIS:** We got everyone up dancing, and then Robbo must have thought, 'Right . . .' He could see it. He could see visually and hear musically what we could do.

**MIKE:** I had a fight with some bloke . . . punched somebody at that gig. There was some fracas in the audience. I guess we all still had a little bit of that attitude: 'They're all cunts and it's us against them,' sort of thing. But it was like the graffiti: you put your name up there. So, we made a big mark with that gig.

**CATHAL:** It just felt that as long as we could show what we had, we'd win it, y'know? And we were so joyous about it, it was infectious.

*

**WOODY:** We'd saved up and bought a van. It was brown: a real kind of shitty, horrible shade of brown. We called it the Saddle Wagon, maybe thinking we were going to pull loads of birds . . . It was more in hope than expectation, because that never happened. We just weren't that kind of band. We were too blokey, I suppose.

**CHRIS:** I knew this right kind of Sid the Sexist type bloke who used to go to women, ''Ere, pick a number between one and three. You've won: get them off, saddle up,' and all that. Women would just tell him to fuck off . . .

So, this all passed into band terminology: pick a number, saddle up. And I called this van the Saddle Wagon. It was a brown Transit – didn't have windows on the side, just windows on the back. Such great days though, because the band would come round my house, and I'd nick all the cushions off the sofas and we'd all be lying on them in the back of this van.

We went up to Liverpool, to play that club, Eric's, and when you're looking out of a back window all the way, you're really dizzy when you get there.

**SUGGS:** We pulled over near Eric's and asked this traffic warden, ''Scuse me, mate, do you know where Eric's is?' He says, 'You from London?' I says, 'Yeah.' He says, 'Eric's? Yeah, just round the corner. But here's a parking ticket because you're on a double yellow line.' Then he walked off.

**MARK:** He gave us a ticket immediately. We were only asking for directions, and it was like, 'Welcome to Liverpool.'

*

CHRIS: On the night, there was a big punch-up in Eric's. It was a real classic, just things flying across the room.

MARK: A big fucking fight, people throwing glasses. As we're playing, there's glasses flying through the air.

CHRIS: Simon Birdsall took a walk through it, pissed, with just stuff whizzing past his head. There was a real proper old-school bouncer, and he was just going *boof* and chinning people and laying them out flat. Chalky called him the Gentleman Charmer.

MARK: We played one gig in Manchester, in a place called The Factory in the middle of this huge housing estate in Hulme. It was literally a one-storey hut – a community centre or something – that someone had decided to put gigs on in.

CHRIS: It was a scary flipping place. On the way there, because we were going to Manchester, Chalky and Toks had these bloody things like iron bars, but covered in rubber. They had affectionately given them names, 'Chalky's Charmer' and 'Toks's Babe'. And just all the way, they kept hitting me and giving me dead arms with these things. So, we get to this place, and it was grim. The people there went, 'Oh, Dexys Midnight Runners were here last week and they got chased down the road.' And we thought Dexys were quite hard, and there was a lot of them, as well.

MARK: The locals hated Cockneys, and they hated us immediately, being from London. Something kicked off and there was a big punch-up. We did literally have to fight our way out of the gig, and it was just nuts.

**CATHAL:** They bottled Si Birdsall and the police turned up and went, 'Fuck off, you southern bastards.'

**CHRIS:** When 'The Prince' came out, we did an interview with *Sounds* where the writer Robbi Millar first mentioned in the press 'the nutty sound of Madness'. That was a phrase that Thommo thought up, and I tried to explain in this interview that we wanted that sort of nutty kind of sound of fairgrounds and *Steptoe and Son* and Kilburn and the High-Roads.

**CATHAL:** Lee had written 'That Nutty Sound' in bleach on the back of a Levi's jacket. It seemed to fit the music, and it looked great. There was a definite almost carnival kind of vibe to the presentation. Lee liked to wear the old light-up bowtie and all that.

**MARK:** 2 Tone was really starting to become a big thing in the music press. It was becoming one of those sort of monolithic movements that you had, all the way through from rock'n'roll to psychedelia to punk. We'd put 'The Prince' out, and it'd got played on the radio, and of course, because 2 Tone was so monolithic, people were buying the record.

It started going up the charts, and we were like, 'Wow.' Then we heard there was a chance of going on *Top of the Pops*. Rick Rogers, The Specials' manager, had an office above Holts, the shoe shop in Camden Town, and it was like, 'Right, you've got to come down here on Wednesday morning because at *Top of the Pops* they're going to look at the charts. They have a meeting and then they pick the bands that're going to go on.'

We had to be there really early: like 8, 9 o'clock in the morning. We all got there, we were all ready, and then we got the phone call: 'Sorry.' Secret Affair had got a couple of places higher in the charts or something, and they had picked them to go on instead.

CHRIS: So, we all went home, dejected.

MARK: When you think about bands, it's all about serendipity. Can you imagine what a story that would have been? That you had been there, you were told to go home, and then that was it, and then the band fell apart . . . So, that early journey is perilous, in that respect. There are so many stories of bands where an event like that just kills them stone dead.

But then, a couple of weeks later, we went through the whole process again. This time, though, they said, 'Right, you're on.'

WOODY: My mum wasn't allowed to be floor manager at *Top of the Pops* that week, because of us. They could not be seen to have any sense of nepotism going on. They had to be seen to be doing the right thing, because you've got to remember that this was the era of brown envelopes filled with money and the bribing and fixing of the charts. If anyone had heard that my mum worked there and we were on *Top of the Pops* for any other reason than we were chosen independently, then the BBC would have been in deep shit.

But I suppose because I'd been down there and seen it all before, the idea of actually going on *Top of the Pops* didn't affect me. The illusion that was *Top of the Pops* wasn't new to me. The studio was a lot smaller than you imagined.

MARK: I think we were relatively cool about going on television, in a way. Mind you, I suppose I was still 17 and Chris was 23. Which is quite a difference at that time. And our youthful arrogance was masking quite a lot of our insecurities.

The studio was tiny, and they had the crowd, which they herded around from stage to stage, because there wasn't a lot of them. They were literally pushing and pushing these people around.

It was hysterical to us that the drum kit was one of those where all the cymbals are dead and all the toms have mats on them. We were just laughing at how cheap it was, because when you're in the studio doing it, all you can hear is sort of '*Clunk, clunk, clunk.*'

LEE: I'd got this suit on that I got out the old Swiss Cottage Oxfam shop: wide parallels, sharp collars, very forties American-looking. The first time we were on, I never took my saxophone. I thought, 'Well, I know we're miming . . .' So, I took a toy saxophone along, and half the keys had snapped off it.

I think I must have taken it because I probably had to get a Tube down there or something. We were still on 2 Tone, so they weren't going to bring any motors round for us. The home-made sax case I had at the time was made of thick timber, and I'd plastered front covers of Superman comics on it. It weighed a ton, and the handle would cut into your hand.

WOODY: I loved the way Lee brought the little plastic sax out, taking the piss. Just superb.

*

**SUGGS:** I mean, we still had this mentality where we were really famous in our own minds: it was Suggs, Mr B, Kix, and everybody knew us round where we all hung out. It wasn't like we were stuck for people who'd recognise us. So, we weren't like, 'Oh, my God, we're on *Top of the Pops*.' It was just like, 'You're lucky to fucking have us here.' Youthful arrogance . . .

**LEE:** You almost needed an A-Z to find your way about the Television Centre. All the floors sort of looked the same. I wandered off to use one of the toilets . . . I was really bursting to go. I went in a cubicle in the gents and there was a hole in the wall, about the circumference of a golf ball, with a drawing of a person's hair and face. It was done very artistically. And I thought, 'Is this what I think it's meant to be for? Serious?' I've peeped down and there's someone in the toilet next to me, waiting to give me a blow job. I was like, 'Fuck this!'

**CHRIS:** They had this BBC bar, and there was this old boy on the door, looked like Jimmy Edwards, and he was like, 'You can't come in here.' Then, we worked out – it was like bunking in the cinema – that if you went outside and climbed up the fire escape, round and through this window, you were in the bar. Plus, it was really cheap. So, we were all in this bar, and when we came out, we were flicking the guy on the door the old V-signs and all that.

**CATHAL:** Illusions were shattered by the realisation that it was a tiny studio where people were being herded around like cattle; that all the microphones were fake, that the cymbals were plastic. It was like, 'Oh.' A real let-down. But, all of a sudden, you're in the world of TV. I was on speed. I was so, so nervous.

SUGGS: We just took a load of sulphate and got pissed and the rest is history.

MIKE: It was mind-blowing, I guess. Suddenly we were becoming recognised. I felt that change, with my family and stuff. They were proud about it, I suppose. But we were on a journey, and the fact that there were seven of us, we were travelling within our little group. It was brilliant and inspiring and gratifying to suddenly be on *Top of the Pops* and all that.

CHRIS: It was great, because the viewing figures were, like, twenty million or something. If you went on there, you were going to go up the charts.

MARK: After you'd done it, you had the realisation that you'd actually been on telly. My mum and dad couldn't believe it.

Things widen out from having your mates at gigs to having people you don't know at gigs . . . then all of a sudden, people are coming up to your mum and dad, going, 'Oh, we saw your son on the television.' You feel a strange responsibility when you actually realise that this is what you're going to do, and you have to be really good at doing it. For all our arsing around, I think we all realised that. Because it is that inverse thing of not wanting people to go, 'I saw you on telly and you're rubbish and the song's really shit.'

The idea of 2 Tone was fantastic and we wanted to be part of it and the idea of it. But I don't know if we ever thought that we had to write songs in that style, as it were. We'd done one single on 2 Tone and I suppose we felt it was time to move on.

**SUGGS:** Dave Robinson from Stiff took us down the pub and said, 'I believe in what you can do. Look, I'll give you a really nice percentage. I won't give you a load of money up front, but I will back you and I will really do what I think the band needs to be done.' It was the best thing that ever happened to us.

**CHRIS:** I liked him because he could see something beyond ska and flipping 2 Tone. He could see longevity.

**MIKE:** We were big fans of quite a few bands on Stiff, and the way they were presenting them. We liked their off-the-wall advertising, the funny little jokes, all that sort of stuff. They weren't part of the system, but outside it and being a bit different. Breaking the rules and being unconventional, and at the same time, being very successful.

Dave Robinson saw something in us, and he projected that. He was magnifying what we had already. Which made us be able to then think, 'Yeah, it's not bad what we're doing.' And we were able to develop it. He saw something. The rest of them record companies didn't see anything.

The other thing about Stiff Records, and Dave really, was that it was all about being spontaneous: it was all, 'Do it quick. You don't have to fuck around in the studio. Get it done and put it out.' He was like, 'Once you've got that success, you just keep releasing songs.'

*

**WOODY:** I thought Dave was absolutely brilliant, because you could tell that there was a side of him that you would not trust him as far as you could chuck him. He just seemed so dodgy. But then, he had the charm of the Irish about him. And the thing was, it was upheld by his ability to not bullshit. The bullshit had gone. He knew our names; he knew what instruments we played; he had seen us; he knew our songs. He had a clear vision of the kind of album he wanted us to make.

**LEE:** It wasn't the size of the record company; it was the style of the record company. Stiff was very funky, and it just ticked all the boxes of what we wanted. But really, I think what attracted us, other than the acts that they had on there, was that it was intimate: you got to see the guvnor. You got to see Dave Robinson, the main man, which you wouldn't have got with a major. That was right up our street. And it was also him saying, 'Yeah, you can have artistic control.'

**MARK:** We really liked Dave's openness and his casual confidence. It was very much like, 'It's not a problem making a record. You'll make a good record: it'll be fine.' So, it was instilling a bit of confidence in you, as well.

**CHRIS:** When we signed with Stiff, Robbo said, 'Alright, I'm going to give you ten grand, so you can all give your jobs up.' He gave us this cheque, which I took to look after.

People that lived in the flats beside me used to come round to see it: 'Look at this, ten grand, ten grand!' It was like the Million Pound Note . . . We had to open an account, at Williams & Glyn's Bank in Camden. Other bank managers took one look at us and went, 'You oiks.' But the manager down there was really nice: 'Come in.' So, we banked with them and we all gave our jobs up.

**SUGGS:** You'd get other bands or lawyers talking about, 'You want a big advance.' But we were already doing alright, fucking about, and we were going to survive. As I said, all my friends always had a tenner in their pockets, regardless. A big injection of money wasn't going to blur our kind of perception of what life was.

We were like, 'What if we do sell a lot of records? We've already done quite well with this "The Prince" thing. What about if it does take off? Fuck the big advance, let's try and get a bigger percentage of the cut at the end of the day.' Just pure market trading instinct. It's like, 'Hang on a minute: he's selling them socks for 50p, but he's got them for two quid over there . . . so there must be somewhere in the middle here.' And that was what we were going by.

It didn't matter to me, putting a load of money in my bank account. What was more important to me was hanging about with my mates and doing the best we could. I thought, 'If we've got this far, let's just see what happens next.'

**WOODY:** When we'd hit *Top of the Pops*, and we'd signed to Stiff Records, I did think, 'Shit, I can't get off now. I'm here, and this is really happening, and this is my life . . . Blimey, I've arrived.' I had mixed feelings about it, because again, you kind of go, 'Is it really for me? Well, there's no turning back now.'

**CATHAL:** I wasn't made a band member. When they signed to Stiff, I had to wait outside. Then Robbo came out and went to me, 'You're on a £20 a week retainer.' I was happy, 'cause I just wanted to be involved. It was never about the money. But I think it was the record company and the management and people around the band that saw me as being a part of it, more than the band did.

**WOODY:** Our gig at Aylesbury Friars in September '79 was a real pivotal point in the band for Cathal.

**MARK:** We started to get the odd gig out of town and we went up there and played with Secret Affair. We were on first and Cathal was coming from Kent somewhere where he'd been working, but he got delayed.

**CATHAL:** I was working then in Ashford, Kent, for Chartered Consolidated, a diamond mining concern, and caught the train up. I was late, but I'd travelled up in the suit to be ready to go straight on stage.

**SUGGS:** That was a pretty big moment. We'd gone onstage and we hadn't done 'One Step Beyond', which had become a clarion call for the band. So, we'd started the gig and it was a little flat. Then Cathal turned up in a Johnson's suit with a blue pork pie hat, and the crowd parted . . .

**WOODY:** It was one of those kind of fabled entrances.

**LEE:** It was like the parting of the sea and, y'know, Chas Smash has arrived! There was a light in the distance, glowing!

*

CATHAL: It really was that biblical thing – the sea parted, I walked through the middle of the crowd and onto the stage and we went straight into 'One Step Beyond'. The great thing about that introduction to 'One Step Beyond' was you immediately went *wallop*. It was a great, explosive start.

SUGGS: We started again, doing 'One Step Beyond', and the crowd went completely fucking mad.

MARK: It was definitely the moment where we realised he added to the whole experience of it all. We felt that the people there were going, 'Where is he and why aren't you doing that song we've heard about?' When Cathal was onstage with us, it was quite a phenomenon, really. It could tire you out, just watching him.

CHRIS: We were thinking, 'Y'know, he's a bit of a valuable asset.'

CATHAL: After that, Dave Robinson was able to say to the band, 'Look, he's part of it . . . really part of it.' Thank fuck.

WOODY: I did really feel that we were missing something without him. There was just something about his presence. Especially live, he just made us complete.

SUGGS: We went down to TW Studios in Fulham to record *One Step Beyond* . . . , the album, and Clive Langer brought in Alan Winstanley as the co-producer. They were a great combination of Alan being someone who was really technical and focused and Clive being someone who was just very much into the feel and the arrangements. Together, they worked very, very well. I was one of the few people who used to hang around when they were doing their thing. I used to love being in the studio, just seeing how this whole thing worked. Sitting there with my banana milk and my steak and kidney pie.

MARK: The album was done at TW Studios, and at Eden Studios in Acton, which Stiff had used quite a bit. Alan was brought in initially to engineer it, because he'd worked on The Stranglers' first album, but he'd also done things like 'Knock on Wood', Amii Stewart. So, he'd done a lot of different work. He then got coerced into helping produce it with Clive, working as a team together.

For a band so young and so early on in their career, we had all the songs sorted out. There was no arsing around in the studio: it was pretty much laying the songs down, as they were, with a few being afforded some overdubs and stuff.

If you're prepared, it takes a lot of the demons away when you're recording. I mean, some bands do like to go in the studio and spend time just trying to work things up and get a feel. But I think we always felt better when we were prepared and we went in and actually just did it. We liked to get the momentum going.

CHRIS: Yeah, it was the classic: 'Let's go and record your live set.' Clive lived above Swanky Modes, in Camden, and he had this tiny little skinny van. We used to squash in the back of this van and he'd drive us over there to the studio.

MIKE: There wasn't a lot of money then. We still hadn't had much success, and it was all very questionable what was going to happen. So, the record company wasn't digging that deep in their pocket, I don't think. I guess we had a certain budget and Clive Langer was working within that. But then again, we'd been playing these songs and we knew them, so we just had to go in and record them. It wasn't too complicated.

CHRIS: We bashed through it. Alan was a really good engineer. Clive wouldn't mind something a bit wild, but then Alan would be like, 'Oh, y'know . . . maybe not.' I used to drive Alan mad with my crap guitar playing or having to do things again and again. One thing that happened was that Clive got Suggs to sing 'Bed & Breakfast Man' and 'My Girl', so that was my last stint on lead vocals. Lee passed the audition and sung 'Razor Blade Alley' and 'Land of Hope and Glory'.

WOODY: Alan Winstanley was very particular about the sound, and he would spend a long time getting it right. Clive was more on the creative side, but Alan would temper Clive's creativity. Because Clive would be going, 'Yeah! Then I can hear this going off!' and Alan would be saying, 'I like it as it is. We don't have to go that bonkers.' Clive did go off on a tangent. I don't want to make him out to be a kind of mad professor, but I think if it wasn't for Alan, it would've been a bit less commercial, maybe a little bit more off-kilter at times. Whereas Clive didn't mind occasional clashing notes, because it was exciting, Alan would be like, 'Ooh, not sure about that.'

SUGGS: The Specials had been in TW Studios before us. Literally, you could smell them in the room. They'd left some bits of tape which me and Alan found. They were only about three-foot-long, and by the time you put them on the tape machine and played them, you just heard one snare drum: '*Bownk*!' We were trying to work out what sort of sound they were making. All we got was, '*Bownk*!' 'We've got the secret to The Specials' mix!' 'No, we've got one snare drum . . .' But that's how close we were on their tails.

The album was done quickly, but Alan would often go, 'Look, Clive, just fuck off for five minutes, while I try and actually balance this crazy shit we've just put down.' Things like 'Night Boat to Cairo', Clive said, 'I think it would be really nice to get some Egyptian strings on it.' Then he calls the string arranger and he thinks he hears Clive say, 'Gypsy strings.' He turns up playing this stuff and Alan's going, 'What the hell is this?'

**LEE:** I got on very well with Alan. He had a very dry sense of humour, and he could see he had a job on his hands, untangling all the parts . . .

Brass was normally the last thing to go on the tape, and there just wasn't something right with the sound of the sax. I mean, I'd sort of noticed it, but being as I'd played it out of tune since I started playing, I didn't really know it was a big deal. But to seasoned, fine-tuned ears, like Alan's and Clive's, it was very much out of tune. And, of course, nobody knew how to tune the saxophone. I didn't know until we made the second album that you had to move the mouthpiece . . . as simple as that. You just twist the mouthpiece on the crook of the sax to tune it. Instead of it being on an inch and a quarter, mine was on about a quarter of an inch, to the point of where it wobbled. All I had to do was move it, but I didn't know.

So, the whole album was basically recorded with three tracks of saxophone on every song, to try and make it sound half in tune. But it gave it that nutty sound, which was good. The sound of a stolen out-of-tune sax . . .

**WOODY:** I mean, the results were brilliant. The one song that changed everything for me was 'In the Middle of the Night'. Because I don't know how I used to play it, but I certainly didn't play it the way that Clive asked me to play it, which was really simple: no rolls, just bare minimum stuff. And it felt so uncomfortable, I can't tell you: 'This is not right.' Of course, the end recording is amazing, because it's got so much space. As soon as I heard it, I kind of went, 'Oh, shit, this is brilliant. I want to play less, because it's so effective.' So, there was a lot to learn.

**LEE:** 'In the Middle of the Night', that's one of my favourites. I got into the lyric; it was different, quirky, off the beaten track, a song about a knicker thief. Langer put me in the street outside the studio to record the newspaper seller bit at the start. They put the microphone out in the road and I did the old, 'Paper, sir? *Evening Standard?*'

**MARK:** As Chris says, the 'Bed & Breakfast Man' was John Hasler. It's interesting, that song, because it shows another trait of Madness. It's quite jaunty, sort of happy and up, but it's actually got quite a melancholy story to it. Because John did have a lot of trouble with his dad, and he did have to go and stay at people's houses, and that was quite sad, really. And again, you can see John's influence on the band, as well. He's there, not only in managing the band or writing some of the songs, but he appears as a character in that song as well.

\*

CATHAL: 'Chipmunks Are Go!' at the end of the album was nothing more than a Marine chant that my dad used to sing: 'One, two, three, four, we're the chipmunks, hear us roar.' I mean, Dad was very Americanised. I said to my mum once, 'Is Dad American?' She said, 'He's never fucking been there . . .' But Dad kind of looked a bit like John Wayne. Anyway, 'Chipmunks Are Go!' was that. It was nothing, really.

WOODY: When it came to the songwriting splits and the publishing, the lawyer who was involved in the first negotiations with Stiff was absolutely adamant that we sort out an arrangement within the band. He said, that in his experience, the one thing that always split up bands was the publishing: who wrote what. So, he said, 'Give something to everyone and don't budge from that. Make sure that you're happy with it, though.' It was seven people in the band at that time and the system was that if you wrote a song, you'd get 50 per cent of the publishing. The other 50 per cent was split between everyone. So, if I wrote a song, I'd get 50 per cent of the publishing and I'd get one-seventh of the other 50 per cent.

SUGGS: I think the cut of how we split the music was great – 50 per cent to anyone who was in the band and 50 per cent to the writers. It was another miracle that we came up with, just off the top of our heads.

LEE: It was one of the better moves that we made, coming to that agreement. I thought that was very fair, because obviously it stopped people in the band from moonlighting. It drew everyone back in.

*

**CHRIS:** It's a good way to do things. Because, I mean, I can't count the amount of songs I've written that weren't much good, and then Thommo does a really good sax bit, or Mike does a good keyboard part . . . something that makes it better. And in the same way, someone else can come along with a song, and unless it's really terrible, I will do my utmost to make it better. Everyone in the band is like that.

**WOODY:** I've had kind of moral dilemmas of 'Do I take a percentage of a song that I had no part of writing?' But that song would never be what it is today without the work that we put into it. Because we've usually changed it completely, out of all recognition.

**SUGGS:** 'Bed & Breakfast Man' was going to be the second single. We thought that was more in keeping with the general vibe of the band than 'One Step Beyond', which Dave Robinson wanted to put out as the next single.

Specifically, for me, my problem with it was that we'd already done a tribute to Prince Buster, 'The Prince'. So why would we want our second single to be a cover of a Prince Buster song? That's all I thought: 'We're just going to end up as a fucking Prince Buster tribute band.'

The thing was that we'd had this idea – I don't know if we'd seen it from the Kilburns or James Brown – where you had a little funny bit of music when you came on stage. 'One Step Beyond' was just this funny little bit of music with Cathal going, 'Hey you . . . don't watch that . . .' So, we never thought of it as a song. We just thought of it as basically an announcement.

\*

**WOODY:** Also, Suggs was going, 'Hang on, this is an instrumental. Where am I in it, what do I do?' And Cathal's now a part of the whole set-up, so you kind of thought, 'Well, you've got Cathal and Suggs – what, are they going to just dance?' It didn't feel right. We'd got loads of other songs, so why couldn't we just put one of them out? But Dave was really adamant.

The thing was that the version of 'One Step Beyond' that we'd recorded was too short to be a single. So, Dave got hold of it, and he thought, 'Well, we can just edit the tape and double the length of the song.'

**MARK:** Robbo, without us knowing, rings up the studio one night, when they're mixing, and says, 'It's too short. Just do a copy of their version and literally pin the two of them together.' He sped it up a little bit, as well. We weren't too happy about that.

**MIKE:** Robbo got Alan to put it through this machine, a Harmoniser. Alan said, 'What I could do is run out a rough copy for you, so you can get an idea of what it sounds like. I'll do it through the Harmoniser, and if it sounds good, we'll do a proper quality version of it.' He sent it over to Robbo to listen to, and the next thing he heard, Robbo was printing up the singles: they were getting pressed. Fuck the proper version!

**LEE:** I thought it was a brilliant, priceless move. He just went ahead, in the dark of night, *snip*, got Alan to weave his magic on it and made it into the single it was. The next thing, it's in the racks, being sold. You bastard! But that's what we would have done, I suppose, if we were a record company.

*

**WOODY:** We had a very, very heated, long discussion with Dave about it. We weren't happy at all, but he was going, 'Look, if this doesn't work out, then dump me. I believe in it so strongly: you will not regret it.' But we were really, really, *really* not happy. Good bloody thing it was a hit. Because it might not have been.

**SUGGS:** Dave had very clear opinions about what would make it into the charts, which was the last, the most distasteful thing to ever talk about: having a hit. For me, anyway.

**MIKE:** When it came out, the BBC said they didn't want to play it. There was some old bod there who said that the saxophone was out of tune, and they weren't going to discredit the BBC by playing some sort of awful thing. I mean, it wasn't good news, hearing somebody at the BBC saying, 'We can't play this, it's out of tune.' So, I don't know if that might have affected it . . . I mean, it got to number 7.

**CHRIS:** Obviously the majors had bigger distribution, so Stiff, they really had to graft. After that, we just thought, 'Right, Robbo can pick the singles.' Because he would have such a driving kind of energy: that's the single, everyone at Stiff knew it was a single, the plugger knew it was a single, Radio 1 knew it was a single, so, y'know, *bosh*. It wasn't like, 'Oh, we might do this remix' kind of thing. But that, 'One Step Beyond', kind of cemented that set-up.

**CATHAL:** The first time I got a proper look-in as far as the band was concerned was when I did 'One Step Beyond' for the album and the single. So, I'm eternally grateful to Robbo.

*

**SUGGS:** I think it was a mutual thing, between us and Stiff, that we were kind of marketed as 'the Nutty Boys from Camden Town'. Camden Market itself was exploding. It had gone from being a few hippies selling patchouli oil to suddenly this fashionable corner of London. Then you've got the punk thing coming out of there, all them amazing record shops, The Clash rehearsing there. And we were spending a lot of time in Camden Town. It would have been harder to go, 'We come from Islington' or 'We come from Hampstead'. It was just a phrase that suited our particular moment in time.

**MARK:** I think Camden Town is the geographical epicentre of the band. Maybe that's a bit of a poncey way of putting it. But, funnily enough, Camden Town is in the middle of where we all lived in the areas around it. Then you had the fact that we played at The Dublin Castle, obviously.

**WOODY:** Most of the band were on the periphery of Camden, so I suppose it was a fair thing to say. I always thought of it as we were all pretty much from the borough of Camden.

**SUGGS:** The fact was that by this point I was actually living at Swanky Modes in Camden. That's when I was starting to really get into songwriting, and I wrote 'One Better Day' – which wouldn't come out till years later – about Arlington House, the local hostel for the homeless.

Of course, a lot of my songs were about Camden Town, but I started making notes about Arlington House. I had this idea of 'One Better Day', like when you say, 'He's seen better days.' And then the idea was, well, 'When was that day?' And then that also became the idea that these two homeless people meet each other and fall in love and . . . why shouldn't they have another better day?

Hanging around in the pubs in Camden Town, you would see all these characters, like the Shroud, this guy dressed in full undertaker's gear. Or the Captain, who used to be in the Royal Bank of Scotland with his flies undone, barking orders at all the staff in there. The twelve hundred men who lived at Arlington House had all dropped out of society, often wearing the same gear they'd dropped out in. You'd get the four geezers in the launderette in Parkway in their jackets and underpants with their only pair of trousers going round and round in the washing machine. It was not destitute, Camden, but it was rough. And then you had all these navvies waiting outside the bank for the Murphy's builders' lorries, like *On the Waterfront*. 'You . . . you . . . not you . . .'

**CHRIS:** After we signed to Stiff, we'd go over to their office in Alexander Street in Westbourne Green. It was an old house, and Robbo's office was in the basement. They had these pigeon-holes, with albums in. We were like, 'Oh! Aladdin's cave . . . ', and we'd be nicking all these albums. A flipping big pile of Ian Dury albums.

**SUGGS:** We were still outsiders. Going in the offices of Stiff . . . they didn't really like us. We were just uncontrollable herberts. They had all this post-pub rock thing going on there, and here we are, just complete berks, thinking we're the bollocks and stealing everything we can get our hands on.

*

**LEE:** Stiff Records, we used to spend a lot of time there, so they were very weary of us. And I mean, I suppose our image could be quite intimidating: particularly Cathal and Suggs, and probably meself. So, we were looked at side-on. We used to give some of the staff a bit of a nightmare, just turning up in our DMs, bomber jackets and shaved heads and basically having a bit of a free-for-all with their back catalogue.

**SUGGS:** One time, Lee and Cathal, they backed the van into Stiff Records and stole all the merchandise and practically every thing that Stiff Records owned, and set up a stall in Camden Market.

**LEE:** He's a fucking liar! Fuck off! No, again, that's a myth. But, yeah, I'd go there demanding two boxes of our records for my 'extended family'. I probably gave a dozen of those away, and the rest I kept until I had my house broken into, and they got taken . . . probably to Camden Market! But no, I never set up a stall . . .

## CHAPTER 13

# NUTTY TRAIN DEPARTING

**SUGGS:** Ah, the fucking Nutty Train. It started with that photograph of Kilburn and the High-Roads where they're all standing at the bus stop, turned sideways. There were some very early photographs done of us walking down Exmouth Market in Clerkenwell where we're almost in a line. Of course, it takes so long to get seven people into a photograph, and sometimes when you're just walking in a line, it's easier, and then obviously you start to think, 'Well, if you compress that, it gets even easier still' And then it became a big thing, the Nutty Train. Where that name came from, fuck only knows.

**CHRIS:** I always say that the Nutty Train was my idea. There was a Dave Allen sketch where this guy's walking along the road and then someone comes out of a house and goes straight behind him. Then, these guys all slowly come out of their houses and they're all walking, squashed together like a Nutty Train. And they walk into this place and the joke at the end is that it's a sardine factory. I always used to think it'd be funny if we walked along like that.

MIKE: For me, it wasn't really the sardine sketch or the Kilburns at the bus stop. It was that 'Paul Hangs Loose' photograph on the back of the Kilburns' *Handsome* album; the picture of this bloke in a mad pose, a bit *Monty Python* sort of thing. I guess I was thinking of that. Maybe everybody else behind me was thinking, 'This is like the sardine sketch', or 'This is the Kilburns at the bus stop', and I'm at the front, thinking, 'This is "Paul Hangs Loose".'

MARK: When we did it for the album cover of *One Step Beyond . . .*, Cameron McVey took the picture. We knew it was going to be black and white and just us against a plain white backdrop. He did a few snaps of the band just standing, like bands do, looking tough, in various poses. Then we tried us all standing in a line, Nutty Train-style. We really worked it out, about the heights of the band members, going from tallest to shortest, Mike to Lee.

SUGGS: We were trying to do it in motion, going past the camera. But we couldn't actually do it moving and take a photograph of it at the same time. It was like, 'Oh, fucking hell, it's cut his head off . . . cut his foot off . . .' So, we stopped and said, 'Why don't we just stand still?'

MARK: Then we did it properly. We perfected the shape of it and everything.

MIKE: We were hanging onto this rail behind us while we were doing it, to make it look proper and not half-hearted. To get it right, which was the same story, really, with the music. Having fun is great, but if you ain't got the shot, you're going to have a shit album cover.

LEE: It was like a ballet barre we were holding onto. Somehow, they painted that out. But I had to lean back quite a long way. The photo session lasted for about an hour and a half, and it took its toll on your back. I was hanging on for dear life. That was certainly a painful experience when we done it for the photo session.

CATHAL: I was on the back cover of the album, not the front. I don't think I was fully accepted for a while. I was half-in, half-out. Which didn't help. I didn't know what was going on, but I loved it.

MARK: At that point, Cathal's not part of it; but he is part of it, in a way, as well, I suppose you could say.

WOODY: They did a separate session with Cathal, and stuck him on the back, pulling all the shapes and stuff. I mean, they were really iconic shapes that he brought to it.

CHRIS: We had a small UK tour coming up and Stiff decided we needed a chaperone. They sent a guy to meet us called Kellogs – longish hair and a Hawaiian shirt. He didn't fit in with us, for sure. But he came to rehearsals and was obviously quite professional. He became our tour manager, and he had to keep Chalky and Toks under control too.

*

**SUGGS:** We made the video for 'One Step Beyond' with an American geezer called Chuck Statler. He'd done all the videos for Devo and we'd seen that one for '(I Can't Get No) Satisfaction'. We liked that: it was that element of being wacky, but not zany. It had a sort of a darkness to it, like when the baby sticks the fork in the toaster, *szzzzz*. So, we thought, 'We like this bloke.'

The main performances for 'One Step Beyond' were done in the Hope & Anchor. Then Chuck came on the road with us, this crazed American, and we had a great old time. We'd just drive around, filming bits.

**LEE:** Chuck Statler used to moon along the motorway. He'd be in one van, we'd be in the other, and he'd just have his arse sticking out the window. In the video for 'One Step Beyond', we finally got the Nutty Train down pat. We filmed it in Leeds when we were up there on tour, and we finally got to fine-tune it, in that bit when we're coming out the barber's shop.

**MIKE:** Chuck was up for filming funny things. So, all of our sort of funny ideas, he was up for doing them. We did all this counting and stuff with the Nutty Train; we had all these ways of getting the troop in line. Certain people in the band were into it. Cathal was into it, and everybody else just went along with it.

**CATHAL:** There was a sense of pride and us really being a unit. When we were doing the Nutty Train up in Leeds in public, we didn't give a fuck how silly we looked. We felt strong. It felt really strong what we were doing.

Lee was always trying to do something wackier. Mike, once you got him going, he was throwing all these shapes and pulling faces that came out of nowhere, and you thought, 'Fuck, that's so cool.' We were happy to go over and over everything, again and again and again, because we were enjoying it.

WOODY: I was not at all comfortable with doing the Nutty Train. I felt really stupid. And it was also very, very, very difficult to do, apart from anything else. Barso was really particular about which arm to use and he would go, 'No, you've got to put your hand like this,' and it was just like, 'Oh, come on!' Poor Lee and myself, because we were at the back, by the time the shock wave had got to us, it was completely out of time.

I mean, to be honest, anything to do with choreography and dancing, I really hate with a vengeance. I'd be more than happy just to sit behind my drum kit and get on with the job.

CHRIS: Chuck was great, and we kind of learnt, you need a cameraman, you need a sound man and you need a lighting man . . . That's all you need.

Chalky was a really good dancer, and he's in the 'One Step Beyond' video, in that bit where he's in the street dancing, wearing a white vest. Toks is leaning on the wall, because he said, 'I ain't going to dance unless you pay me . . .'

MARK: The 'One Step Beyond' video really did capture what was going on at the time; with the dancing and the look and everything. It felt odd sometimes, doing the Nutty Train, but then it kind of felt quite good in a way. I mean, it felt part of the whole thing. It was really different.

\*

WOODY: Even though we were now signed to Stiff, we were still asked to do the 2 Tone UK tour, with The Specials and The Selecter. Brighton was the first gig, on 19 October, which was also my 19th birthday. We met outside the Roundhouse in Camden, and got on the coach.

MARK: Suggs turned up with his touring luggage: one white carrier bag.

I said, 'Where's your gear?'

'In there, mate,' he said, jiggling the bag up and down and pulling out a wad of £20 notes. 'That's all you need to go on tour!'

I admired his bravado, but how did he know? He'd never been on tour himself . . .

WOODY: I had a little bottle of whisky. But I just wasn't a very good drinker, so I got halfway through it and was completely drunk out of me head. I needed a piss, and there were no toilets on that coach at all, and it was absolutely rammed, so I had to go in the back and piss into a flipping Coke can. And, of course, try and get your wee in one of those – wee everywhere . . . it was just horrible. Then, of course, you put it down and it spilt over, and it was like, 'Oh, fucking hell . . .'

MARK: The coach was literally one of those take-the-OAPs-to-the-seaside coaches, with a driver, in a shirt, tie and jacket. Then he saw all us getting on . . .

WOODY: There was loads of people smoking dope on the coach, and it was kind of like a day out to the seaside. On Brighton beach, the three bands did this photo session for *The Face*, with

Chalkie Davies, which ended up being a kind of iconic photograph of us all.

MARK: It's just such a lovely photograph, and there we all are. You look at that and it's really kind of precious in a way, because you just think, 'God, this is the kind of start of it all,' and suddenly there we were, in the middle of it all. You knew it was going to explode.

The 2 Tone tour was a rolling explosion, with every gig more manic and wild than the last one. And as it went on, it picked up and dragged along more and more people with it. For a few months, it became the focus and cultural centre of everything.

LEE: We were only a few gigs into the tour, and Neville from the Specials and myself got into trouble at the Watford Gap Services, was it?

WOODY: I know exactly where it was. It was Leicester Forest East on the M1.

CHRIS: We go in the service station, and Thommo's clowning around, and he starts jumping on the tables.

MARK: Lee got on a table and then started throwing food around or something. It was just stupid stuff.

CHRIS: It was little old ladies working there, probably looking at the guys from The Specials and The Selecter, and thinking, 'It's black people, I'm going to ring the police . . .'

*

**SUGGS:** All I know is, the Old Bill turned up. Lee had stolen some stuff out of the motorway service station.

**LEE:** I mean, I might have taken a pork pie . . .

But on leaving, in the car park, we was approached by a couple of security guys, and I was mocking the feller that wanted to have a word with me, by running backwards pretty quick. He couldn't keep up, so he was pretty angry.

**CHRIS:** We're all outside and suddenly all these police vans screech up.

**WOODY:** All I saw was these chase scenes, everywhere around us, like Benny Hill. But it was terrible, because no white member of any band was being chased. It was all the black members. And it was just so unnecessary.

**CHRIS:** Neville and Lynval from The Specials were slammed up against the windscreen.

**LEE:** The next thing, I was being thrown into a police car and hearing some punches being thrown outside. I went to get out to help Neville and got a whack in the face from one of the police.

**CHRIS:** So, it was chaos, but nobody got arrested.

**LEE:** The coppers were maybe hoping to get a football crowd in or something, and they thought, 'Right, these'll do . . .' Y'know, we fitted that criteria – a gang of lads being a bit boisterous, looking a bit different. They were letting off a bit of steam with us, using us as punch bags . . .

**MIKE:** It was very primitive, bare essentials, on that tour. Dodgy hotels and little bed and breakfasts and stuff. But then, we were young blokes: we'd hardly been out of north London, so it was very exciting to be off around the country. And then playing the gigs every day: I guess it was quite hard, but then, there's that joy and exuberance. I mean, we didn't really think about it, but I guess we were learning loads through that whole process.

**MARK:** As the tour went on, more and more people ended up on the bus – friends, crew, journalists. I mean, it was amazing, really. Sometimes we had people sitting in the gangways.

One night, we were up north somewhere, and we were all on the coach with various people, and bottles rolling around and people had had a drink. So, someone decides that they're hungry, and Jerry taps the coach driver and says, 'Stop here,' at this fish and chip shop. Everyone on the coach gets out, and this guy behind the counter at the chip shop can't quite kind of believe it. At about eleven-thirty at night, a coach party of people descend on him. And the order was something like thirty-six cod and chips, four rock and chips, an Irn Bru, two Twixes . . . He just couldn't believe it, because he made, like, a fortune for him on a wet Tuesday night.

**CATHAL:** I liked my spliff, and I ended up sitting with Rico Rodriguez and Neville from The Specials a lot. Rico would go down to London, pick up some grass, then we'd sit with him and roll it up in newspaper, so he could sell it in £1 deals. It was just for the bands. It was just about having enough, because you were in areas you didn't know, and you weren't sure where to get any. Maybe promoters could have scored, but it never occurred to us. We were just all looking after ourselves. I mean, we were thrown out of a few hotels because a lot of the guys in the bands would be walking in, openly smoking spliffs.

It was one massive crew on the bus: it felt great. Lee would be playing his compilation tapes, there'd be lots of spliff. It was really fantastic. And you felt, at the gigs, that between The Specials, The Selecter and Madness, like we were something socialist and rebellious. It had all those kind of revolutionary vibes to it.

**WOODY:** At the same time, there was a lot of in-fighting in the bands. There was quite a lot of that going on in The Selecter as well as The Specials . . . a lot of falling out. And the band that seemed to stay together more than anyone else was us. I don't know why. But the tour was bloody tough going, and it was really messy.

**SUGGS:** That was the greatest time of my life, the 2 Tone tour. The most tremendous incredible time. As we were going round the country, every day the tour manager would be getting off at a service station, calling the venue and the promoter would be going, 'Look, there's a riot going on outside and it's four hours before the gig. I'm going to have to find a bigger venue . . .'

Literally anything and everything could happen. Stage invasions, stages collapsing. The Bridlington mods versus the Bridlington skins, and a bit of NF thrown in. Every night was just chaos. The bands themselves fighting with each other backstage.

They were rough times, man. It was just this raw energy that was flying around. The amount of times we had to jump offstage and break up fights in the audience and all that. You just thought it was the way it was. My wife was in Deaf School and I used to go on the road with them and think, 'Fucking hell, it can just be, like, playing music at gigs, without people throwing bottles at you.'

MIKE: In that period, there was a lot of fighting at gigs. The police were cracking down on the football matches and they were starting to put the football hooligans away. I think Margaret Thatcher decided that enough was enough and she wanted to stop the British hooligan syndrome. So, they started spreading into other areas of youth culture, like gigs and stuff. There was a bit of fighting spilled over from that, I think.

I was never really scared, or it didn't feel threatening. But there were definitely some nasty types sometimes turned up. A certain amount of unruly elements in the crowd would just come for trouble, to fight. There'd be an element out there that you'd need to watch out for. The bands tried to shout them down from the stage, often. The Specials would just stop playing. Terry Hall used to throw a hissy fit and refuse to play. They would turn all the lights on, and take the steam out of their kettle, I suppose, by putting the spotlight on them and saying, 'What the fuck are you doing, you fucking idiots? We're here to enjoy ourselves, we're here to dance.' We used to do it slightly differently, but still you'd try and maybe sometimes have somebody removed.

MARK: Normally what would happen is the whole crowd would start clapping and that would be a way to get the idiots out of the building. The bouncers would come in and try and throw them out.

*

MIKE: But, in general, because we were packing them in every night, it was great. We all used to come out at the end of the gig, and we'd all be dancing on the stage, and half the audience would come up onstage as well. Jerry Dammers always invited a stage invasion. It was obviously part of his sort of socialist philosophy, getting all the punters on stage: 'Why shouldn't they be onstage? There is no stage . . . there is no barrier!' So, it was all good fun.

CHRIS: Chalky and Toks had this rubber chicken that they'd picked up somewhere. Neville from The Specials was a right tough nut and he used to come out for 'Gangsters' and fire a starting pistol. So, one night, he fired the starting pistol and we threw the chicken up. This chicken landed on the stage in front of Neville and I had to avoid him bashing me up . . .

CATHAL: There was definitely a sense that Neville was trying to outdo me, with the moves. I'd be doing combat rolls, jumping off speakers, and all this shit onstage. Just trying to go as wild as possible. I mean, the whole stage would be moving. You'd be in gigs, and you'd see the balconies going up and down. You'd think, 'Fuck, it's going to go.' There was always a stage invasion and it was very hairy. But we learnt very early on to be unthreatened by that, and welcoming.

It was also just the growth of people suddenly dressing like us. I mean, it was an amazing time. The Specials' music was kind of recognising the concrete jungle vibe, and Madness were about the joyous aspect, so it was kind of different to the punk thing. Madness's thing was a window on our reality; a celebration of our culture.

I actually thought, on the 2 Tone tour, that The Selecter were the best band. I enjoyed them the most. Their show was fantastic.

Over time, I maybe appreciated The Specials' music more. But, The Selecter . . . the tunes were absolute killer.

One gig we played on the 2 Tone tour, the promoter put the ticket price up, and we all refused en masse to go on unless they reduced the price and returned money. They wanted to be greedy and we were trying to keep to an affordability for kids. There were definitely aspects of socialism. There was a feeling that a lot of the audience were socialists; that they were racially aware.

**WOODY:** The stage invasions at the end got more and more extreme, and it was just a big party atmosphere.

Mind you, Hatfield Poly – that was a horrendous gig. It got invaded by people that had razor blades and started attacking everyone.

**CHRIS:** We had a security guy called Steve English, who was massive. He'd done the Sex Pistols and was a bit of a legend. He said to me there was something dodgy about the Hatfield venue – no security there and some of the windows were left open.

**LEE:** I'd went for a wander about in the crowd. And then the doors burst open . . . three doors in a row, *bap bap bap*. About twenty people came in with these balaclavas on, shouting, 'We're the Anti-Nazi league . . . you fascists . . .' They were lining people up and there was this kid next to me who actually wet himself.

**CHRIS:** They said they were the Anti-Nazi League. But, really, they wanted to hurt people and they dressed it up like that.

*

MARK: They just wanted to come in and cause havoc basically. Indiscriminately hitting everyone they could. Now, whether they were anti-fascists, or local football hooligans, we were never sure. But it was really, really nasty. Just mayhem, generally. We were standing there watching The Selecter, and you didn't know whether or not you could leg it, because it was happening all around you, so it was difficult. We just stood there and then this guy came charging up to us. He had a chair and he was ready to take a swing. And it's probably the first and last time I said it . . . but I said, 'Listen, man, we're with the band,' and it completely disarmed him. He just went, 'Oh, alright then,' and then he ran off.

LEE: They had Stanley knives, batons and I think I might have even seen a machete at one point. They were just attacking the merchandise stalls, smashing everything up with these baseball bats. The noise and the aggression just completely threw you. I felt like a dead weight, and just couldn't move. Everything was spinning out of control, and it was all going off around you, but you were in this vacuum.

MIKE: I mean, it was just a violent bunch of fucking idiots who turned up. They were some sort of political group who for some reason thought cutting people with a razorblade would do something or other.

MARK: It was horrible, and in the aftermath of it, there was people bleeding, people with black eyes. Just chaos.

WOODY: There were literally people with noses split in two and great big gashes on their heads. But I did feel like I was in almost this bubble of protection. I just drifted to the dressing room while it was all going off, and I helped look after people that were injured who were coming backstage.

MARK: We had to decide very quickly whether the gig was going to continue or not. The Specials came on and played, and we played as well, but they were both very short sets.

CHRIS: I really didn't want to go on, and Chalky and Toks said, 'You've gotta.' I wasn't scared, I was just upset.

Kellogs wasn't at this date, because he had some family business to deal with. Then, Dave Robinson sacked him for not being there, which we thought was very unfair, as it wasn't his fault. We got him reinstated, 'cause we'd grown to like him.

SUGGS: All in the space of being on that tour, we were having a hit with 'One Step Beyond', The Specials were having a hit with 'A Message to You, Rudy' and The Selecter were having a hit with 'On My Radio'. Then we all appeared on the same edition of *Top of the Pops*. It was fantastic. That particular *Top of the Pops* was just great for us, because it was like, 'Here we go again, and now this really is happening.'

CHRIS: During the tour, the Selecter single, 'On My Radio', started going up the charts. So, they started saying they should be above us on the bill. Then 'One Step Beyond' was released and shot up the charts to number 3. So that was that. We did 'One Step Beyond' on *Top of the Pops* and we walked through the audience, and it was like, bang – whoosh. 'Game over!'

But, for us to get to the next gig in Cardiff after doing *Top of the Pops*, we had to hire a plane. Obviously, it meant we had to get to an airport, get the plane, then at the other end, get to the venue. And this plane was terrifying, because it was tiny. You just felt you were hanging in the air, and I thought, 'I'm not supposed to be in this.' Anyway, we fly to Cardiff and we get to the venue and The Specials, who'd just gone and got the train, arrived about ten minutes later . . .

**MIKE:** We left the 2 Tone tour early, 'cause Dave Robinson had some idea that he wanted us to get to America before The Specials. He thought that whoever got to America first was going to be the one that they all thought started the ska thing over there. And he wanted it to be Madness. So, he took us off the tour for that. He went, 'Well, you've done the 2 Tone tour now . . . you don't actually have to do the whole thing.'

**LEE:** The last gig we done on the 2 Tone tour was in Ayr, before Dexys Midnight Runners joined it to replace us. That was a sad day. We all had our bags with us, and we walked across the back of the stage as The Specials were playing, waving goodbye to the chaps.

**CHRIS:** They were playing 'Blank Expression', and I said, 'Come on,' and we all got our suitcases and did a Nutty Train behind the guys in the band who were at the front of the stage. They turned round and they were in hysterics.

**LEE:** It definitely felt like the end of an era. I wasn't thinking, 'It ain't going to be as enjoyable as this ever again,' because it was, in a different way. But you never forget your first tour . . .

*

MARK: They were great, riotous gigs. It was brilliant, because you could really feel the momentum building. You knew you were really onto something.

But we didn't go straight to America. We did three gigs over three nights in November '79 at the Electric Ballroom in Camden.

SUGGS: At the Electric Ballroom, we had Red Beans and Rice supporting us who were our local R&B band and really great. A couple of them were black and, one of the nights, this sea of skinheads turned up. It was right at the height of it all. It was just the epicentre of whatever that thing was. Red Beans and Rice went onstage and there was Sieg Heiling going on at the front.

LEE: There was an NF element and us being seen as an all-white skinhead band, we were, like, prime meat for their propaganda.

WOODY: There were all these Sieg Heiling skinheads, and it was horrible. It was like going to a Nazi rally. And yet, you knew that it wasn't everyone. It was only a kind of small minority, but they were very prevalent.

MARK: It was just a fractious gig all round. It was absolutely dreadful. Suggs and Cathal came on to try and calm it down, but . . . yeah, it was terrible.

SUGGS: Me and Cathal went onstage and these skinheads were throwing shit everywhere. We jumped in the crowd and then we thought, 'Oh, fucking hell . . . hold on . . . What have we done here? Let's get back out again quick.'

All that skinheady NF contingent attached itself to us. We were white and we were skinheady-looking geezers. But, really, it was so ironic because we were playing the music of Jamaica. Or trying to. That's what we thought we were doing anyway.

The skinhead thing had mutated into a kind of NF thing at West Ham and places like that. But it was also part of that whole phenomenon that they were really coming down on football hooliganism at that time. So, gangs would attach themselves to a band, almost like they would a football team. 'Cause then they could go on 'away matches'. You'd have this gang following you around. So, like, Secret Affair would have the Glory Boys, which was basically the West Ham firm. It was just a very bizarre time.

We knew some kids from King's Cross who were Tuinal-ed up, fucking swastika-on-their-forehead-the-wrong-way-round type characters. They were the lowest rung of the social ladder. I know obviously that's not acceptable. But it was just a bit of that kind of thing that there was just this scum sort of element of kids. We used to say, 'The ones you need to worry about are the geezers at the back with the bank manager's hairdo and the fucking moustache.' These kids were just the scummy whatever at the front. And then in the end, progressively, we got more vociferous that we were gonna deal with it. We couldn't have it, as it became more serious, really. We had some naïve idea that we could change them . . .

CATHAL: There was a gig we played in Covent Garden, at the Rock Garden, and there was a kid there handing out British Movement flyers. I said to him, 'Look, you've got a picture of Hitler here and you've got the English flag. You do realise that British soldiers died fighting Hitler?' He was like, 'Oh, I hadn't thought about that.' I think there was a lot of poor kids out there who had nothing to hang onto. It was the beginning of the end of youth clubs, there was nothing for a lot of impoverished youth, and that's a recruiting ground for extremists.

**WOODY:** Our gigs were being used for idiots to ruin. We were up against that kind of attitude and getting linked in with it. You were going, 'What the fuck?' There were a lot of kind of politically based bands, but all we wanted to do was to be known for writing about everyday life. It was as simple as that. Many of our own band members had followed skinhead fashion. They weren't racists.

But we weren't a band that made political statements. I believed that we had no right whatsoever to say what you could and couldn't do, in the sense of fashion. A lot of people were saying, 'You should ban these people from your gigs.' You'd go, 'How can you?' You're then judging someone on their appearance, completely. How could you say all skinheads were racist? Of course, they weren't. That was a ridiculous thing to say. You could condemn racists. But racism was something that we fought in our own way by paying tribute to all those wonderful black artists and being part of the 2 Tone thing.

**MARK:** There was an *NME* article that came out and it basically alluded to the fact that there was a right-wing element following us that we were sympathetic to. It couldn't have been further from the truth: everyone was into reggae and black music. I think that article definitely knocked us at the time, being quite young as well, because we thought it was unfair. It also made us a little bit cynical about the press. We felt we'd been stitched up.

**CATHAL:** Yeah, the infamous interview that went all weird. I said, 'What does it matter . . . Who cares what their political views are? We don't ask them, like we don't ask them if they're Conservative or Labour as they come through the door. There's no difference . . . they're all kids.' What I was trying to say was, 'You can't stop people coming through the door. You can't tell their politics by the way they look. You can't stop anyone coming in because of their haircut.' But it sounded like I was saying we wouldn't stop them coming in.

I got myself in a lot of trouble. I upset band members by trying to express a point which didn't come across. I felt really green. It was the early days of being interviewed . . . you're nervous. There's all that awkwardness of representing the band and a movement in some way, the 2 Tone thing, which was a reaction against the racism that was everywhere. On television, and in common usage everywhere in the country, racist terms were used all the time. But yeah, I was . . . not ashamed . . . but really embarrassed about the whole thing.

**SUGGS:** It was so just intrinsically involved in what were just very violent times generally. But, for us to stop them coming in, it would've been like saying, 'We're not gonna have any punks . . .' Y'know, 'Are we not gonna have any skinheads at all?' We were just a bit naïve, really, I think.

**CATHAL:** After that, we hired an ex-SAS guy who would literally just walk into the crowd. He was, like, 6'2", and he'd go up to these troublesome skins and just tie them up with their braces.

But the racist element came and went really quickly. I think it was the death throes of the depression of the seventies. The success of the band pretty quickly moved us more into a younger market . . . a pop market.

# CHAPTER 14

# UNCLE SAM

**CATHAL:** Going to America ... no one was that confident. There was a feeling of being threatened by the communication and language – that 'Hey, gee, how are ya?' kind of thing. But there was an excitement to it. There was a real groundswell there for the British sound, for the 2 Tone thing. They loved it.

**MARK:** We'd signed to Sire Records in America. Dave Robinson at Stiff and Seymour Stein of Sire had somehow worked out a band-sharing agreement.

At this point, for the band, it just seemed like one thing after another, one thing after another: we were doing bigger gigs in the UK, we were on telly a little bit more, and then they said, 'Right, you're going to America ...'

Having loved that Ian Hunter book, *Diary of a Rock'n'Roll Star*, about his tour of America, for me it was just amazing ... that I would actually go and experience this after having read about it. I was just 18. And I know everyone always says it, but it's true – that moment when you make that drive in from the airport in New York and you see the Manhattan skyline, it's just mind-blowing.

CHRIS: We were on Sire because Seymour really liked us, and we really liked Seymour. He was an absolute character. His knowledge of music was incredible and Sire was a cool label.

Anyway, we go to America, and I was so excited. We all were. Even things like Schlitz beer . . . on the first New York Dolls' album cover, they had a tin of Schlitz beer, and it looked so exotic. Of course, when I actually got to taste it, it was like pish . . .

Going to New York, we'd all been told, 'It's going to be cold . . . it's November', so we all had Crombies on. We were staying at this hotel called the Iroquois. We got there, and it was all marble, and there was an old black guy cleaning shoes in the lobby. It was exactly what you imagined it might be: 'Ah, this is fantastic . . .' Then you got out the lift, and it was like, 'Oh, my God.' It was a right old skank-house.

LEE: Yeah, it was rough and ready. The beds were clean, but there was a lot of cockroaches in the bathroom. It was a cockroach's second home or something.

CHRIS: All the doors would rattle, because the rooms had been broken into hundreds of times. I was sharing a room with Mike, and that was an experience in itself. I came back once and he was washing his underpants in the sink. I kid you not.

CATHAL: We went out one night and got back to the Iroquois and I said, 'Look, I've forgotten my key . . . Can you give me a pass key?' It was an off-duty cop, sitting in the security box, bulletproof glass, and he wouldn't get out of the box: 'No, sir.' I said, 'Well, I'm going to kick the door in and I'll pay for it in the morning.' He said, 'Sure, no problem.' So, I went upstairs, kicked the door . . . and the door didn't go . . . the fucking whole frame went in. It was so old, the hotel. I mean, I'm sure it's a snazzy gaff now.

CHRIS: Kellogs from Stiff was still looking after us. He went, 'Go to this bar, everybody goes there . . .' So, we go to this bar and I'm thinking, 'Oh, there's not many women in here . . . ', and it was a gay bar, y'know. They were just such a laugh . . . they thought we were Marines or something because we all had really short hair and the Crombies on. Everybody there liked Woody. They were saying to him, 'Stick your cock in this drink,' and we're going, 'Do it, Woody,' and we're buying them drinks and stuff.

Kellogs told me that he went to Seymour Stein's office, which he had in Warner Bros. Records, and his secretary was on the floor with a load of Madness posters, cutting the bottom off the posters, where it said: 'Stiff Records'. So, there wasn't much funding.

SUGGS: New York in 1979 was just like in the movies: *The Warriors, Mean Streets, Taxi Driver*. Steam coming out of the subway vents, street lights not working, potholes. We embraced it. People would say, 'Don't go down there,' and that's exactly where we went. There was no notion of the danger. I mean, it wasn't just us coming from where we came from, but it was that sort of arrogance, that everything was ours for the taking. It wasn't the other way round! We were certainly not for the taking . . .

*

MARK: New York had gone bankrupt, almost, a few years earlier, so it was still really grimy and there was rubbish everywhere. But we had that youthful innocence, confidence and arrogance. Me and Chris walked miles around New York. We just wanted to see every bit of it. The gigs there were really late. Sometimes, we didn't play till two in the morning in a club, so we'd spend the days just walking, walking, walking, going everywhere, looking at everything, at any time of the day or night. We wandered through some of the worst areas, without a care. All around the Lower East Side and Alphabet City, where it was really dodgy. It'd be, like, four in the morning we'd be wandering around, but we'd be going, 'Ah, fuck it.'

LEE: You know the little people in that film *Time Bandits*? I felt like one of them in New York. I mean, even the manhole covers were the size of the front of an old steam train. And yeah it was still really rough there. Sinkholes in the roads, through the volume of traffic there, I suppose. I don't know. But it was a bit grim.

I did like to go off on me own and I got lost one time. I mean, how do you get lost in New York, when it's all a grid? You've just got to find the corner of Lexington or whatever and the number of the street you're looking for. But I got lost and it was quite scary. Fuck knows where I was. Somewhere in Manhattan, in the ghetto.

Maybe I'd had a bit of speed sulphate and I'd just gone wandering. But I never took the all-important matchbook from the hotel so I'd know the address, and I couldn't pronounce the name of the hotel either. So, I phoned up the operator, trying to find out where it was. My accent obviously pissed off this woman. She thought I was a crank caller. She couldn't understand me.

I was like, 'Excuse me, I'm lost, and I'm looking for my hotel.'

'What? You're looking for a hotel?'

'Yeah, I think I'm staying in Euro . . . it's got a French name, it's very French, you know, bonsoir . . .'

I just heard, 'Brrrrrrrr' – she hung up. I thought, 'Fuck.' I'm walking about in a dogtooth Harrington, quite short hair, DMs, Sta-Prest or whatever, lost in New York. You're from London, so you are streetwise, but now you're in this city that's magnified by ten times for its iffiness. Somehow, in the end, I found my way back.

SUGGS: There were all these crazy characters out there. I saw some of my pals, like Chris Sullivan and Robert Elms, who were temporarily living out there, basically on the streets. They just kept their clothes in a bag in one of them big bins outside. Unless they pulled a bird, they wouldn't have anywhere to stay that night. We ended up in some mad apartments. In this one guy's place, Cathal was skinning up and he put out twelve skins and emptied this guy's whole box of weed into it. The bloke's going, 'Oh, no, man, don't do that. That's my whole month's supply.'

CATHAL: Me and Suggs were invited to dinner by Seymour Stein to Rodney Dangerfield's comedy club. Then The Pretenders turned up, so we were relegated to sitting in the fucking bar, while he had dinner with them, because they'd sold more records. Which was a real great introduction to how it worked . . .

MARK: We played three or four clubs in New York in pretty quick succession. The Mudd Club was one of them, which was a really trendy club. We got there, and they had these shutters that they could pull down over the stage, for some reason. So, we said, 'Well, why don't we come on with the shutters down, and then we could just, like, lift them up and start playing?' From my memory, it wasn't to a lot of people. David Byrne from Talking Heads was there. He came in the dressing room afterwards, which was a little room on the side of the stage. He went, 'That was a good show,' and that's all he really said.

CHRIS: Maybe he was a bit intimidated. I saw him leaving, which was a shame, 'cause I'd have liked to have met him. But it was really late at night, and we were jet-lagged and pissed and God knows what, and I thought, 'I'm going to die.' We were in this dressing room and it was chaos. Woody was sitting in this chair and these girls were cutting his hair. It was all just crazy, and we were the new flipping thing in town. I stayed in The Mudd Club and met a girl who told me it was her 22nd birthday, so I helped her celebrate in style, as it were. She told me I was 'devilishly handsome', which caused a lot of piss-taking.

MIKE: The whole thing was all a bit chaotic really. People kept disappearing ... meeting Americans and going off into different directions. So, we'd had this sense of belonging together, but then everybody was getting into these other situations, which was exciting and everything, but a bit dispersing as well.

We did go together to see the Statue of Liberty and it's, like, tiny. You expect it to be really big. So, everything was a bit, in some ways, smaller, or a bit different, or a bigger mess than I'd thought. You had this idea of the Empire State Building, but then it was like 'Where is it?', and it's in the middle of all these office blocks and everything.

I mean, I don't know ... I was finding it a bit difficult, I think. I was not really comfortable socially, so I wasn't able to really let myself go. I was a little bit shy and self-conscious, so for me, suddenly meeting all these new people and everything was hard. But that was maybe a personal thing with me. Although what we're all going through affects the band, because we're all in the band.

SUGGS: We were definitely fish out of water, and it just wasn't making any sense being there. It didn't seem we were relating to anybody through what we understood from back home. It was kind of like the audiences were coming to see this funny novelty band. And we did feel like a funny novelty thing. Our accents and what we were singing about and the music we were playing was so out-of-step with what was going on in New York, or America.

CHRIS: After New York, John Hasler, who was still our manager, went home. He'd come over with us, but Kellogs, who was the more experienced music industry bloke, was edging him out. I think John felt a bit out of his depth, which was fair enough, really.

MARK: But it was just absolutely amazing to be there and to see all these cities that you'd heard about. We played at The Paradise Club in Boston and there ended up being a vinyl bootleg of it. But the problem with the bootleg was that it was taped at slightly the wrong speed, so we sounded a bit Mickey Mouse.

CHRIS: It was recorded off the radio or something, because you heard this guy going, 'Now, the band is coming on . . . it's Chrissy Boy, and Snuggs . . .'

SUGGS: I think it was in Boston or Philadelphia that as we were walking towards the stage, someone gave Mike a spliff. Then he passed it down the line to the rest of us, and it was so fucking strong. I saw Mike's face change and he turned round and headed back for the dressing room, and then we all did. We were used to Moroccan hash, and this was pure super-strong American weed. Fuck that for a laugh! But then, after a while, we pulled ourselves together and did the gig.

**WOODY:** In San Francisco, we played with the Dead Kennedys. Earlier that day, someone had passed around just this single-skin joint, and I only took, like, one or two puffs on it. Oh, my God, it completely spaced me out. It was like a totally different thing from back home. I kind of thought, 'I can take it.' But no. It absolutely wiped me out.

The gig was very interesting, because I felt like I had tree trunks instead of drum sticks in my hands. Time was the weird thing . . . time didn't exist! Playing 'My Girl', I was just thinking, 'It's going on for ever and ever and ever. It must be the end now,' and we'd only got as far as Mike's solo. So, after that gig, I went, 'Never again. I just don't need it in my life.'

**MARK:** That club in San Francisco was The Mabuhay, or Fab Mab, as it was called. Me and Lee got chatted up there by a huge transvestite. This guy . . . he/she was, like, 6'4", and looked like they could have played American football. Massive, the squarest jaw ever, and under the makeup was stubble. We fought over him: there was a terrible cat fight! And I backed off. But it was all just part of the experience, because that never happened to me in London.

Kellogs had done tours of America before, and he had friends everywhere. When we were in San Francisco, he said, 'Come out to Marin County. I've got some friends out there.' So, me and Woody drove out with him. Marin County was absolutely beautiful, and we showed up at this farmhouse place, and it was obviously, like, a commune. We weren't so far away from the hippies and hippie communes and hippie ideals. This woman came out, and Kellogs said, 'This is Girl.' And I was like, 'Oh, hello, Girl. Is that your real name – Girl?' But it was also the contrast between the hustle of the east coast and the laidback, childlike – but not childish – lifestyle of the west coast. Which, coming from London, was very different for us.

CATHAL: On the tour bus, the roadies were like, 'Let's put *Deep Throat* on the video.' We were like, 'Fuck off, we want to see *Chitty Chitty Bang Bang.*' Seriously!

WOODY: We went to New York and Boston and Philadelphia and San Francisco and then, when we got to Los Angeles, it was all sunshine and palm trees. I thought, 'Fucking hell, this is amazing.'

MARK: It was completely different. It was laid-back, the sun was out, totally different atmosphere.

We were staying at the Tropicana in LA, where Tom Waits lived for a bit in the seventies. It was one of those motels that had kitchens in the rooms, and it was all based around a terrible swimming pool, which was painted black, so it gave it a really weird, murky, deep, dark appearance. Anyway, we camped out there at the Tropicana. It was a well-known place for parties, so people would just show up. Then it had the famous Duke's Coffee Shop below it, where you'd go for breakfast.

*

SUGGS: It was that breakfast thing in America: 'You can have anything you want.' You'd be like 'What?', and just talking about the eggs for about an hour: over easy, sunny side up . . .

WOODY: I was trying desperately to cling on to my vegetarianism, which included not eating eggs, and that was really difficult. I ate cheese, so it was basically chips or pizza, and that was about it. In America, basically I was starving, pretty much, until we hit Los Angeles. Good old Bedders kind of held my hand and said, 'Look, just try some eggs, because you need to eat properly.' It was a lovely moment, actually. I felt really grateful to him, because I had a friend who was understanding that although, morally, eating eggs didn't sit well with me, I was starving to death. He said, 'Give it a go,' and I had an omelette in Duke's.

CATHAL: I existed totally on banana milkshakes and fry-ups, because they were just brilliant.

MARK: We used to go to Barney's Beanery in West Hollywood as well, to play pool and just sort of hang around.

CATHAL: Every time we got a packet of cigarettes in Barney's Beanery, they'd give you a printed matchbook and it had on it, 'Faggots stay out'.

SUGGS: Incredible, really, for that to be going on in California, not that long ago . . .

MARK: All the time that we were in LA, we were living in T-shirts – it was November, but it was warm. Everyone you met there had a car, so they'd offer you a lift: 'I'm going that way, get in.' We only had one hire car or something, just to get people in the band around.

**SUGGS:** I fell off the back of this open-top rental car. Lee was driving and I tumbled off on the freeway, nearly got run over.

I mean, we had a lot of fun. We did two shows a night at the Whisky a Go Go. It was, like, one at midnight and one at two in the morning – the foolishness of youth – wearing the same clothes that were still wet from the first show.

**CHRIS:** Two sets a night, for three nights. We wrote stuff on the dressing room wall, slagging The Specials off, because we knew they were coming there on tour after us.

**CATHAL:** At the Whisky a Go Go, as a promo gimmick, they bought an old banger and painted it black-and-white check and they raffled it off. But whoever won it didn't want to pick it up. Over there, you threw away cars like that on the side of the highway. So, there were no takers.

Rodney Bingenheimer was the DJ there, and he'd been promoting us. Me and Suggs went back to his house and he had an autographed copy of an Elvis album. He'd been around.

Another night, I went to see the Dead Kennedys play at the Whisky, and a load of military turned up and nearly started a riot, because they were like, 'This is disrespectful.'

**WOODY:** Our gigs were just full-on partying, to excessive degrees.

**MARK:** The audiences definitely had heard some of the records. I think they had their eye on what was happening in the UK, so they sort of knew us, and we went down pretty well, really. Don't forget, we were playing stuff really, really fast. They had the surf punk thing going on over there at that time, and we kind of fell in with that. We were lumped in with the punk bands.

WOODY: There was this really weird thing that kids did at the gigs: a dance called the Worm. They used to get up on the stage, then fall down on it with their arms down by their sides, and their legs together, and wriggle like a worm. Your first instinct, of course, was to kick them off: 'Fucking get off the stage.' But that just exacerbated it. The more you kicked them or tried to get them off the stage, the more they seemed to love it. You were just thinking, 'What the fuck is going on?'

SUGGS: We were there in LA for about a week or more, so it was the first time in America that we could actually just spread out a bit. Kellogs had holed himself up in a room with a secretary, and we never seen him for three days. Every now and then, we'd bang on his door and he'd throw an empty Jack Daniel's bottle at us. Suddenly there was a lot of cocaine about. It wasn't our thing. We weren't rock'n'roll in that way. But a lot of the people around us, the managers and the tour managers, were all really incredibly excitable, day and night.

We did have this thing called the Eight O'Clock Club, though. We'd stay up till 8 o'clock every morning, letting off fire extinguishers and all that carry-on. Just being teenagers, basically.

MARK: We met The Go-Go's in LA. They were brilliant, and we got on with them immediately. It was fantastic, because they knew everywhere to go, so we'd go out on trips with them and they'd introduce us to lots of other musicians there. And The Go-Go's certainly liked to drink . . .

LEE: Back at the Tropicana, after the gigs, they'd come back, and you'd have every Tom, Dick and Harry dancing about the Astro-Turf around the swimming pool.

CHRIS: So, we hung out with The Go-Go's, and Bedders, he was seeing the drummer, Gina. I thought, 'That guitarist Jane's rather nice . . .', so I kind of ended up with her. Y'know, we extended English hospitality.

SUGGS: It was hilarious: at one point it almost seemed we were all knocking about with one of The Go-Go's. The odd thing was, there was four of them and seven of us . . .

CHRIS: But they were a flipping brilliant band. We didn't like them just because of, y'know, romantic, ahem, connections.

MIKE: When we played in LA, everyone was totally out of it . . . but does that matter? I don't know. You almost got the feeling sometimes like it didn't. You thought you could do anything. You could go up there and just shit on the stage and it'd be like, 'Ahh! Madness made it to LA!' I guess the performances were good. But touring America takes its toll.

WOODY: I'd already been starving hungry, gaunt, knackered, absolutely frazzled to fuck from the 2 Tone tour. And then in America, I really felt just dreadful most of the time. Clinging on for dear life, really. Being in these amazing places, but kind of missing home.

## CHAPTER 15

# WHEN WE WAS WE

SUGGS: Another big turning point for the band was when we put out 'My Girl' as the third single. 'Cause we hadn't really appealed to girls up to that point. We loved 2 Tone, but we didn't just want to be a ska band.

MIKE: There were a lot of arguments between us about the ska thing: 'We can't be a one-trick pony. We don't want to keep repeating ourselves.' Maybe we over-embraced it a little bit at a certain point, so then we wanted to slightly disassociate ourselves from it.

'My Girl' was a very important song in our career, because up to then it could have been seen like we were just sort of ska enthusiasts. We felt like we had something else to offer, and that song took us away from ska. It felt like something a bit different and original. So maybe people thought, 'Whoa, this band has got something else to say.'

*

**SUGGS:** 'My Girl' changed the demographic again into real pop. And then it was *Smash Hits* and we were all over the place.

**WOODY:** We moved very quickly from doing sweaty clubs with a lot of very scary-looking skinheads, and then the crowds got younger. At first, it was a bit kind of, 'Oh my God, we've become a boy band.' But it was alright. We kind of related to the kids who were watching us, 'cause we'd been kids ourselves actually not that many years before.

**LEE:** 'My Girl' comes out, and suddenly we've not got the NF at our gigs – we've got teen girls. It's gone from boneheads in string vests to teeny-boppers. Now we've got the handbags replacing the beer bottles and a waft of fucking Charlie perfume coming up towards the stage!

I mean, it was just one of those things. Directly after 'My Girl', because it was moving so fast, we had a moment where at the gigs, you did see gooey-eyed girls at the front. But it was briefly lived.

**SUGGS:** We'd had that gang, the Totts and Whets, who used to follow us around, and these people started drifting away: our hardcore fans who had been there from the beginning. We'd been this tough-lads, outsider kind of thing, and all of a sudden, it became this public thing. We became a pop band, and that wasn't the intention. But I just thought 'My Girl' was a brilliant song, so I didn't see it like that.

**WOODY:** Even though Madness were getting bigger, it wasn't very hard to keep our feet on the ground because, to be honest, the amount of piss-taking in the band was ruthless. You didn't have much chance to be an airy fairy, up-your-own-arse type of individual anyway. You'd soon be taken down a peg or seven.

**MARK:** We made a video for 'My Girl' at The Dublin Castle. It was the first one that Dave Robinson directed, who would of course go on to direct a lot of the videos. I think he decided to do it himself because it was cheaper . . .

**SUGGS:** Robbo got The Dublin Castle for nishpence! And production values: nought.

**CATHAL:** 'Another cheap video,' as we used to say! Very simple. Just dead simple.

**MARK:** We had to fit on the tiny stage at The Dublin Castle. It was a straight performance. For one bit of the video, we decided all to sing one line each, for some reason: we just made that up there and then on the day. So, it's a pretty straight representation of the band – how we looked at the time, how we used to line up on the stage at The Dublin Castle.

**MIKE:** It's that moment where you freeze something into history. I always felt like, 'Make an effort at this moment, because this is going to always remain. So, let's organise and whip ourselves up and do something good.' We used to create magic moments. Every time we done one of those videos, it would be, magical, in an ordinary kind of way.

**WOODY:** Years later, Clive Langer and Alan Winstanley produced 'Absolute Beginners' for David Bowie, and Clive told me a story that Bowie had told him about 'Ashes to Ashes', which came out only a few months after 'My Girl'.

Bowie had said that he'd been looking for a drummer to do the 'My Girl' beats on 'Ashes to Ashes' and he couldn't find one that had the same feeling as me. He'd said, 'There's something about the feel that's really great, and none of the American drummers could do it.' Clive went to me, 'Woody, you do realise that if you put "Ashes to Ashes" up against "My Girl", it's exactly the same?'

Anyway, it kind of inflated my ego and pissed me off at the same time. I thought, 'David Bowie could have fucking asked me!'

MIKE: Well, I don't want to tell you about what I stole off Bowie! I mean, I think everybody steals a bit. But, in a month of Sundays, you wouldn't recognise that 'My Girl' influence on 'Ashes to Ashes'. So, job well done, I'd say.

SUGGS: Suddenly becoming famous was a bit of a shock, because we went off like a packet of crackers. You might get shouted at in the street or have people coming up to you. But it wasn't like you were being followed around by the paparazzi. There wasn't any instance where it got unbearable.

CHRIS: When we got a bit famous, I often used to go to this market near where I lived with my wife and Matthew, my son, and people would go, 'Alright, Chris?' And I didn't know them. Then you'd hear them go, 'Oh, he's got really big-headed . . .' But I thought, 'Well, I don't even know you.' Bearing in mind, we were getting really big, and I was still living in this council flat, and my name and address was in the phone book. It wasn't like money started rolling in the door.

CATHAL: The fame happened so quick. It's an odd thing, standing on stage every night with people in front of you, all dressed and moving like you, copying you.

I'd be at my piano at the window of my gaff in Holloway and faces would pop up in the window, looking in. It was weird. Or I had someone shouting at me at a bus stop in Archway once: 'One Step Beyond!' I was like, 'Fucking hell.' But you're so busy, you're not getting the real feeling of what it means. Because you're in it, you don't have an objective view. It was building and building, without us really realising.

MARK: You kind of rolled with it. You didn't give anything much thought. Youth helps, 'cause you feel that you're pretty indestructible and you're just swept along on the wave of the whole thing.

But, what an amazing end to my teens. Fame didn't really affect me much, 'cause I was very good at hiding in plain sight. Being a Londoner, you just kind of wandered around. I never had any bother. People were always pretty nice if they came up to you. It was always when I was on the Tube or on the bus.

LEE: It affected the neighbours more than anything else. They were all like, 'Whoo!' They see you in a different way. You're stood there right in front of them, but you're also on TV. I stayed in a block of flats right near William Ellis School, Parliament Hill. You'd get kids coming up and they'd be knocking on the door. One day I'd be fine with it. Another day, I'd be like, 'Fuck off.' It depended what mood you were in.

MIKE: You'd go in a shop and people'd start laughing and giggling and pointing and shit. And I was only the keyboard player. But who would have guessed? Me on *Top of the Pops*, writing hits and stuff. So, it was very exciting. It was what we wanted and, suddenly, we got it. It was unbelievable, really.

WOODY: It was really surprising. You're famous, but you're still the same person inside. People used to say, 'Hello, Woody,' and you'd kind of go, 'How does that person know who I am?' Then you'd realise, of course, that you're on *Top of the Pops* and your face is on the back of *Jackie* magazine.

There was one day I was walking down the street and this girl stopped, looked at me and went, 'You're in that band, Madness, aren't you?' I went, 'Yeah, I am,' and she went, 'You're shit.' Fucking brilliant.

SUGGS: We played this big gig at the Lyceum just after Christmas, '79. One of the things I used to love was wandering about in the crowd, before the gig started, to get the vibe. And obviously, as you became more famous, it became more and more difficult. By the time we got to this Lyceum gig, it was impossible. I just couldn't move for people going, 'It's Suggs, it's Suggs, it's Suggs.' Our sound men and lighting men were all hippies, so me and Cathal got a couple of hippie wigs, and we went through the crowd – taking our lives in our hands, for sure – until we got to the safety of the mixing desk and we took the wigs off.

*

**LEE:** The very first edition of *Top of the Pops* of 1980 started with Madness doing 'My Girl'. We were all done up in dinner suits, cleanly shaved. I didn't even have sunglasses on. We thought it was a pretty good idea to all dress up in dinner suits, even though I was normally against that, looking smart, in me early years. We were like a bunch of Bryan Ferrys up there.

**SUGGS:** I think it was Dave Robinson's idea. But Ian Dury and the Blockheads had done it as well, with 'Hit Me with Your Rhythm Stick'. They'd gone on *Top of the Pops* in black tuxedoes and bow ties, and it was just the last thing you'd expect the Blockheads to be wearing. So, that somehow impacted on the idea that the last thing you'd expect was Madness in white tuxedoes.

I mean, the connotations are your Bryan Ferrys and your Humphrey Bogarts. It's got some sort of gravitas, wearing a white tuxedo. In my mind, anyway. But yeah, it was all part of this time of change. Robbo had this idea that we could go from being ska yobbos to a pop band, and that happened right in that moment in time on the first *Top of the Pops* in 1980.

Mind you, when I say we weren't yobbos any more . . . When 'My Girl' came out and we performed on that New Year's show, me and Lee were still nicking scooters. We nicked this Lambretta from outside Caledonian Road swimming baths, and we were wheeling it across the road and we got stopped by the police. This copper says, 'What are you up to, sunshine?' And then he goes, 'Here, you're that fella who does that wriggly head stuff on *Top of the Pops*, in't you?'

But, I mean, I think that Cathal was the first one to say, 'Madness is like some dysfunctional family.' We were, for sure.

We had gravitated together. It felt like something that definitely Freud or whoever would look back over with me and go, 'Of course, you were looking for a father figure.' Whoever that might be: Lee, Mike, or Chris. Because they were all slightly older than me, so I looked up to them, definitely.

**CHRIS:** Who was saying that we were a dysfunctional family? My psychiatrist?! But yeah, somebody said to us once, 'That's why you got together, because you were all sort of parentless.'

I think it's sort of true. Mike's dad left when he was very young. My parents split up when I was twelve or something like that. So, when you were at school, it was a bit of a stigma, I suppose. Everybody else, they've got a mum and a dad. But it wasn't like I thought, 'Right, I'm only going to start a band with people to feel like I'm part of a family.' It was just circumstance.

**WOODY:** Isn't it funny? I knew nothing about Chrissy Boy's mum. I knew absolutely nothing about Mike's dad. It sounds really weird, that I've known these people most of my life and I'd never even gone there.

**CATHAL:** Lots of absentee parents. And strong and unusual mother figures! I think the band, what it's done for us, the opportunities it's given us, the joy it's given people ... I mean, it's absolutely incredible. It's so hard to express it. Maybe there's the psychological aspect of we'd found something which made us happy. We'd found something where we belonged.

**MARK:** I don't know if all bands do it, but this is what our band does – we talk about these waypoints quite a lot, actually. You've got this shared existence. You've got this shared memory, and it's the equivalent of people going, 'Are you alright?' But we do it by going, 'Do you remember when we were in . . . ? What did you do there? Did you do that or was it someone else?' And one of us will remember exactly what happened. So, it's interesting: I think the band do use that shared, collective memory a lot, to ground us and place us, and then I think it enables us to move on.

MIKE: Madness was like a new family for us, definitely. And we were all going off into a whole different world. All these experiences we were going through, there was a common thread that we were all still the same and we'd all been there together down the years.

Although, it got pretty difficult, I think: being so young and suddenly getting caught up in that whole thing and being set apart from other people and stuff. I found it a bit difficult in the end, having the spotlight on you.

LEE: To me, it was more a gang thing than a family. I mean, I'd always been in a gang, going as far back as, like, where I used to live, Denyer House. The Aldenham Glamour Boys was a gang thing. Then, in the band, we was living out of each other's pockets.

But yeah, to me it was like still being in a gang, but with the added privilege of doing something we enjoyed, which was playing music.

The biggest thing I learned, though, is that if you sit down and if you get rid of all the distractions and crap out the way . . . lock yourself down somewhere . . . bolt yourself down and put your mind to it, you can do almost anything. And that was certainly the case when I first met Mike and Chris.

But no way did I ever think it would last as long as it has done.

**SUGGS:** I don't remember ever thinking about whether it was going to last. Not me, anyway. I didn't care.

You see this polished Madness thing that's been going for 40 years, and people would think, 'Course you knew.' But I didn't have a clue. I wasn't taking it the slightest bit serious. That's why I'd got thrown out the band at the start, because I just thought it was a laugh and just something to do – hanging about with pretty cool geezers. The idea that I was ever going to make a career out of it was totally beyond my comprehension.

**CHRIS:** I knew I had great friends in the band, that we were like a kind of gang. And you were living for the moment. But, even right up to now, we still argue, we disagree. But, that's Madness, mate.

**WOODY:** We always used to use that Andy Warhol phrase, '15 minutes of fame'. But we used to say about us that we'd only have 10 minutes of fame! I told you we were cynical . . . But that's good: I think that's healthy. That's probably what kept us going.

**MARK:** I said to Woody at the time, 'If we can make three albums, it will be absolutely brilliant. If we can last that long, it'll be great.' He went, 'Yeah, yeah, I hope we can . . .' Then, for the next five years after, it was non-stop.

**CATHAL:** We just saw it all differently from other bands, I think, because of that gang and family thing. Everyone was trying to amuse each other the whole time. I don't think the band were comfortable in a lot of things, and there was a process of making each other comfortable.

But I don't think the impact of what Madness meant to people hit us until years later. I think initially it was because we had people like Chalky and Toks, who were very grounding, taking the piss out of everyone. Then, Chrissy Boy with his nicknames for everyone. There was no star trip going on. There was no delusion at that time. It was all really us against the world, but not in an aggressive way. It was just: 'This is our thing.'

MIKE: We did feel like we were established, to an extent, after 'My Girl'. That we'd cracked it, and it wasn't like a flash in the pan. We'd set it up pretty good, I think, to continue.

But we never had a magic plan how to sustain it, 20 years, 30 years, 40 years on.

We weren't really thinking about the future. It was all meant to be, predestined, sort of thing. It all happened so quickly, and it all happened so easily. It was like a motorbike ready to go and we jumped on, *rarrrr* and we were off, full speed, and that's where this book ends.

# APPENDIX I: THE PHOTO BOOTH

## What was happening?

1. **Cathal:** Helping Mr Hasler with some Kundalini breath work.
2. **Mike:** With Lee in Yarmouth, met a couple of girls whose dad owned a tug boat.
3. **Mike:** Me and Lee.
4. **Mike:** The classic Roxy Music pose.
5. **Mike:** Long summer days.
6. **Mike:** The moody Ted look.
7. **Mike:** Yarmouth with Lee.
8. **Mike:** Me and the man with the Teflon quiff Tony Hilton fighting for the front row.
9. **Lee:** Bryan Ferry.
10. **Chris:** Leather jacket £15, Queen's Crescent; bumfluff moustache; free haircut by El Thommo.
11. **Mike:** Warming up for the Brian Ferry look.
12. **Chris:** Thommo in Levi's coat with faux fur, lolz.
13. **Cathal:** Chrissy Boy fiddles with my brain. Most enjoyable.
14. **Chris:** Jacket Oxfam – £5; jumper Chelsea Girl – free; Roxy Music badge – £1.50.
15. **Mike:** On the 'Streets of San Francisco'.
16. **Cathal:** Probably the most handsome member of the band!
17. **Mike:** Jostling for the front row with Simon Birdsall.
18. **Lee:** Haircut by Chrissy Boy – £1.50.
19. **Mike:** Hmmmm.
20. **Chris:** Jacket as in pic 14. Barnet very long. Cigarette Gold Leaf.
21. **Chris:** Hat Kangol – free. Single Sex Pistols – free. Jumper M and S – free.
22. **Mike:** Karl Malden and Michael Douglas cleaning up Frisco.
23. **Mike:** Don't get up – there's one more!
24. **Mike:** With my new Ray Bans.
25. **Chris:** Best haircut ever from 'Keep Your Hair On'. Shirt Levi's – free.

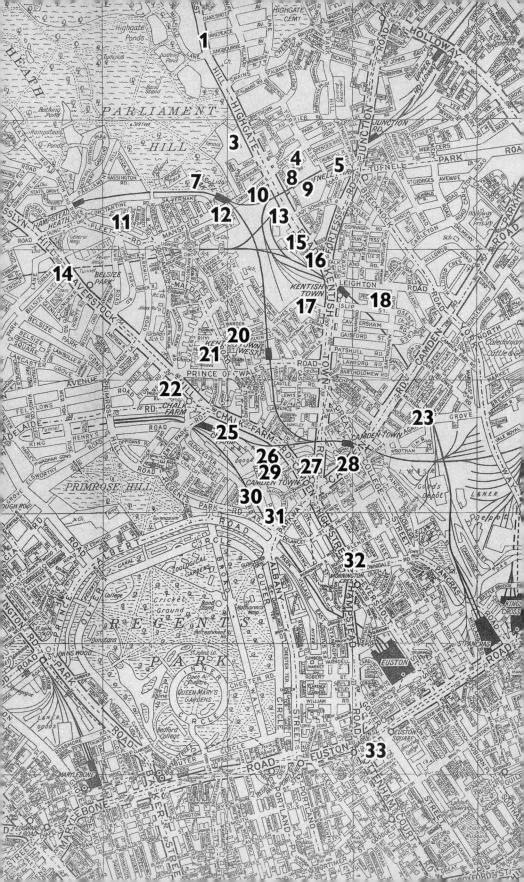

# APPENDIX II: WHERE WE WAS

## Our Neighbourhood

1. Langbourne Mews. Earlier Lee home.
2. The Rainbow Theatre, Finsbury Park.
3. William Ellis School, Highgate Road, NW5. School of Mark Bedford, John Hasler, Gary Dovey, Clive Langer.
4. Chetwynd Road, NW5. Home of Mike.
5. Acland Burghley School.
6. Hornsey Road, N7. Home of Mark Bedford.
7. Parliament Hill playground.
8. Denyer House. Home of Lee.
9. 'Tammo Land' (Ingestre Road, NW5). Lee's hangout.
10. Mortimer Terrace, NW5. Home of Chris. Jumping Trains.
11. Agincourt Road, NW3. Later home of Woody.
12. Gospel Oak Station. 'The Magic Line'. Graffiti. Jumping Trains.
13. The Aldenham Youth Club, Highgate Road, NW5.
14. Hampstead Town Hall, NW3.
15. The Forum venue, Highgate Road, NW5.
16. The Street Disco aka the Bull & Gate pub, Highgate Road, NW5.
17. Holmes Road Police Station.
18. The Forties, Islip Street, NW5. Earlier Lee home.
19. Georges Road, Holloway, N7. Later home of Woody.
20. Kentish Town West Station/Talacre. Trains. Adventure playground.
21. Penshurst, Prince of Wales Road. Later home of Chris.
22. Haverstock School, Haverstock Hill, Chalk Farm. School of Woody and Lee.
23. Stratford Villas, NW1. Home of Woody.
24. Hope & Anchor pub, Upper Street, N1.
25. The Roundhouse venue.
26. Blind Alley gig, Camden Lock, NW1.
27. Holt's shoe shop, Rock On Records & 2Tone Records office.
28. Swanky Modes clothes shop. Later home of Suggs.
29. Dingwalls venue & Camden Market.
30. London Film-Makers' Co-op gig.
31. The Dublin Castle pub.
32. The Music Machine venue.
33. Home of Suggs.

# A Bit Further North

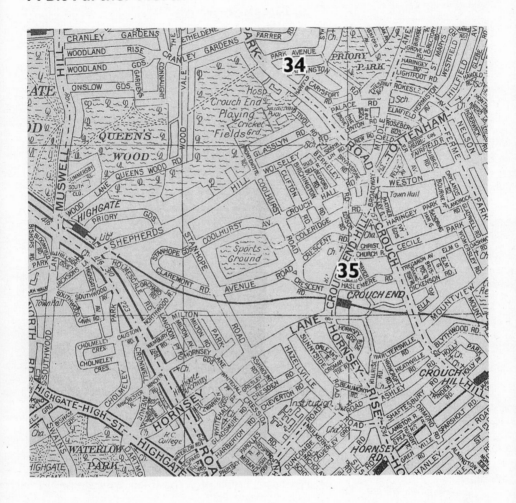

34. Park Avenue South, Muswell Hill. Home of Mike.
35. Hornsey College of Art, Crouch Hill. Mike and Mark.

# A Bit Further West

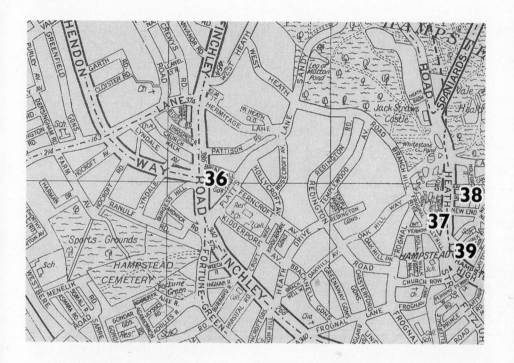

36. The Basement Rehearsal Room (pictured on the cover), below The Dentist Surgery, Finchley Road.
37. The Holly Bush.
38. Duke of Hamilton.
39. The Flask.

# ACKNOWLEDGEMENTS

Madness would like to thank:

Dave Robinson, John Curd, Clive Langer, Alan Winstanley, John Eichler, Jerry Dammers, Rob Dikens, John Hasler, Gavin Rodgers, Kerstin Rodgers, The Totts and Whets, Sonnie Rae, Prince Nutty, Chalkie and Toks, Mathew Sztump, Andy McDonald, Maureen, Debbie, Spike, Elsa Birdsall, Steve Hedges, Rick Rodgers and all at Trigger, Paul Conroy, Annie Pitts and Nigel Dick at Stiff Records, Ben Barson for lending out his gear and room, Pat Barson for letting us rehearse in her house, Fiona Richmond and her dad for letting us use the Dentist's basement, Wandsworth Harry for loyalty above and beyond the call of duty, Jamie Spencer aka "Kenny Pipe", Fred Rowe, Humphrey Ocean, Gid London, Miranda Joyce, Matt O'Casey, Clare Muller, Alison Weir, Arabella Weir, Christina Weir, Susi Molteno.

And Goodnight, God Bless
Ian Dury, John 'Kellogs' Kalinowski, Alex Harvey, Stiff Records, Alo Conlon, Gary Dovey, Frank Murray.

# *BEFORE WE WAS WE*
# ACKNOWLEDGMENTS

With special thanks to:

Tom Doyle, Paul Agar, Lorna Russell, Michelle Warner, Jess Barnfield and all at Ebury Publishing, Hugh Gadsdon, Garry Blackburn, Katy Ellis, Tony Murphy, Jamie Chalmers, Julian Turton, Colin Young, Jim O'Gara, Kate Dosanjh, Gary Pettet, Martin Hampton, Barnes Tenser, Stuart Preston and all at MFL, Harry Wandsworth.

# INDEX